Levant

Also by Anissa Helou

Lebanese Cuisine
Street Cafe Morocco
Mediterranean Street Food
The Fifth Quarter, an Offal Cookbook
Modern Mezze
Savory Baking from the Mediterranean

Levant

Recipes and memories from the Middle East

Anissa Helou

HarperCollins*Publishers*

HarperCollins*Publishers*
77–85 Fulham Palace Road,
Hammersmith, London W6 8JB

www.harpercollins.co.uk

First published by HarperCollins*Publishers* 2013

1 3 5 7 9 10 8 6 4 2

A catalogue record of this book is
available from the British Library

ISBN 978-0-00-731343-3

Printed and bound in Great Britain by
Clays Ltd, St Ives plc

MIX
Paper from
responsible sources
FSC® C007454

FSC is a non-profit international organisation established
to promote the responsible management of the world's forests.
Products carrying the FSC label are independently certified
to assure consumers that they come from forests that are managed
to meet the social, economic and ecological needs
of present and future generations.

Find out more about HarperCollins and the environment at
www.harpercollins.co.uk/green

Contents

*For my mother and late father,
who taught me to love food.*

Also for my late grandmother and Aunt Zahiyeh.

*And for my siblings who were the first to share
with me all those delicious dishes
we grew up with.*

Levant

*S*oleil levant means 'rising sun' in French and 'Levant' – the land to the east, where the sun rises – is the word that came to describe the eastern Mediterranean at a time when the Mediterranean, which links three continents, Europe, Asia and Africa, was the centre of the world.

The term became current in the late sixteenth century with the creation of the English Levant Company that traded with the Ottoman Empire. A century later, the French set up the Companie du Levant for the same purpose and during the eighteenth and nineteenth centuries 'Levant' became widely used by travellers in their accounts of the region, although not always referring to the same countries.

My Levant encompasses my own home countries, Lebanon and Syria, which were called the Levant States by the French when they had a mandate over them from 1920 to 1946 – as a child, I spent the school year in Lebanon, in Beirut, and my summers in Mashta el-Helou in Syria. The term Levant for me also includes Turkey, Jordan, Palestine and northern Iran. Inclusion of the latter may be controversial, but Iranian cooking is the mother cuisine of the region. The Abbassid caliphs, who ruled from the eighth to the thirteenth centuries, favoured Persian cooks, and as their empire expanded, they took them along, which explains the sweeping influence of Persian cuisine over the cooking of the Middle East and North Africa. This, I think, gives me licence to include some of Iran's classic northern dishes. The non-inclusion of Israel may be construed as controversial too, but as everyone knows, Israel is a very young state and many dishes that are now described as Israeli were originally, and still are, Palestinian, Lebanese or Egyptian, and I prefer to give the original rather than the assumed version of a dish where I can. Another country I could have included is Cyprus, which some historians and travel writers regard as part of the Levant. I have chosen not to include dishes from Cyprus in this book simply because this is a personal compilation of favourite recipes rather than a scholarly work, and as such I have made my own, very selective choice.

Most of the essential ingredients – be they grains, pulses, nuts and spices or seasonal produce – are common to the region as a whole. Many dishes are also shared between different countries,

Anissa standing in front of one side of al-Dar in Mashta el-Helou, her father's ancestral home in Syria.

while just as many are specific to one country or another. Equally, when dishes are shared, there is enough of a difference in the way they are prepared to single them out as belonging to a particular country.

Even the dominant flavours can be defined from one country to another. There are no combinations of sweet and savoury in Lebanon where the emphasis is on tart, fresh flavours. By contrast, complex or intriguing flavours are preferred in Turkey, northern Syria and Iran where dishes combine meat with fruit, and in some cases fruit juice, to create enticing sweet-savoury mixtures. Jordan and Palestine favour more subdued flavours and their dishes tend to be higher in fat, as do those from southern Syria. And Iran is the only region where rice is king, whereas burghul and *frikeh* ('burnt' green wheat that is dried and either cracked or left whole) are the staple elsewhere.

The main staple in the Levant is bread, an essential part of meals, but this too varies from one country to another. In Lebanon, a very thin, large pita is the most common type, used to scoop up

food and to make wraps. Even though the country is tiny, there
are regional variations, including *marqûq*, a very large, paper-thin
mountain bread baked over a *saj* (a kind of inverted wok), and
mishtah, a flatbread from the south that is flavoured with spices
and has added cracked wheat (*jrish*). Both are single-layered
whereas further north you will find *tabuneh*, which is double-
layered like pita but larger and thinner. Neither *mishtah* nor
tabuneh tend to be found outside their region; indeed, I never knew
them when I lived in Lebanon, discovering them only a few years
ago when I was researching my book on savoury baking.

In Syria, the common bread, at least in rural areas, is *tannur*, a
large, round single-layered loaf that takes its name from the *tannur*
that was the original pit oven, built either below or above ground.
Pita is common in cities and small towns where there are
commercial bakeries. A few bakeries make *marqûq* although the
bread is not as common in Syria as it is in Lebanon. Jordan and
Palestine have more or less the same type of bread, including
shraak, which is like *marqûq*, and *tabûn*, which is similar to *tannur*
but baked in a regular wood-fired oven. As for Turkey, the choice
tends to be between *pide*, a long, oval, spongy flatbread, and *lavash*
or *yufka*, a cross between *marqûq* and *tannur* that is baked over a
flat *saj*. Some regional Turkish bakeries offer a round flat loaf with
deep indentations all over the top called *tırmaklı ekmek*, while
many sell a fat, baguette-like bread that is used for sandwiches.
Iran has three main types, all flat and each reserved for a specific
meal. *Nan-e taftun* (similar to *nan-e lavash*) is the most common,
a large, thin rectangular loaf that is used to scoop up food or to
wrap around cheese and herbs or kebabs at lunch or dinner. *Nan-e
barbari*, a thicker loaf resembling Turkish *pide* but made thinner
and much larger, is normally eaten for breakfast, with cheese and
omelettes or jam and butter. There is a sweet version made with
milk and a little sugar which is served at teatime. My favourite is
nan-e sangak, a large flat loaf made with a mixture of white and
wholewheat flour and marked with distinctive indentations on the
bottom as a result of being baked in a wood-fired oven lined with
pebbles. It is found in *dizi* restaurants where they specialise in one
meat and vegetable stew served in individual containers called *dizi*.

Each neighbourhood has at least one bakery, which is always
mobbed just before mealtimes by customers eager to buy fresh
bread to eat with their meals. The neighbourhood bakeries are
also where people who do not have an oven bring their food to be
cooked. Nowadays this applies more in small towns and villages

but it can still be seen in large cities too. Not so long ago I stopped at lunchtime at a bakery in Gaziantep in south-eastern Turkey and noticed people collecting baked dishes that had been lined up in the window on the slats where loaves are normally spread to cool. One man walked away with a fabulous-looking dish full of anchovies while a woman picked up a baking dish brimming with the Turkish equivalent of ratatouille. I also saw a man bring in a dish of marinated chicken pieces wedged between vegetables to be cooked for the family meal that night.

Throughout the Levant the accent is on seasonality with cooks rarely using produce that is out of season. Meat is almost always an adjunct to vegetables rather than the other way round; it is only in dishes such as *kibbeh* or *kafta* or when it is being grilled that meat takes centre stage. Even then, grilled meat is always served with a mound of fresh herbs and salads to add freshness. And in almost all cooked dishes, especially one-pot meals, the ratio of meat to vegetables, grains or pulses is smaller. In winter, when people didn't have easy access to transport or refrigeration, and with insufficient grazing to maintain their flocks, they ate or cooked with preserved meat (*qawarma*, a kind of confit of minced

Anissa's maternal grandmother and aunt in their kitchen in Beirut.

lamb). In summer, when there is bountiful produce, cooks have always made sure they don't let any of it go to waste, preserving it – usually by drying or pickling – to use during the fallow winter months.

In fact, there is a strong philosophy of no waste throughout the Levant. I still remember watching with fascination as my mother and grandmother prepared stuffed aubergines or courgettes, marvelling at their dexterity as they cored the vegetables and how careful they were not to waste anything. Once they had loosened the core inside each aubergine, they would gently squeeze it out in one piece and lay it on the bottom of the pan in which they cooked the vegetables. Once cooked, the stuffed vegetables would be arranged on a serving platter and the juicy cores gently scooped out to serve on the side. My mother and grandmother were less careful with the courgette cores, however, which they chopped up and squeezed dry to use in frittatas. I'm sure that if they could have thought of a way to use the stalks, they would have. My aunt in Syria was just as frugal, using every scrap of food, and when she couldn't incorporate leftovers into a dish or make one out of them, she fed them to her cows or chickens. Sustainable living long before it became a buzzword.

But the philosophy of no waste is not the only reason why you should want to explore the food of the Levant. It really fits in with contemporary life being naturally healthy, economical, and on the whole simple to prepare. Some readers may wonder at all the specialist ingredients, but given today's interest in global cooking, you will find most of these on supermarket shelves. Admittedly what is available in supermarkets may not be the best of its kind, but with Lebanese and Turkish cuisine becoming more and more popular, specialist shops offering a range of different and better-quality brands are popping up everywhere, not to mention online stores.

Another appealing aspect of Levantine cuisine is the vegetarian repertoire, which is both large and exciting thanks to the bountiful produce of the region and the wide range of vegetable dishes cooked in olive oil, the main fat used in cooking. Known in Arabic as *bil-zeyt* and in Turkish as *zeytinyağlı*, these are usually served as starters although they are also eaten as a main course by Christians during Lent and on Friday when good Christians abstain from eating meat.

And because the diet is vegetable-based, with meat playing a supporting role, you can produce a beautiful meal on a modest budget. You can also use minced meat without worrying about appearing cheap because minced meat provides the basis of some of the most elegant Levantine dishes. No self-respecting cook would buy it ready-minced, however. Instead, he/she will instruct the butcher to prepare a choice cut of meat, skinning it and trimming it of fat before mincing it to just the right degree.

It's true that some dishes like stuffed vegetables or *kibbeh* are time-consuming to prepare, but many others like dips or even flatbreads are simple to make, and with today's accent on casual eating what better than a meal made up of mezze dishes to enjoy with your family and/or friends. A proper mezze spread remains the preserve of restaurants, but you can still whip up an impressive mezze at home by preparing three or four dishes yourself – a dip, a salad, a savoury pastry and a vegetable cooked in olive oil and tomatoes, perhaps also some grilled chicken wings – then supplement the spread with shop-bought items like feta cheese drizzled with olive oil and sprinkled with fresh or dried herbs, toasted nuts (or fresh when they are in season), olives, crudités and bread of course. Much more convivial than a regular three-course meal. To finish, you can offer an amazing assortment of baklava or a sweet you have made yourself, although Levantines rarely conclude their meals with a sweet dessert, however fond they are of them – and they are famous for their sweet tooth. They normally end the meal with coffee or tea and fruit, reserving sweets to enjoy with more coffee or tea in between meals either on their own or when they have visitors.

Another advantage is that many of the dishes can be prepared well ahead of time and either served at room temperature – a very common way of serving most vegetarian dishes – or reheated to serve on the day, which makes Levantine food ideal for contemporary cooks with busy lives.

The Levant is changing fast, both because of the spread of modern technology and because of the Arab Spring, which in Syria has tragically led to the killing of thousands and the destruction of much of the country. I have not been back since the beginning of the uprising, which sadly morphed into a civil war owing to the government's brutality and intransigence – their refusal to accept that people would want to liberate themselves from a repressive regime. One day I will return, although when I do I fear I may not find many of the people I describe in this book. Perhaps even some culinary traditions will have vanished too. This happened when

A sexy ambulant greengrocer in Ouzai in Beirut, Lebanon.

I returned to Lebanon after the long civil war that tore the country apart. Other countries have escaped such violence and destruction, but things are changing elsewhere too. Iran is now an Islamic republic suffering under the weight of strict sanctions, while Turkey and Jordan are developing at great speed. Meanwhile, Palestine is being eroded and may eventually exist only in name. All these changes make it even more pressing for me to record Levantine culinary traditions that have either disappeared or are at risk of disappearing.

When I started out in adult life, cooking was the last thing I wanted to do, but this book, which brings together my favourite recipes from the Levant, is in a way the culmination of my liberation from my former attitude to cooking which I equated with being domesticated. It includes stories from my childhood and youth growing up in Lebanon and Syria as well as anecdotes from my culinary travels throughout the region. I hope these accounts will inspire you to cook the dishes and visit the region itself, although you may have to wait before you visit Syria, and even Iran is not the easiest place to travel in, especially if you are

9

a woman. The other countries I mention here are safe, however, and definitely worth exploring if you haven't done so already.

Tasting the food in situ and seeing the ingredients in the markets – the vibrant spices and mounds of fresh produce – will make you appreciate the different cuisines of the Levant even more. All of which brings me to say a few words about the ingredients needed for the recipes. We are all aware now about the difference the quality of ingredients makes to a dish, especially if it is one that you haven't made before. Many of the essential ingredients that I call for in the recipes will last in your kitchen cupboard and I would urge you to source them carefully to achieve the best results.

I would also recommend you follow the recipe carefully too. I still remember, when tabbuleh became fashionable, how many recipes advocated soaking the burghul. I couldn't understand why cookbook writers would advise such a step as we normally rinse and drain the burghul and use it straight away. Later, I developed my own method of letting the burghul sit after rinsing and draining so that it fluffs up and absorbs just the right amount of dressing. Then I realised that the soaking instructions were because the writers were using coarse-grade burghul which we reserve for cooking only, using the fine-grade variety that doesn't need any soaking for salads and *kibbeh*. In fact, soaking fine-grade burghul makes it mushy. This is only one example but it illustrates the importance of sourcing the ingredients properly. So, go to a specialist store, buy the best you can afford, having read the recipe carefully, and you will be rewarded with superior results that will impress your family and friends.

And finally a word about the transliteration and spelling of foreign terms. There are many different ways of transliterating Arabic and, browsing online or looking through other books, you will see different spellings for the same word or recipe name. I have relied both on a classic form of transliteration and a phonetic one to transcribe words as I would say them in Arabic, whereas I have used only the classic transliteration for Iranian. The Turkish alphabet has been used for words in Turkish.

Anissa Helou
London, February 2013

En Famille

My relationship with family meals has been one of love, hate, then love again. As a child, I loved eating *en famille*, sitting at our large, solid wood dining table in Beirut with my father at one end, my mother at the other and my siblings and I on either side.

We were four girls and a boy. I was in the middle with two older sisters, a younger brother and a baby sister. My two older sisters and I were very close in age, and we formed one camp on one side of the table while my brother and baby sister formed their own on the other side. Throughout the meal, we shifted between conspiratorial conversations within our camp, to silly arguments either within our camp or with my brother's.

My father watched over us kindly while my mother busied herself with the food, telling us to eat if we didn't (not something she had to do often) or to calm down if we got too excited. She also told our maid when to clear up, when to bring more water or the fruit, and so on. My mother was, still is, the most wonderful cook and she prepared delicious meals that we all ate heartily.

However, as much as I loved my mother's food, I loved my grandmother's better. She had been widowed early and lived with my aunt and four uncles in the Christian part of town – we were on the Muslim side – in a large airy flat with beautiful Art Deco furniture. We visited her often. Her kitchen was like ours, with lovely white marble counter tops. And although she cooked like my mother – she did after all teach her everything she knew, the way my mother taught me – she had little touches that made her food even more exquisite. For instance, the Lebanese always cook stuffed vegetables on a bed of bones for a richer sauce. My mother simply washed the bones and lined the pot with them, while my grandmother parboiled and rinsed the bones before using them. This, she said, helped get rid of the scum the bones release during cooking and made for a cleaner and more refined sauce. She had similar sophisticated touches for almost every dish she prepared.

Also, the meals at her house were jollier than at our own. My aunt and uncles were not that much older than us – people married very young in those days – and even though they were no longer of an age to be playmates, they were playful with us.

13

We ate in the kitchen unless *sitto* (granny in Arabic) had guests in which case we moved to the dining room. We often went there early and I would go straight into the kitchen to sit on the white marble counter, right by where my grandmother prepared our lunch. Sometimes, I helped with simple tasks such as bunching up the parsley for the tabbuleh but most times I just looked. My desire to be in the kitchen was not so much to help, nor really to watch the cooking, although I learned a lot by just being there, but rather because I wanted to taste everything. My mother never let me do this at home, insisting that I should wait for my meal, whereas my grandmother always gave us tastes of whatever she was preparing. I do the same, offering tastes to whomever is with me in the kitchen, not to mention my tasting everything as well.

My mother and aunt were in charge of setting the table and they always laid a selection of nibbles called '*zinet el-tawleh*' (decoration of the table so that it looks appetising even before any of the prepared dishes are served). Their 'decoration' consisted of olives, cucumbers and carrots, cut into sticks and seasoned with a little salt and lemon juice, a bowl of hommus or labneh drizzled with olive oil, bright pink home-made turnip pickles (made that colour by adding raw beetroot to the brine), fresh nuts when in season or roasted ones when not, and of course bread. The meal itself consisted of a couple of salads, either tabbuleh or fattush plus a seasonal one such as tomatoes, purslane and meqteh (a kind of wild, pale ridged cucumber) and a main course, often stuffed vegetables, which we loved and which my grandmother regularly made for us. We always finished our meals with fruit.

If we happened to visit on a Sunday, she would grill kebabs. Sunday is barbecue day for pretty much everyone in Lebanon, and on those days, I would abandon my grandmother to be with my uncles on the balcony where they set up the *manqal* (Arabic for the small metal barbecue used throughout the Middle East) to start the charcoal fire.

When we finished eating, we moved to the drawing room for the grown-ups to drink their Turkish coffee but before that one of us girls had to grind the coffee in a beautiful brass grinder. After drinking the coffee, they all turned over their cups to let the dregs drain out, leaving patterns inside each cup that my aunt read to tell each their future. I loved listening to her interpretation of the various patterns. If the coffee dribbled down the side leaving a clear white line, it meant the person had an open road ahead of him/her. If the coffee was thick and the residue stayed on the bottom of the cup, it meant the person's heart was dark and heavy, and if there was a big white patch on the bottom of the cup, there was marriage in the air, and so on.

My aunt was very beautiful with long wavy dark hair like Ava Gardner's. She actually looked like her and when I met Ava Gardner many years later, she told me I looked like her sister; I didn't say it but I immediately thought she must have been the family's ugly duckling! In any case, once my aunt had done her coffee-cup reading, she played music to dance with one of my uncles. And despite my having no sense of rhythm, I would jump up to join them. They were very kind and never resented my interfering with their Paso Doble or Cha-Cha-Cha.

Those were our family meals in the city but I had just as many joyous meals in the mountains where we spent our summers, either in Mashta el-Helou, my father's ancestral home in Syria or in Rechmaya, my maternal grandmother's village in Lebanon. Sometimes, my parents rented a house in one of the Lebanese mountain resort towns for us to spend time on our own.

Then I grew into a moody teenager, and started spending all my time reading in my room. It was around that time that I began to hate family meals, often insisting on eating in my room, which for some reason my mother agreed to.

This antagonistic attitude lasted until I left Lebanon for London. Away from home, my relationship with family meals turned to love again, although not immediately. First, I went through a phase of wanting to eat out all the time and hardly ever cooked at home. Then I started cooking for friends, both European and Lebanese food but it wasn't until I started writing about food that I became interested in family meals again, not only to soak up the warm atmosphere but also to learn more about the different dishes of each of the countries I visited and the customs that surrounded serving and eating them. What was interesting was that in many parts of the Levant and beyond, families gathered around the table pretty much the way we did when I lived in Beirut. Of course, the meals and the order in which the dishes are served change from one country to another but the conviviality, generosity and hospitality are the same, which is not surprising, really. The legacy of the Ottomans as well as common Middle Eastern traditions have yielded similar dining habits throughout the region, not to mention the common ingredients.

Lemony Swiss Chard and Lentil Soup

'ADASS BIL-HAMOD

I don't like soup on the whole, possibly because my mother had this maddening habit of offering to make it whenever any of us were ill. That said, I do like some soups, especially those that don't remind me of the diced vegetable and chicken soup that my mother invariably prepared for the invalid in question. I especially like the following soup and always make it when chard comes into season. We often had it chilled for lunch with not much else other than bread, but you could serve it as a starter followed by a simple roast. The Lebanese tend to resist modernisation in the kitchen and many still crush garlic using a wooden pestle and mortar; some have now adopted a plastic version, but that is their only nod to modern times! I prefer to simplify my life and therefore use a metal garlic crusher, even if the pestle and mortar do a more thorough job, crushing the garlic into a creamy paste that dissolves into the soup, whereas the crusher just pulverises the garlic into tiny pieces that don't emulsify with the liquid in quite the same way.

Serves 4–6

200g (7oz) large green lentils
400g (14oz) Swiss chard
Juice of 2 lemons or to taste
10 garlic cloves, peeled and crushed
150ml (5fl oz) extra-virgin olive oil
Sea salt

Put the lentils in a bowl of water to soak while you prepare the Swiss chard, which you need to trim – the bottom of the stalks are often quite dirty and need to be cut off. Chop both leaves and stalks into thin strips about 1cm (½in) wide.

After they have soaked for about 30 minutes, drain the lentils and put in a large saucepan. Add 1.5 litres (2½ pints) of water and place over a medium-high heat. Bring to the boil then add the chard. Reduce the heat to medium, cover the pot with a lid and let it bubble gently for 15 minutes or until the chard has wilted, at which stage mix the chard in with the lentils and cook, covered, for another 30–45 minutes or until the lentils are tender.

While the soup is cooking, prepare the seasoning by slowly incorporating the lemon juice into the crushed garlic, then gradually mixing in the olive oil. When the lentils and chard are done, stir the mixture into the soup. Season with a little salt and simmer, uncovered, for another 5 minutes. Taste and adjust the seasoning if necessary. Serve at room temperature.

Mini Dumplings and Meatballs Soup

MANTI CORBA

Most people in Turkey make their own *manti* (dumplings) but you can also buy them ready made. They will not be as delicate, nor will they be as small, which is the sign of the best *manti*, but they will be good and you will save considerable time preparing this satisfying soup that is often served at large family gatherings as the first of many courses. I was lucky enough to be invited one day to eat with the in-laws of my friend Nevin Halıcı (see page 29). Her elder brother, Feyzi Bey, is married to a wonderful woman, Bahar, who comes from a family of fine cooks and whose sister Lale, who made the soup, is considered the best of them all. I have adapted her recipe below.

Serves 4

For the filling
125g (4½oz) minced lean lamb
1 very small onion or a shallot, finely chopped
2 tsp pepper paste
Sea salt
¼ tsp black pepper

cont.

For the meatballs
250g (9oz) minced lamb meat
¼ tsp ground allspice

For the dough
75g (2½oz) plain flour
Sea salt

For the soup
½ tbsp extra virgin olive oil
½ tbsp pepper paste (see page 326)
½ tbsp tomato paste
½ tsp finely ground black pepper
½ tbsp dried mint
200g (7oz) cooked chickpeas (½ jar)
Juice of ½ lemon
15g (¾oz) unsalted butter

Put all ingredients for the filling in a bowl. Mix well.

Mix the flour and salt together in a bowl. Gradually add
3 tablespoons water to make a rather stiff dough. Divide the dough
into two and shape each into a ball. Roll the first piece into a very
thin sheet, then cut into small squares about 3cm (1¼in) square for
very small manti, or 6cm (2½in) square for larger ones. Put ¼ or ¾
teaspoon meat filling (depending on the size) in the middle of each
square. Lift the corners of the square and stick together to shape a
neat pouch. Repeat the process with the remaining dough until you
have used all the dough and half the filling.

Mix the remaining filling with the meat. Add the ground allspice
and salt and pepper to taste and mix well. Shape into the smallest
balls you can make, like large marbles, in proportion to the size of
your manti. Place on a tray. Cover loosely with cling film and
refrigerate to firm them up.

Put the olive oil in a big pot and place over a medium heat. Add
the pepper and tomato pastes, the black pepper and 1 teaspoon
dried mint. Stir for a couple of minutes then add 750ml (1⅓ pints)
water and salt to taste. Bring to the boil. Then reduce the heat to
medium-low and let simmer for 10 minutes before adding the
cooked chickpeas, the manti and the meatballs. Add the lemon

juice and let bubble for 20 minutes. Check the water and add a little more if you feel the soup is too thick – the manti will absorb some of it. Just before serving, melt the butter in a pan and add the remaining dried mint. Pour all over the soup and serve immediately.

Mixed Pulses and Grains Soup
MAKHLUTA

Here is an incredibly nourishing soup that we often had at my grandmother's during Lent. She served it with a platter of pickles and bread, of course, and to start with we would have tabbuleh (see page 22) or a cabbage salad. I often prepare it for lunch and make enough to last a few days. Sometimes I flavour the soup with cumin, other times with cinnamon. I also alternate between using seven-spice mixture and allspice, depending on how spicy I want the soup to be; allspice gives it a more subtle taste while the seven-spice mixture makes for a stronger flavour. You can eat it hot in winter or just warm in the summer. It is both versatile and satisfying, and perfect for both vegetarians and vegans!

Serves 4–6

50g (2oz) dried cannellini beans, soaked overnight
   in cold water (enough to cover the beans by
   2–3 fingers) and ½ tsp bicarbonate of soda
75g (2½oz) dried chickpeas, soaked overnight in cold
   water (enough to cover the chickpeas by 2–3 fingers)
   and ½ tsp bicarbonate of soda
150g (5oz) brown lentils, soaked for 30 minutes in cold
   water (enough to cover the lentils by 2–3 fingers)
150ml (5fl oz) extra-virgin olive oil
2 medium-sized onions, peeled and finely chopped
30g (1oz) coarse burghul, rinsed under cold water and
   drained
30g (1oz) short-grain white rice (bomba, Calasparra or
   Egyptian), rinsed under cold water and drained   *cont.*

2 tsp ground cinnamon or ground cumin
2 tsp ground allspice or Lebanese seven-spice mixture
   (see page 331)
½ tsp finely ground black pepper
Sea salt

Rinse the soaked beans and chickpeas under cold water, then drain and put in a large saucepan. Drain the lentils and add to the chickpeas and beans. Add 2.5 litres (4⅓ pints) of water, cover the pan with a lid and place over a medium-high heat. Bring to the boil, then reduce the heat to medium and let the pot bubble gently, covered, for 1 hour or until the pulses are tender.

While the pulses are cooking, put the olive oil and chopped onion into a frying pan and place over a medium heat. Fry the onions, stirring occasionally, until golden.

Add the burghul and rice to the pulses when they are ready. Tip in the fried onions with their oil and season with the spices and a little salt. Let the soup simmer for 15 minutes, then taste and, if needed, adjust both seasoning and consistency to your liking. If the soup is too liquid, boil for a little longer; if too thick, add a little boiling water and simmer for a few more minutes. Serve hot or warm. You can also serve the soup at room temperature.

Green Beans in Tomato Sauce

LUBYEH BIL-ZEYT

The traditional way to serve this dish is by spreading the beans and their sauce on open pita bread: you tear off strips from the dry edges of the bread and use them to scoop up the beans. When you have finished eating the beans, you roll up the sauce-soaked bread to eat like a sandwich with wedges of raw onion. It was my favourite dish of all the ones my mother and grandmother cooked, and in a way it still is, especially when I want to have a taste of home. I always ask my mother to make it for me when I am in

Lebanon. *Lubyeh bil-zeyt* was the first dish I ever cooked. I was 16 at the time and we lived in a small building that my father had bought. My room was on the same floor as the kitchen and dining room, with my parents' on the floor above and my brother's and sisters' on the floor below. I was always the odd one in the family, insisting on having my own room and not wanting to share anything! It made me feel quite grown up to have a whole floor to myself, and one night my two older sisters and I decided to have a midnight feast. I made the green beans while my sisters prepared a chocolate cake. We ate the beans – I kept a little for my mother to taste the next day – and we used most of the chocolate cake in a cake fight that took forever to clear up. We didn't want my parents to be angry at the mayhem we'd created while they were fast asleep. My mother never knew about the cake fight but she was very proud of my culinary efforts and impressed at how, on my first attempt, I'd managed to prepare the beans almost as well as she did!

Serves 4

3 tbsp extra-virgin olive oil
1 medium-sized onion, peeled and finely chopped
6 garlic cloves, unpeeled
400g (14oz) Helda beans or fine green beans
Sea salt
1 × 400g can of Italian cherry tomatoes, drained

Put the olive oil, onion and garlic in a wide saucepan. Place over a medium heat and fry until the onion turns golden.

While the onion is cooking, top, tail and, if necessary, string the beans. Then cut them on the slant in 5–6cm (2–2½in) lengths; if you are using fine beans, simply top and tail them. Rinse under cold water, then add the beans to the onions. Sprinkle with a generous pinch of salt, and cook, covered with a lid, for about 5 minutes, stirring regularly, until they turn bright green and become glossy.

Add the tomatoes and season with a little salt. Mix well and cover the pan, letting the mixture bubble gently for about 20 minutes or until the sauce has thickened and the beans are done to your liking. I like to keep them slightly al dente; my mother cooks them until quite soft. Serve hot, warm or at room temperature, with pita bread.

Tabbuleh

Tabbuleh is basically a parsley and tomato salad with a fair amount of mint and a smattering of burghul and spring onions. However, despite the salad having gone global, it is still rare to see it made properly in the West, with a lot more herbs than burghul. Somehow it is not natural for Westerners to regard parsley as an essential ingredient when they are used to it as a garnish. When I was a child I loved perching on the cool marble worktops in my grandmother's kitchen to help her bunch up the parsley, being very meticulous about aligning the sprigs where the leaves started, so that my grandmother could chop the parsley in neat slivers with a minimum of stalk attached. I also helped my mother in our kitchen, where we had the same worktops – most Lebanese kitchens at that time had white marble work surfaces. And today I chop the parsley exactly as my mother and grandmother did all those years ago. I hate to say it but there are no short cuts. Using a food processor to chop the herbs is not an option because it turns the herbs to mush. You just need to hone your knife skills, which you'll also need for dicing the tomatoes, plus a very sharp knife to avoid crushing them. As a final tip, drain the diced tomatoes before adding them to the salad. This will keep your tabbuleh crisp and make it last longer.

Serves 4–6

30g (1oz) fine burghul
600g (1lb 5oz) firm ripe tomatoes, diced into small cubes
50g (2oz) spring onions (about ½ bunch), trimmed
400g (14oz) flat-leaf parsley, most of the stalk discarded
70g (2½oz) mint, leaves picked from the stalks
¼ tsp ground cinnamon
½ tsp ground allspice or Lebanese seven-spice mixture
  (see page 331)
¼ tsp finely ground black pepper
Sea salt
Juice of 1 lemon or to taste
150ml (5fl oz) extra-virgin olive oil
4 Little Gem lettuces, quartered

Rinse the burghul in several changes of cold water, then drain well and put in a bowl. Stir with a fork every now and then to help fluff it up.

Put the diced tomatoes in a separate bowl and set aside while you thinly slice the spring onions and chop the herbs. A word of warning: do not chop the herbs with a mezzaluna – this will only bruise them. Instead, use a razor-sharp knife and gather as much as you can handle in a bunch and slice them very thin to end up with nice, crisp thin strips.

Drain the tomatoes of their juice and put in a large bowl. Add the spring onions and herbs and sprinkle the soaked burghul all over. Season with the cinnamon, allspice (or seven-spice mixture) and pepper, adding salt to taste. Add the lemon juice and olive oil and mix well. Taste and adjust the seasoning if necessary. Serve immediately with the quartered Little Gem lettuces.

Mushy Lentils and Rice

MUJADDARAH

Mujaddarah is a typical Lenten dish and a great vegetarian option for those who do not eat meat. My grandmother, who was more religious than my mother, often made it on a Friday, when Christians traditionally don't eat meat. I loved watching her fill white soup plates with the smooth brown mixture, then line them up on the white marble counter to let them cool before she handed them out to each of us with a big bowl of lemony cabbage and tomato salad. Like *lubyeh bil-zeyt* (see page 20), *mujaddarah* was one of my favourite family lunch dishes. It is also a typical dish to serve for lunch on spring-cleaning days, when it is put on to cook early in the morning and left to cool while the women of the house set about washing floors and beating the dust out of carpets. I was reminded of this the other day in London when my neighbour's housekeeper started beating the dust out of his drawing-room cushions on the loading bay opposite mine. It was a sound from the past!

Mujaddarah is normally served at room temperature with a salad (see page 28), raw onion and Arabic bread (see page 257) – all classic accompaniments. You can serve it in one big dish or, like my grandmother, in individual soup plates, where it sets like jelly with a very even top. And you can vary the recipe by puréeing the lentils before adding the onions and rice to make *mujaddarah m'saffayeh* ('sieved' *mujaddarah*). Simply drain the lentils, reserving the cooking water, then put them in a food processor and process until smooth. Return to the pan with the cooking water and finish as below.

Serves 4

400g (14oz) brown lentils, soaked for 30 minutes in
  cold water (enough to cover the lentils by
  2–3 fingers)
100ml (3½fl oz) extra-virgin olive oil
3 medium-sized onions, peeled and finely chopped
50g (2oz) short-grain white rice (bomba, Calasparra or
  Egyptian), rinsed under cold water and drained
1 tsp ground cinnamon or ground cumin
1 tsp ground allspice or Lebanese seven-spice mixture
  (see page 331)
½ tsp finely ground black pepper
Sea salt

Drain and rinse the lentils and put in a very large saucepan with 4 litres (7 pints) of water. Bring to the boil, then reduce the heat to medium – give the lentils a good stir in case some have stuck to the bottom of the pan – and leave the pot to bubble gently for 1 hour or until the lentils are tender and the water has reduced by two-thirds.

In the meantime, put the olive oil in a frying pan, place over a medium heat and when the oil is hot, fry the sliced onions until they become soft and transparent. Using a slotted spoon, transfer half of the softened onions onto a plate and continue frying the rest until they caramelise and turn a rich dark brown, without actually letting them burn. Remove with the slotted spoon and place on several layers of kitchen paper, spreading them out in a thin layer so that they drain well and become crisp.

When the lentils are cooked, add the rice to the pan. Tip in the softened onions and their frying oil, and season with the spices and a little salt. Simmer uncovered for 20 minutes, stirring regularly, until the rice is done and the mixture has thickened, but without letting it dry out. Taste and adjust the seasoning if necessary. Immediately pour the lentils and rice into a shallow serving bowl or into four deep plates, and allow to cool. Scatter the caramelised onions over the lentils before serving at room temperature.

Rice and Lentils

MUDARDARAH

The ingredients are more or less the same as for *mujaddarah* (see page 23) but the end result is very different – more like a risotto than a purée. I believe my mother learned to make this dish from my aunt Zahiyeh, with whom we spent our summers in Mashta el-Helou in the Syrian mountains (see page 83). In those days, only members of the family lived there, but now it is an over-developed bustling summer resort where people flock from all over Syria, Lebanon and elsewhere to enjoy the cool mountain breezes, lush vegetation and beautiful views. As for my aunt, she is long gone but I still remember her when I make this dish, and many others besides. She often replaced the rice with burghul. If you decide to make *mudardarah* with burghul instead of rice, you need to use the coarse variety and reduce the quantity to 100g (3½oz) while increasing the quantity of lentils to 200g (7oz). The rest of the recipe remains the same.

Serves 4

150g (5oz) brown lentils, soaked for 30 minutes in cold
   water (enough to cover the lentils by 2–3 fingers)
150ml (5fl oz) extra-virgin olive oil
3 medium-sized onions (about 300g/11oz total
   weight), peeled and thinly sliced

cont.

25

150g (5oz) short-grain white rice (bomba, Calasparra or
    Egyptian), rinsed under cold water and drained
½ tsp ground cinnamon
½ tsp ground allspice or Lebanese seven-spice mixture
    (see page 331)
½ tsp finely ground black pepper
Sea salt

Drain and rinse the lentils, then put in a large saucepan. Add
2 litres (3½ pints) of water and place over a medium-high heat.
Bring to the boil then reduce the heat to medium. Give the lentils
a good stir in case some have stuck to the bottom of the pan, cover
with a lid and simmer for 30–45 minutes or until the lentils are
nearly cooked.

While the lentils are cooking, heat the olive oil in a large frying
pan over a medium heat. (To check that the oil is hot, dip in an
onion slice; if the oil bubbles around it, it is hot enough.) Fry the
sliced onions until they caramelise and turn a rich brown, but
without letting them burn. Remove three-quarters of the onions
with a slotted spoon and leave to drain on a double layer of
kitchen paper. Spread them thinly so that they drain well and
become crispy.

Add the rice to the lentils, then season with the spices and a little
salt and bring back to the boil. Reduce the heat, stir in the onions
left in the frying pan, and their oil, then replace the lid on the
saucepan and simmer for 15 minutes. Turn off the heat, wrap the
lid in a clean tea towel, put it back over the pan and leave to sit
for 5 minutes.

Stir the lentils and rice before transferring to a serving dish. Scatter
the crisped onions over the top before serving hot with a white
cabbage salad (see page 28). You can serve this dish tepid or
even cold, in which case it's best to garnish with the crisped onions
at the last minute or they will go soft in the steam rising from the
lentils.

Pumpkin Dip
MUTABBAL QARA'

This dip comes from my wonderful Palestinian singer friend Reem Kelani, with whom I cooked when I wanted to learn more about Palestinian food. Reem made the dip with pumpkin, although I prefer to use butternut squash because the colour is more intense and the texture creamier and less watery – she also does this now; we seem to have come to the same conclusion separately. If you are going to use pumpkin, however, be sure to buy the right kind and avoid the stringy type. Kabocha, a winter squash rather like butternut that is also known as Japanese pumpkin, is my favourite. Reem made a quick harissa to garnish the dip, using dried pepper flakes and a little tomato paste, but you can use regular harissa or, even better, Turkish or Aleppo pepper paste (see page 313) diluted with a little olive oil.

Serves 6

1kg (2lb 2oz) kabocha or butternut squash, peeled,
    deseeded and cut into chunks
1 garlic clove, peeled and crushed
125ml (4½fl oz) tahini
Juice of 1 lemon or to taste
Sea salt

To garnish
Extra-virgin olive oil
Few sprigs of flat-leaf parsley, most of the stalk discarded,
    finely chopped
Pinch of ground cumin (optional)
Pepper paste (optional) (see page 326)

Steam the squash for about 40 minutes or until very soft. Leave it to drain in a colander until cold, pressing down on it, if necessary, to get rid of excess liquid. Put the cooked squash in a food processor. Add the garlic, tahini, lemon juice and a little salt, and process until smooth. Taste and adjust the seasoning if necessary.

27

Transfer the dip to a shallow serving bowl. Make a groove inside the outside rim of the bowl and drizzle olive oil into the groove. Garnish with some chopped parsley and a pinch of cumin (if using). Spread a spoonful of pepper paste (if using) across the middle and serve with flatbread.

Cabbage and Tomato Salad

SALATET MALFUF WA BANADURAH

One of my favourite salads, this is often served with *mujaddarah* (see page 23). You can make it just with cabbage, simply dressed with lemon juice, crushed garlic and olive oil, or you can add diced tomatoes, which my mother often did in summer when the tomatoes were at their best, and which I've done here, using cherry tomatoes for their more reliable flavour. I no longer add garlic to my dressing because I don't want to impose my garlic breath on others, but I have left it in the recipe for those who prefer to use it. The best cabbage to use here is either pointed spring cabbage, which I buy organic, or the flat Middle Eastern variety, which is even more tender but which you can only find in Lebanese or Turkish shops. I often add a sprinkling of Aleppo pepper to the basic dressing because I like the slight heat it gives the salad.

Serves 4–6

1 pointed spring cabbage (about 500g/1lb 1oz), trimmed
  of any damaged outer leaves and finely shredded
Handful of cherry tomatoes, quartered
1 garlic clove, peeled and crushed (optional)
Juice of 1 lemon or to taste
50ml (2fl oz) extra-virgin olive oil
Sea salt
½ tsp Aleppo pepper (see page 313) (optional)

Put the shredded cabbage and quartered tomatoes in a mixing bowl. Add the crushed garlic (if using), lemon juice and olive oil.

Season with salt and Aleppo pepper (if using) to taste and toss the salad, being careful not to crush the tomatoes. Taste and adjust the seasoning if necessary. Serve immediately.

Turkish Burghul Salad
KISSIR

Kissir is the Turkish version of tabbuleh (see page 22), with burghul and tomatoes being the main ingredients rather than parsley and tomatoes, which form the basis of tabbuleh. I am convinced that *kissir* is at the root of how tabbuleh came to be misinterpreted in the West as a grain salad. A food writer must have confused the two recipes, giving a recipe for *kissir* as one for tabbuleh, and the mistake stuck until very recently when cookbook authors, chefs and ready-meal producers finally understood that tabbuleh is a herb salad and not a grain one. This is not to say that *kissir* is inferior to tabbuleh in any way; it is just as scrumptious and healthy, with an intriguing sweet and sour taste imparted by the pomegranate syrup dressing. You can use lemon juice instead, if you prefer, which will give the salad a more straightforward tart flavour. I have adapted this recipe from one in my friend Nevin Halıcı's *Turkish Cookbook*, though there are many variations. If you want to make it with pepper paste, for instance, omit the Aleppo pepper and stir in 1–2 tablespoons pepper paste (see page 326) with the pomegranate syrup and oil before using to dress the salad.

Serves 4–6

200g (7oz) fine burghul
2 small Spanish onions (about 150g/5oz total weight), peeled and very finely chopped
5 medium-sized firm ripe tomatoes (about 500g/1lb 1oz total weight), deseeded and diced into 1cm (½in) cubes
½ small green bell or Marmara pepper, deseeded and finely diced

cont.

Few sprigs of flat-leaf parsley, most of the stalk
   discarded, finely chopped
4 tbsp extra-virgin olive oil
1 tsp Aleppo pepper (see page 313)
1½ tbsp pomegranate syrup (see page 327) or
   3 tbsp lemon juice
Sea salt to taste

Put the burghul in a large mixing bowl and stir in 200ml (7fl oz) of boiling water a few spoonfuls at a time. Cover with a tea towel and leave to sit for 15 minutes.

When the time is up, stir the chopped onions into the burghul. Add the remaining ingredients and mix well. Taste, adjusting the seasoning if necessary, and serve immediately.

Stuffed Courgettes and Aubergines
MEHSHI KUSSA WA BATINJEN

Mehshi is possibly my all-time favourite dish for eating *en famille* – a homely yet sophisticated recipe that is as delicious as it is utterly satisfying. My grandmother often prepared it for us when we visited for lunch, and my mother always makes it for me when I return to Beirut. It is important to use the pale green courgettes sold in Middle Eastern shops. They are less watery than the regular dark green ones. It is also a good idea to select aubergines and courgettes that are more or less the same size for an elegant presentation; and of course choose ones that are very fresh. In Syria, some people cook the stuffed vegetables in a tomato sauce, but I prefer water, as in the recipe below, placing ripe tomatoes on the bottom of the pan to add both colour and flavour to the resulting sauce. And like my grandmother and mother, I also line the bottom of the pan with bones to enrich the cooking broth, although this is optional. An interesting variation on the courgettes is to use *'ajur*, a variety of gourd that appears in the spring for a very fleeting season. Slightly bitter and with a striped skin, it is used by Syrian cooks to make this dish, stuffed with either rice or *frikeh* ('burnt' cracked wheat – see page 4). Perhaps one day an enterprising gardener will start planting *'ajur* here, in which case I urge you use it as it is more interesting than courgettes with a more distinctive flavour.

Serves 8–10

1.2kg (2lb 10oz) medium-sized pale green courgettes
  (about 20 in total)
1kg (2lb 2oz) small aubergines (about 20 in total)
3–4 lamb bones (optional), rinsed under cold water
300g (11oz) ripe tomatoes, peeled and sliced
1kg (2lb 2oz) plain yoghurt, to serve

For the stuffing
200g (7oz) short-grain white rice (bomba, Calasparra or
  Egyptian), rinsed under cold water and drained
300g (11oz) freshly minced lean lean lamb, from the
  shoulder or shanks (either ask your butcher to mince
  the lamb, or do it yourself using the fine attachment
  on a meat grinder)
1 × 400g can of Italian chopped tomatoes
½ tsp ground cinnamon
1 tsp ground allspice or Lebanese seven-spice mixture
  (see page 331)
1 tsp finely ground black pepper
Fine sea salt

First prepare the courgettes and aubergines. Cut off and discard the stem end of each of the courgettes and shave off the brown skin at the bottom. Cut off and discard the stem ends of the aubergines and remove any husks capping the skin. Next fill a large bowl with cold water in which to plunge the vegetables once they've been cored.

Holding one courgette firmly in your hand with your fingers wrapped around it and the cut top uppermost, insert a narrow apple corer (or a special Lebanese corer, if you can get hold of one) into the cut top and push down as close to the edge as possible

31

(2–3mm/⅛in from the skin) and keep pushing until the corer is halfway down the courgette. Take out, insert the corer again next to the first incision and repeat until you cut a rosette all the way down the courgette, but leaving the bottom intact. Twirl the corer inside the courgette to loosen the pulp, and pull out the first piece. Slide it off the corer into a bowl (saving the pulp to make the courgette omelettes on page 64), then insert again and, with a circular motion, scrape the sides and bottom to remove as much pulp as possible, leaving walls 2–3mm (⅛in) thick. Do this gently and carefully, gradually extracting the pulp, or else you will split the top or pierce the sides or bottom of the courgette.

Plunge the cored courgette in the bowl of cold water, filling the inside with water. Finish coring the courgettes and leave to soak while you core the aubergines the same way. (You can use the aubergine pulp for a variation on the courgette omelettes, remembering to sauté it longer as it won't cook so quickly.) Place the cored aubergines in the bowl of water and leave to soak with the courgettes while you make the stuffing.

Put the rice in a mixing bowl and add the minced meat and chopped tomatoes. Season with the spices and a little salt, and mix together with your hands so that all the ingredients are well blended. Pinch off a little of the mixture and sear in a hot pan to taste, then adjust the seasoning if necessary.

Line the bottom of a very large saucepan, big enough to accommodate comfortably all the stuffed aubergines and courgettes half standing in one layer, with the bones (if using) and sliced tomatoes.

Drain and rinse the aubergines and courgettes under cold water. Take hold of a courgette or aubergine and hold it upright, cupping your hand around it. Scoop up a little of the stuffing with your other hand and gently push it inside the cored vegetable, using your finger to force it down. Every now and then, shake the vegetable in a downward motion to make sure the filling is well inside it (or push the filling in further with your little finger). Fill up to three-quarters, to leave enough room for the rice to expand, and place in the pan with the open end slightly raised – use the bones or tomato pulp to prop it up.

Continue filling and arranging both the aubergines and the courgettes, first lining them around the side of the pan, then filling up the inside, until you have used up both vegetables and stuffing. (If you have a little stuffing left over, cook it separately in double its volume of water and serve it on the side.)

Pour a little water in the empty stuffing bowl, swirl it around to extract the last bits of flavouring and pour over the vegetables to barely cover them. (The level of the water should come to about 2cm/¾in below the tops of the vegetables.) Add a little salt, bearing in mind that the stuffing is already seasoned. Cover the pan with a lid and place over a high heat. Bring to the boil then reduce the heat to medium and let the stuffed vegetables bubble gently for 45 minutes or until it is done. Two-thirds of the way through, taste the broth and add more salt if necessary.

Once done, let the courgettes and aubergines sit, covered, for about 10 minutes before transferring to a serving dish. The best way to lift the soft, cooked vegetables intact is to carefully lever them out using your hand and a spoon. Cool the fingers of one hand in cold water and gently pull away one stuffed vegetable while sliding the spoon underneath it. Lift the vegetable, holding it against the spoon with your fingers, and place on a serving platter. Repeat with the remaining vegetables, arranging them on the plate. Ladle the sauce into a sauceboat and spoon the yoghurt into a bowl and serve with the hot stuffed vegetables, along with some pita bread.

Stuffed Swiss Chard
MEHSHI SILQ BIL-ZEYT

Traditionally this vegetarian stuffing includes chickpeas, which are soaked overnight, skinned and split. I don't like their crunchy bite, finding it an unpleasant contrast to the melting rice and velvety leaves, and so I always make mine without chickpeas. I even made my mother stop using them! In the south of Lebanon, they leave out the lemon juice and olive oil and increase the amount of sumac to 3 tablespoons. I have never tried it that way, but I can't imagine it to be an improvement, as this recipe, which is my mother's, is perfect as it is.

Serves 4

1kg (2lb 2oz) Swiss chard (about 2 bunches, as sold in
  Middle Eastern shops)
1 large ripe tomato, sliced

For the stuffing
150g (5oz) short-grain white rice (bomba, Calasparra or
  Egyptian), rinsed under cold water and drained
300g (11oz) firm ripe tomatoes, diced into 5mm (½in)
  cubes
50g (2oz) spring onions (about ½ bunch), trimmed and
  finely chopped
100g (3½oz) flat-leaf parsley (about ½ bunch), most of
  the stalk discarded, chopped medium-fine
50g (2oz) mint (about ¼ bunch), leaves picked from the
  stalks and chopped medium-fine
2 tbsp ground sumac (see page 331)
¼ tsp ground cinnamon
½ tsp ground allspice or Lebanese seven-spice mixture
  (see page 331)
¼ tsp finely ground black pepper
Sea salt
Juice of 1 large lemon or to taste
150ml (5fl oz) extra-virgin olive oil

First prepare the Swiss chard. Cut off the stalks and then cut each leaf into three pieces: first cut across the top third of the leaf, taking where the spine becomes thin and pliable as a dividing line, then slice off and remove the thick spine, leaving two more pieces of chard leaf. The cut pieces should make rolls 8–15cm (3–6in) long. Some leaves may be too small to cut in three, in which case simply cut them in two, again taking where the spine becomes thin as a dividing line. Slice off the back of the thick spine of the bottom parts without breaking the leaf and reserve the stems and stalks to line the bottom of the pan (or save the stalks, if in good condition, to make a salad).

Arrange the cut leaves, smooth side down, in neat layers inside a colander. Then run boiling water over them to soften them. Allow the leaves to drain while you line the bottom of a large saucepan – big enough to hold the stuffed leaves – with the tomato slices and stems and stalks from the chard leaves.

Next make the stuffing. Place the rice in a mixing bowl and add the diced tomatoes, spring onions, parsley and mint. Season with the sumac, cinnamon, allspice (or seven-spice mixture) and pepper, adding salt to taste. Add the lemon juice and olive oil and mix well – the stuffing should look like a salad. Taste and adjust the seasoning if necessary.

To stuff the chard leaves, first remove any damaged leaves from the colander and lay them over the stalks and tomato slices in the pan. Next take one of the undamaged leaves and lay it, smooth side down, on your work surface with the cut side nearest to you and the veins running away from you. Spread 1 teaspoon of stuffing (or more depending on the size of the leaf) in a long, thin and slightly raised line, the thickness of your little finger, along the side facing you, about 1cm (½in) from the edge (leaving a narrow strip) and from the end of the leaf on either side.

Fold the narrow strip of leaf over the stuffing and roll into a flat and loosely packed roll so that the rice has enough room to expand. Flatten the empty edges, then carefully lift the rolled leaf and lay over the tomatoes with the loose flap facing down. Continue stuffing, rolling and arranging the stuffed leaves side by side, forming one layer at a time, until you have used up the leaves and/or the stuffing. If you have any stuffing left over, put it in a small pan, cover with water and cook over a low heat to serve on the side. Use any leftover leaves to cover the rolled ones.

Pour enough water into the pan to just cover the stuffed leaves and add a little salt, bearing in mind that the stuffing is already seasoned. Cover the leaves with an overturned heatproof plate to stop them from unrolling during cooking. Then cover the pan with a lid and place over a high heat. Bring to the boil, then reduce the heat to medium and let the pot bubble gently for 45 minutes or until the stuffing is done (see next step). Two-thirds of the way through cooking, taste the broth to check the salt content, adding more if necessary.

35

When the 45 minutes are up, it is a good idea to taste a filled leaf to make sure the rice is done. If it is cooked through, turn off the heat and allow to cool before transferring the leaves delicately to a serving dish. I usually pick them up with my fingers to keep them intact; if you don't like using your fingers, you could use a spoon instead – you may need two spoons for the longest leaves. Serve at room temperature.

Stuffed Vine Leaves on a Bed of Lamb Chops

MEHSHI WARAQ 'ENAB BIL-KASTALETTAH

Stuffed vine leaves are best when prepared with fresh leaves, but the season (late spring/early summer) is short. Frozen leaves are the next best option, although these are normally prepared at home and not available to buy. Failing that, you need to resort to preserved vine leaves. I prefer those that are vacuum packed because they are less salty than those preserved in brine. Often both are widely available, however, and can be bought all year round. Preserved leaves are bigger than fresh ones. When using those preserved in brine, be sparing with the salt. They remain quite salty even after rinsing under cold water. You need to allow a fair amount of time to prepare this dish, although this will depend largely on the speed at which you roll the vine leaves. A practised cook will stuff and roll the leaves in the recipe below in an hour, while a novice or less practised cook may take nearly twice as long. I belong to the latter camp not because I am a novice but mainly because I don't prepare the dish that often. As a result, I am rather slow at rolling the leaves. Regardless, it is a wonderful party piece and well worth the effort.

Serves 4

8 thin lamb chops (about 600g/1lb 5oz total weight),
    most of the fatty bits trimmed
Sea salt
1 cinnamon stick
200g (7oz) medium-sized fresh or preserved vine leaves
Stock from cooking the lamb chops
Juice of 1 lemon or to taste

For the stuffing
125g (4½oz) short-grain white rice (bomba, Calasparra or
    Egyptian), rinsed under cold water and drained
200g (7oz) freshly minced lean lamb, from the shoulder or
    neck (either ask your butcher to mince the lamb or do it
    yourself using the fine attachment on a meat grinder)
2 tbsp water
¼ tsp ground cinnamon
½ tsp ground allspice or Lebanese seven-spice mixture
    (see page 331)
¼ tsp finely ground black pepper

Put the lamb chops in a saucepan, cover with water and place over
a medium heat. As the water is about to boil, skim away any scum
that rises to the surface, then add a little salt and the cinnamon.
Cover the pan with a lid, reduce the heat and let the stock bubble
gently for 15 minutes. Lift the chops out onto a plate, strain and
reserve the stock for later.

Meanwhile, make the stuffing. Place the rice in a mixing bowl,
add the minced meat and water and season with the spices and
a little salt. Mix with your hands to blend well. Pinch off a little
mixture and sear in a hot pan to taste, then adjust the seasoning
if necessary.

Choose a pan with straight sides and large enough to arrange
the lamb chops in a tight even layer on the bottom. Put the vine
leaves (fresh or preserved) in a colander and run boiling water over
them. This will soften them and make them easier to roll. If you
are using preserved leaves, rinse these beforehand in cold water,
at least a couple of times, in order to get rid of some of the
briny taste.

Take one vine leaf, cut and discard any stem and lay it flat on your work surface, smooth side down with the stem end nearest to you. Arrange ½–1½ teaspoons of stuffing, depending on the size of the leaf, in a thin raised line along the side of the leaf facing you. The line should be thinner than your little finger, set about 1.5cm (⅝in) away from the edge of the leaf and from the end of the leaf on either side. Fold each side over the rice, in a line that slightly tapers towards the bottom, then fold and tuck the top edges over the stuffing and roll from the stem end, neatly but loosely in order to leave enough space for the rice to expand during cooking.

Place the rolled leaf, loose edge down, over the lamb chops, on one side of the pan. Continue filling, rolling and arranging the vine leaves, side by side, lining the sides of the pan first and making one layer at a time, until you used all the leaves. If you have any leftover stuffing, put it in a small pan, add an equivalent amount of water and cook for 20 minutes to serve on the side.

Pour some, or all, of the reserved stock over the rolled leaves until they are barely immersed. If you do not have enough stock, add water. Add a little salt, bearing in mind the saltiness of the vine leaves, and shake the pan to swirl the water and dissolve the salt. Put an overturned heatproof plate over the leaves, to stop them from unrolling during cooking, cover the pan with a lid and place over a medium-high heat. Bring to the boil, then reduce the heat to medium and let the pot bubble gently for 50 minutes. Add the lemon juice and cook for another 10 minutes. It is a good idea to test one vine leaf, before you take them off the heat, to make sure the rice is properly cooked. Remove from the heat and leave to sit, covered, on a work surface for about 10 minutes.

The traditional way of serving this dish is to turn out the contents of the pan onto a serving platter as if it were a cake, and this is why you need a pan with straight sides. You'll also need to wear heatproof gloves while performing this operation. First pour out the cooking juices into a bowl while holding back the stuffed vine leaves using the plate covering them. Remove the plate and place a big round, flat serving platter over the top of the pan. Hold it firmly against the pan with the flat of one hand. Slide the pan slowly over the edge of the work surface and put your other hand underneath it. Lift the pan off and quickly turn it upside down, then slide the platter onto your worktop and slowly lift the pan off to uncover a 'cake' of cooked stuffed vine leaves topped with the juicy lamb chops.

Alternatively, you can spoon the rolled leaves out, a few at a time, and arrange them in neat layers in a serving dish, putting the lamb chops on top or all around them. Baste with some of the cooking juice and serve immediately with a bowl of yoghurt.

Citrusy Petits Pois, Carrot and Lamb Stew

YAKHNET BAZELLA WA JAZAR

I was always delighted when my mother announced that we had *yakhneh* (stew) for lunch and in particular when it was this delectable one with its unusual taste of orange peel that is so well suited to the carrots and peas. (For more on the use of citrus peel in Levantine cooking, see page 317.) I now make it quite differently from my mother, however, using Chantenay carrots which are small enough to keep whole for a prettier presentation. If I can't find any, I simply cut larger carrots in half across then again in half lengthways. I also use frozen petits pois that I thaw in boiling water, drain and add to the stew at the very end to keep the vivid colour. To thicken the sauce and keep it tasting fresh, I use canned cherry tomatoes that I first drain thoroughly to minimise the cooking time. My mother, like everyone in Lebanon, uses fresh tomatoes. I would probably do the same if I lived in a country where the tomatoes are good. Sadly, this is not the case in England except possibly for two months of the year at the height of summer.

Serves 4–6

50g (2oz) unsalted butter
1 medium-sized onion, peeled and finely chopped
2 lamb shanks

cont.

2 × 400g cans of Italian cherry tomatoes, drained
Peel of 1 small unwaxed orange
6–8cm (2½–3in) strip of unwaxed lemon peel
½ tsp ground cinnamon
½ tsp ground allspice or Lebanese seven-spice mixture
  (see page 331)
¼ tsp finely ground black pepper
Sea salt
300g (11oz) Chanteney or baby carrots
500g (1lb 1oz) frozen petits pois, defrosted (or fresh
  when in season)

Melt the butter in a large saucepan over a medium-high heat.
Add the onion and sauté until golden, then place the meat in the
pan and brown on all sides.

Add the tomatoes, orange and lemon peel, and season with the
spices and a little salt. Bring to the boil, then reduce the heat to
low, cover the pan with a lid and cook for 45 minutes, stirring
occasionally.

Add the carrots and simmer, covered, for 10 minutes then discard
the orange and lemon peel. By now the sauce should have
thickened. If it hasn't, uncover the pan and boil until it is quite
thick. Add the petits pois and simmer for another 5 minutes or
until the peas are done. Serve hot, either with good bread or with
vermicelli rice (see below).

Vermicelli Rice

REZZ BIL-SH'AYRIYEH

Here is a fun variation on regular rice in which toasted vermicelli
is cooked with the rice. Vermicelli rice is normally served with
meats cooked in a yoghurt or tahini sauce, but I like to serve it
with the carrot and pea stew on page 39.

Serves 6

25g (1oz) unsalted butter
30g (1oz) dried vermicelli, broken into pieces about
    2cm (¾in) long
200g (7oz) white short-grain white rice (bomba,
    Calasparra or Egyptian), rinsed under cold water
    and drained
Sea salt

Melt the butter in a saucepan over a medium heat. Add the
vermicelli and fry, stirring constantly, until the pasta is golden
brown. Add the rice and mix well.

Pour in 400ml (14fl oz) of water and season with salt. Bring to
the boil, then reduce the heat to low, cover the pan with a lid and
simmer for 15 minutes or until the rice is done and the water
completely absorbed. Wrap the lid in a clean tea towel, replace
over the pan and leave to sit for 5 minutes. Serve hot.

Kibbeh Pie

KIBBEH BIL-SANIYEH

Sadly, I have just lost my Lebanese butcher in London who
prepared the mince for my *kibbeh*. Taken from a leg of lamb that is
first boned, skinned and trimmed of fat, the meat is passed twice
through the fine attachment of a meat grinder. It seems a crime to
mince meat from such a luxurious joint, but minced meat is not
considered a cheap option in the Levant. Quite the opposite. Some
of the most celebratory dishes, including *kibbeh*, are made with it,
and the meat for these dishes is always chosen from a very lean
part, namely the top of the leg. The fillet is normally reserved for
kebabs (see page 323) or to make *bastirma* (a type of spiced cured
meat). There are dozens of different ways of preparing *kibbeh*; this
is one of my favourites.

41

Serves 4–6

For the stuffing
60g (2oz) pine nuts
200g (7oz) lamb from the leg, boned, skinned and
    trimmed of fat
60g (2oz) unsalted butter, plus extra for greasing
5 medium-sized onions (about 500g/1lb 1oz total weight),
    peeled and finely chopped
1 tsp pomegranate syrup (see page 327)
2 tsp ground cinnamon
2 tsp ground allspice or Lebanese seven-spice mixture
    (see page 331)
½ tsp finely ground black pepper
Sea salt

For the *kibbeh*
500g (1lb 1oz) lamb from the leg, boned, skinned and
    trimmed of fat
1 medium-sized onion, peeled and quartered
2 tsp ground cinnamon
2 tsp ground allspice or Lebanese seven-spice mixture
    (see page 331)
½ tsp finely ground black pepper
200g (7oz) fine burghul, rinsed under cold water and
    drained
Baking dish measuring 25cm (10in) in diameter and
    5cm (2in) deep

To make the stuffing, first preheat the oven to 220°C (425°F),
gas mark 7.

Spread the pine nuts on a non-stick baking sheet and toast in the
oven for 5–7 minutes or until golden brown. Remove from the
oven and set aside. Leave the oven switched on for baking the pie,
reducing the heat to 200°C (400°F), gas mark 6.

To prepare the meat for the stuffing and the *kibbeh*, first put the
lamb through a fine mincer, or ask your butcher to do this for you,
if you prefer. You can mince the meat in a blender but you have to
be careful not to process it too much or it will become too smooth
and not only lose texture but also be more difficult to shape,

especially if you are making *kibbeh* balls. Once you have minced the lamb, drag a serrated knife through the meat to catch any sizeable bits of ligament. Wipe these off the blade and drag the knife through the meat a few more times until you stop picking up any further pieces.

Melt the butter in a large frying pan. Add the chopped onions and fry, stirring regularly, until lightly golden. Add 200g (7oz) of minced lamb and cook – mashing and stirring it with a wooden spoon or fork to break up the lumps – until it loses all traces of pink. Take off the heat and add the pomegranate syrup. Season with the spices and a little salt, then stir in the toasted pine nuts. Pinch off a little of the mixture and sear in a hot pan to taste, then adjust the seasoning if necessary.

Next make the *kibbeh*. Put the quartered onion in a blender and process until completely pulverised. Add the remaining 500g (1lb 1oz) of minced meat, along with the spices and a little salt, and blend until smooth. If your blender is not big enough to take the onion and meat in one go, process them in two equal-sized batches. Prepare a bowl of lightly salted cold water and have it to hand before transferring the meat to a mixing bowl.

Add the burghul to the meat and mix together with your hand, dipping it every now and then in the salted water to moisten your hand and add a little water to the *kibbeh* to soften it. Knead for about 3 minutes or until you have a smooth mixture. Pinch off a little of the *kibbeh* and sear in a hot pan to taste, adjusting the seasoning if necessary.

Grease the baking dish with a knob of butter and divide the *kibbeh* into two equal-sized pieces. Moisten your hands in the salted water and pinch off a handful of *kibbeh* from one piece. Flatten it between your palms, to a thickness of about 5mm (¼in), and place it on the bottom of the baking dish, along one side. Smooth it down evenly with your fingers. Pinch off another handful from the same piece, flatten and lay next to the first piece, slightly overlapping it. Dip your fingers in the water and smooth the pieces together until the joint disappears, to ensure that they don't come apart during cooking. Continue the above process until you have finished the first half of *kibbeh* and covered the bottom of the dish. Then go over the whole layer with moistened fingers to even it out.

43

Spread the stuffing evenly over the *kibbeh* and then lay the other half of the *kibbeh* over the stuffing in the same way as above. You might find the top layer slightly more difficult to do as you will be laying it over the loose stuffing instead of the smooth surface of the baking dish, but you will soon get the hang of it.

Cut the pie into quarters, then with a sharp knife make shallow incisions to draw a geometric pattern – such as small lozenges, squares or thin stripes – across the top of each quarter. The decorative work is time consuming and can be omitted without affecting the taste, although the presentation will not be so attractive or as traditional. After you have finished decorating the pie, make a hole in the middle with your finger, going all the way through. Place a knob of butter over the hole and one on each quarter of the pie.

Bake in the oven for 15 minutes. Let the pie sit for a few minutes before serving hot with a yoghurt and cucumber dip (see page 215).

Kibbeh Balls in Yoghurt Sauce

KIBBEH BI-LABNIYEH

Kibbeh freezes very well. You could make the balls well ahead of time and freeze them, so that all you have to do on the day is to make the yoghurt sauce. Before serving, drop the just-thawed *kibbeh* balls into the hot yoghurt, where they will cook in minutes. You can also vary the sauce by replacing the coriander with fresh or dried mint, for which you will need 30g (1oz) of the fresh leaves, finely chopped, or 3 tablespoons of the dried herb. I very rarely use mint in my yoghurt sauce as I like the taste of coriander and find that it works with both the cooked yoghurt and the various meats or stuffed vegetables that are cooked in the sauce.

Serves 4–6

1 quantity of cooked *kibbeh* (see page 42)
1 quantity of cooked *kibbeh* stuffing (see page 42)

For the yoghurt sauce
25g (1oz) unsalted butter
100g (3½oz) fresh coriander (about ½ bunch), most of
   the stalk discarded, finely chopped
7 large garlic cloves, peeled and crushed
1kg (2lb 2oz) plain yoghurt (preferably goat's)
1 medium-sized organic egg, whisked
Sea salt

Divide the *kibbeh* into 20 equal-sized pieces and roll them into balls, each the size of a large plum. Lightly moisten your hands in salted water (dipping them in the bowl of water used during the preparation of the *kibbeh*) and place a *kibbeh* ball in the palm of one hand. With the index finger of your other hand burrow a hole into the ball while rotating it – this makes the hollowing out easier and more even. You should produce a thin meat shell resembling a topless egg. Be careful not to pierce the bottom or sides of the *kibbeh* shell.

Put 1½–2 teaspoons of stuffing inside the *kibbeh* shell, gently pushing the stuffing in with a finger, then pinch the open edges together. Cupping your hands around the *kibbeh* ball, gently shape it into an ovoid ball with slightly pointed ends. Put the finished ball on a non-stick baking sheet. Continue making the balls until you have used up both *kibbeh* mixture and stuffing – if you have any stuffing left, serve it warm on the side or topped with fried eggs. Place the *kibbeh* balls in the fridge or freezer, if you have the space, to firm them up.

To make the yoghurt sauce, first melt the butter in a frying pan over a medium heat. Add the chopped coriander and crushed garlic and sauté for 1 minute or until the mixture becomes aromatic, then remove from the heat, cover with a clean tea towel and set aside.

Put the yoghurt in a large heavy-based saucepan. Add the whisked egg and a little salt. Mix well and place over a medium heat. Bring to the boil, stirring constantly to help prevent the yoghurt from curdling. (Goat's milk yoghurt, which I always use, is less likely to curdle, but it still does if you are not careful.) When the yoghurt has come to the boil, reduce the heat to low and simmer for 3 minutes, still stirring.

Carefully slide the *kibbeh* balls into the sauce and simmer for 10–15 minutes, stirring very regularly to stop the yoghurt curdling. Add the coriander and garlic mixture and simmer for another minute or so. Serve hot with vermicelli rice (see page 40) or with good bread.

Lentils and Aubergines Cooked in Pomegranate Juice

RUMMANIYYAH

There is a wonderful moment in the autumn when you can buy ready-squeezed pomegranate juice in the markets in both Aleppo and Damascus that home cooks use to make this delicious vegetarian dish. I doubt you will find this in the West, however, so you will need to squeeze your own. You also need to make sure you are using sour pomegranates and not the sweet ones. If you do not have access to fresh pomegranate juice, use a combination of pomegranate syrup (see page 327) and lemon juice (3 tablespoons of pomegranate syrup to 80ml/3fl oz of lemon juice) and dilute in 1 cup of water.

Serves 5–6

200g (7oz) brown lentils, soaked for 30 minutes in cold
    water (enough to cover the lentils by 2–3 fingers)
Seeds from 3 sour pomegranates, plus extra to garnish
50g (2oz) unbleached plain flour
1 tbsp fennel seeds
2 whole dried red chillis or 2 tsp dried chilli flakes
5 garlic cloves, peeled

Sea salt
2 medium-sized onions, peeled, one finely chopped and
   the other thinly sliced
120ml (4½fl oz) extra-virgin olive oil
500g (1lb 1oz) aubergines, cut into 2.5cm (1in) cubes
1 tsp ground cumin
2 tbsp tahini

Drain the lentils and boil in 500ml (18fl oz) of water for approximately 15 minutes. Strain, reserving the water, and set aside.

Put the pomegranate seeds in a food processor. Add 2 tablespoons of water and process until the seeds are completely pulverised. Strain and mix with the flour until you have a smooth mixture.

Crush the fennel seeds and dried chilli with a pestle and mortar, then add the garlic and 1 teaspoon of salt and pound until you have a smooth paste.

In a large saucepan, sauté the chopped onions in half the olive oil until golden. Add the aubergines and continue to sauté until soft and wilted. This will take about 10 minutes.

Tip in the lentils and their water and let the mixture bubble gently for about 7 minutes. Then slowly add the pomegranate juice and flour mixture while stirring continuously. Add the crushed spices and cumin and keep stirring until thickened. Next add the tahini and continue stirring for another 5 minutes. Take off the heat, pour into a large serving bowl or 5–6 individual ones and leave to cool.

In a separate pan, fry the sliced onion in the remaining olive oil until golden. Garnish the serving bowl (or individual bowls) with the fried onions. Scatter pomegranate seeds all over and serve at room temperature with Arabic bread (see page 257) and olives.

Kibbeh Balls with Quince in a Fresh Pomegranate Sauce

KIBBEH SFARJALIYEH

Syrians love cooking with fresh pomegranate juice when pomegranates are in season. There are market stalls that sell only pomegranates, both the sour type, which is called *leffan*, and the sweet type, which is eaten as it is or juiced and sold in the juice bars. Syrians are keen on fresh produce and rarely prepare dishes outside of the season in which particular fruits or vegetables are at their best. Some home cooks freeze fresh pomegranate juice to use out of season, but quince doesn't freeze very well, which makes this *kibbeh* dish one that is special for autumn, when quinces are in season. More like a soup than a stew, it has a very delicate sweet and sour flavour.

Serves 4–6

250g (9oz) lamb, taken from the shanks
5 cardamom pods
1 cinnamon stick
5 peppercorns
1 medium-sized onion, peeled and studded with
   4 cloves
Sea salt

For the sauce
Seeds from 1kg (2lb 2oz) sour pomegranates
50g (2oz) golden caster sugar
1.5kg (3lb 5oz) quinces, cored, peeled and cut into
   wedges

For the *kibbeh* balls
100g (3½oz) cold unsalted butter, diced into 2cm (¾in)
   cubes
½ tsp ground cinnamon
½ tsp allspice
½ quantity of uncooked *kibbeh* (see page 42)

First make the sauce. Put the pomegranate seeds in a food processor with 2 tablespoons water and process until the seeds are completely pulverised. Next put the sugar and 125ml (4½fl oz) of water in a large saucepan. Add the wedges of quince and place over a medium heat.

Cover the pan with a lid and cook for 15 minutes, shaking the pan every now and then to coat the quince in the syrup. Add the pomegranate juice, lower the heat to medium-low and simmer for another hour or until the quinces are tender. By then they should have turned a beautiful pink colour.

Meanwhile, make the *kibbeh* balls. Put the butter cubes in a mixing bowl, add the cinnamon and allspice and gently toss to evenly coat the butter with the spices. Prepare a bowl of lightly salted cold water and have it to hand.

Divide the ½ quantity of *kibbeh* into 12 pieces and roll them into balls, each the size of a walnut. Lightly moisten your hands in the salted water and place one *kibbeh* ball in the palm of one hand. With the index finger of your other hand burrow a hole into the ball while rotating it – this makes the hollowing out easier and more even – taking care not to pierce the bottom or sides of the *kibbeh* shell.

Place a cube of seasoned butter into the *kibbeh* shell and seal the meat around the butter. Gently roll the *kibbeh* to create a round ball a little smaller than a ping-pong ball. Finish making the *kibbeh* balls and refrigerate to firm them up.

Put the lamb in another saucepan and cover with water. Place over a medium heat and bring to the boil. As the water is coming to the boil, skim any scum that rises to the surface. Add the spices, onion and some salt and simmer, covered with a lid, for 1 hour. Strain the meat, onion and spices, reserving the cooking broth, and discard the spices and onion.

Place the cooked lamb in a clean pan, add the strained stock with the cooked quinces and their juice, and place over a medium-low heat. When the cooking broth is simmering, carefully drop in the *kibbeh* balls and taste the broth, adding more sugar if it is too sour. Adjust the salt, if needed, and simmer for 5 minutes. Serve very hot in soup plates, making sure each diner gets equal amounts of lamb, quince and *kibbeh*.

Chicken Fatteh

FATTET DJEJ

Fatta means 'to break into pieces' in Arabic, and *fatteh* (also known as *fatta* depending on the country or the accent) describes a composite dish made up of pieces of toasted pita topped with meat, vegetables and/or pulses, covered with yoghurt and garnished with toasted pine nuts. The dish is a typical street breakfast in Lebanon, although it is eaten at other times of day too, and there are many variations depending on the time it is served, the region or the family. Here I give a version of the dish using chicken, but you can easily make it with lamb instead. Replace the chicken with a shoulder of lamb, skinned and trimmed of fat, or 1kg (2lb 2oz) neck fillets, and prepare in the same way, bearing in mind that you may have to cook the lamb for a little longer. The traditional method is to use dried chickpeas that you soak and then cook with the meat, but I like to simplify things if I can and I now use ready-cooked chickpeas that are preserved in brine in a jar without any preservatives. All I do is rinse them well before adding them to the stock and cooked meat to heat them through. In that time, they absorb the taste of the stock and you won't know the difference between chickpeas you've cooked from scratch and ready-cooked ones.

Serves 4

1 medium-sized chicken (about 1.5kg/3lb 5oz)
1 cinnamon stick
Coarse sea salt
1 large round pita bread, opened at the seams
    (see page 234)
100g (3½oz) pine nuts

1 × 675g jar of chickpeas preserved in salted water
    (475g/16½oz drained weight), rinsed under cold water
    and drained
1 garlic clove, peeled and crushed
Handful of mint leaves, crushed with the garlic (optional)
1kg (2lb 2oz) plain yoghurt

Put the chicken in a large saucepan, add 1.25 litres (2¼ pints)
of water and place over a medium heat. As the water comes to the
boil, skim any scum that rises to the surface. Once it has come
to the boil, reduce the heat, then add the cinnamon stick and
1 tablespoon of salt and cover the pan with a lid. Let the stock
bubble gently for 45 minutes or until the chicken is done.

Meanwhile, preheat the oven to 220°C (425°F), gas mark 7.

Toast the bread in the oven until golden brown, then remove and
allow to cool. Spread the pine nuts on a baking sheet and toast
them in the oven at the same time for 5–7 minutes or until golden
brown.

Remove the chicken from the saucepan and strain the stock into
a clean pan. Then skin the chicken and take the meat off the bone
before cutting it into bite-sized pieces. Add these to the stock
together with the chickpeas and place over a low heat.

Mix the crushed garlic (and mint, if using) into the yoghurt and
add salt to taste.

Break the toasted bread into bite-sized pieces and spread over the
bottom of a serving dish. Spread the hot chicken pieces and
chickpeas over the bread. (You can at this stage add a little stock,
although I prefer not to because I like the bread to stay crisp.)
Cover with the yoghurt and garnish with the toasted pine nuts,
then serve immediately.

Lentil Kibbeh

MERCIMEKLI KÖFTE

Here is a very simple vegetarian version of *kibbeh* (see page 42) that is claimed by both Turks and Armenians, which is not surprising given that south-eastern Turkey had a sizeable Armenian community until they were deported and subsequently killed at the beginning of the twentieth century. The dish remains, though, and you will also find it in Lebanon and Syria among the Armenian community in those countries, where it is very much part of the culinary repertoire. I was given the following recipe by a wonderful Turkish home cook, Belgin, who does cookery demonstrations for groups that I bring to her house. We start in her kitchen before moving to her dining room for a lavish and exquisite lunch. I always ask her to start with this *köfte* (the term the Turks use for *kibbeh*, while the Lebanese use the word *kafta* to describe a particular mixture of minced meat, herbs and onions that is either grilled, stewed or baked or even eaten raw). I love snacking on the patties, eating them with my hand while waiting for the other dishes to be ready.

Serves 4–6

200g (7oz) red lentils, rinsed under cold water and
    drained
175g (6oz) fine burghul, rinsed under cold water
    and drained
80ml (3fl oz) extra-virgin olive oil, plus extra for drizzling
2 medium-sized onions (about 200g/7oz total weight),
    peeled and finely chopped
100g (3½oz) pepper paste (see page 326)
100g (3½oz) organic tomato paste (see page 332)
1 tsp ground cumin
Sea salt

To serve
Little Gem lettuce leaves
Few sprigs of flat-leaf parsley, most of the stalk discarded,
    finely chopped

Put the lentils in a saucepan, add 500ml (18fl oz) of water and place over a medium heat. Bring to the boil then lower the heat and simmer for 30 minutes or until the lentils are mushy and the water has almost evaporated. Add the burghul and mix in well, then cover the pan with a lid and let it sit while you fry the onion.

Put the olive oil and chopped onions in a frying pan and cook over a medium heat, stirring regularly, until the onions are golden and very soft. Add the pepper paste and tomato paste and mix in well.

Transfer the lentils and burghul mixture to a mixing bowl. Add the onion mixture and mix to a smooth paste with your hand (wearing a glove as the mixture may dye your hand red). Add the cumin and a little salt and mix again, adding a little water if the mixture is too stiff. Taste and adjust the seasoning if necessary. Then, just as you would for the *kibbeh* balls on page 42, pinch off pieces to make medium-sized oval patties, which you indent by gently squeezing the patties with your fingers.

Arrange the lettuce leaves on a round platter and place a piece of *kibbeh* on each. Drizzle with olive oil, sprinkle with parsley and serve immediately.

Raw Kibbeh with a Spicy Burghul and Herb Topping

KIBBEH FRAKEH

All the time I lived in Lebanon, I never knew about many regional dishes eaten elsewhere that are very different from the ones we ate at home or in restaurants. Every now and then my mother would mention a dish and say that she didn't know how to make it because it was not from where her mother's family came from, the Chouf Mountains. She hardly ever cooked outside of her region's repertoire, which was basically classic mountain cookery. It wasn't until I met Nayla Audi, one of my great friends in Lebanon whose

53

family comes from the south, that I started to find out more about southern specialities, including this very particular way of preparing raw *kibbeh*. But even in the south, people have their own family or village variation on *frakeh* (basically the same as *kibbeh* in its raw state on page 42, but the burghul is mixed with wild herbs and spices), as I later found out from another friend, Hammoude Jouni, whose family is from Saida, whereas Nayla's father's family is from Kfar Rumman, very close to the Israeli border. The house is a lovely old square stone structure built around an inner courtyard, and next to it is the family cemetery where all her relatives are buried. Seeing the cemetery reminded me of my aunt Zahiyeh's mausoleum for her husband which was behind her house. Sunday lunches in Kfar Rumman are wonderful affairs with the whole family tucking into a mezze of different types of *kibbeh*, including *frakeh*. For the following recipe, you can also spread the mixture of burghul, herbs and spices over the raw meat without pre-mixing. The taste is different and meatier, which I prefer.

Serves 4–6

1 small onion, peeled and quartered
50g (2oz) flat-leaf parsley, most of the stalk discarded
30g (1oz) marjoram, leaves picked from the stalks
Small handful of basil leaves, plus extra to serve
2 dried rosebuds (see page 328)
Zest of ½ unwaxed lemon
Zest of ½ unwaxed orange
100g (3½oz) fine burghul, rinsed under cold water and
    drained
Sea salt
Finely ground black pepper
300g (11oz) freshly minced lean lamb, from the top
    part of the leg (either ask your butcher to mince the
    lamb or do it yourself using the fine attachment on
    a meat grinder)
Extra-virgin olive oil for drizzling

Put the onion, herbs and rosebuds in a food processor and process until very fine. Transfer to a large bowl, then add the lemon and orange zest and burghul. Season with salt and pepper to taste and mix well.

Pour some cold water into a medium-sized bowl, add a little salt and stir to dissolve. You will use this for dipping your hands in as you combine the meat with the burghul and herb mixture or *tahwicheh* (which means 'foraging' in Arabic).

Add the minced meat to the herb mixture and mix well, using your hand and dipping it every now and then in the bowl of salted water. Divide the meat into 16 pieces and form each into a torpedo-shaped patty with your hands. Squeeze each patty slightly to make indentations in the mixture with your fingers.

Arrange the patties in a circle on a serving platter, piling the basil leaves in the middle of the plate. Serve immediately with olive oil for those who would like to drizzle some over their *kibbeh*.

Lamb Cooked in its Mother's Milk

LABAN EMMOH

I love the name of this dish, which in Arabic means the milk of its mother, although it is not entirely accurate because the lamb is actually cooked in yoghurt and not in milk! I am guessing that the name derives from the traditional practice of making yoghurt from sheep's milk before using it in a number of dishes where meat or vegetables or even eggs are cooked in yoghurt, or served topped with yoghurt. This group of dishes is a real favourite of mine, especially in summer when you can serve them just warm, which is perfect on hot days.

Serves 4

4 lamb shanks
Coarse sea salt
400g (14oz) baby onions (about 16 in total),
    peeled

cont.

For the yoghurt sauce
25g (1oz) unsalted butter
100g (3½oz) fresh coriander (about ½ bunch), most of the
    stalk discarded, finely chopped
7 large garlic cloves, peeled and crushed
1kg (2lb 2oz) plain yoghurt (preferably goat's)
1 medium-sized organic egg, whisked

Put the shanks in a large saucepan, add 1.25 litres (2¼ pints) of
water and place over a medium heat. Bring to the boil, skimming
away any scum that rises to the surface, and add 1 tablespoon
of salt. Reduce the heat, cover the pan and let it bubble gently for
45 minutes. Add the peeled onions and simmer for another
15 minutes or until both onions and meat are done.

Meanwhile, make the yoghurt sauce. First melt the butter in a
frying pan over a medium heat. Add the chopped coriander and
crushed garlic and sauté for 1 minute or until the mixture becomes
aromatic, then remove from the heat, cover with a clean tea towel
and set aside.

Put the yoghurt in a large heavy-based saucepan. Add the whisked
egg and a little salt. Mix well and place over a medium heat. Bring
to the boil, stirring constantly to help prevent the yoghurt from
curdling. When the yoghurt has come to the boil, reduce the heat
to low and simmer for 3 minutes, still stirring.

Use tongs to remove the shanks from the broth and slide them into
the yoghurt. Then use a slotted spoon to transfer the onions from
the broth into the yoghurt sauce. Add the sautéd coriander and
garlic and simmer, stirring very regularly to stop the yoghurt from
curdling, for another 10 minutes. Serve hot with vermicelli rice
(see page 40) or good bread.

Stuffed Breast of Lamb

DOLE' MEHSHI

My mother always changed the menu for our Christmas meals.
One year she would make turkey, using the same stuffing as the
one below, which also goes well with chicken. Another year she
would make *kibbeh bil-saniyeh* (see page 41) and another year
she would make breast of lamb. This is the bit of meat that covers
the ribs and as a result is quite fatty. It tends to be large (if the lamb
is quite old, which is how it is sold in Lebanon) and triangular in
shape, and there are two ways of stuffing it. One is to fold it in half
and sew it all around the edges, leaving a large enough opening
through which you insert the rice, meat and nut stuffing before
sewing the opening shut; the other method (the one given here) is
to make a pocket between the skin and the meat that you then stuff
with the rice mixture and sew shut. The presentation is probably
more appealing if you keep the breast as it is and don't fold it.
In either case, stuffed breast is a great variation on the more classic
stuffed turkey. You could also use a neck fillet or a boned shoulder.
Both will have a lot more meat on them.

Serves 8

1 side of a breast of lamb (ask your butcher to
    slice off the rib bones and to make the pocket
    between the skin and the meat)
1 tbsp vegetable oil
1 cinnamon stick
1 bay leaf
1 medium-sized onion, peeled and studded
    with 8 cloves

For the stuffing
100g (3½oz) pine nuts
100g (3½oz) blanched almond halves
300g (11oz) freshly minced lean lamb, from the
    shoulder or shanks (either ask your butcher to
    mince the lamb or do it yourself using the fine
    attachment on a meat grinder)

cont.

1 tsp allspice or Lebanese seven-spice mixture (see
   page 331)
1 tsp ground cinnamon
¼ tsp finely ground black pepper
Sea salt
400g (14oz) short-grain white rice (bomba, Calasparra
   or Egyptian), rinsed under cold water and
   drained

First make the stuffing. Preheat the oven to 220°C (425°F),
gas mark 7.

Spread the pine nuts and almonds on separate baking sheets and
toast in the oven, 5–6 minutes for the pine nuts and 7–8 minutes
for the almonds, until they turn golden brown. Remove from the
oven and set aside.

Put the mince in a non-stick saucepan large enough for cooking the
rice, and sauté over a medium heat until the meat has lost all traces
of pink. Add the spices and some salt, then add the toasted nuts
(reserving a little for garnish) and the rice. Mix well, then pour in
650ml (just over 1 pint) of water and a little more salt. Bring to
the boil, then lower the heat and simmer for 10 minutes. Remove
from the heat and allow to cool slightly.

Start sewing one side of the opening of the pocket in the lamb
breast and stuff the pocket with the rice mixture. You want to use
about one-third of the rice, reserving the rest for serving with the
lamb. Spread the rice evenly inside the pocket, align the edges of
the breast and sew the opening shut.

Heat the vegetable oil in a large saucepan over a medium heat.
Delicately transfer the stuffed breast to the pan and brown on both
sides. Pour in 1.5 litres (2½ pints) of water and add the cinnamon
stick, bay leaf and the clove-studded onion. Bring to the boil,
skimming away any scum that rises to the surface, then reduce
the heat, cover the pan with a lid and let it bubble gently for about
1½ hours.

Remove the breast from the pan and let it rest for 5 minutes before
serving. Alternatively, if you want the meat to have a more golden
colour, you can transfer it to a baking dish and bake it in the oven

(preheated to 200°C/400°F/gas mark 6) for 10–15 minutes or until golden. Leave to rest for 5 minutes once cooked.

Meanwhile, add a little broth from cooking the lamb to the remaining rice mixture, and cook over a low heat until the rice is completely done and very hot. Slice the breast into thick slices, being careful not to break up the rice stuffing, and serve with the remaining rice on the side.

Dumplings in Yoghurt Sauce
SHISH BARAK

There is a recipe for this dish, also known as *shushbarak*, in a fifteenth-century Syrian cookery book called *Kitab al-Tibakhah* (*The Book of Cookery*), written by Ibn al-Mabrad or Ibn al-Mubarrad, a legal scholar from Damascus. The author gives these instructions: 'You take minced meat and stuff it in dough rolled out like cut *tutmaj* [unfilled dumplings cooked in yoghurt]. It is cooked in water until done. Then take [it] off the fire and put yoghurt, garlic and mint in it.' This is more like the Turkish or Armenian *manti* (see page 17), in which the dumplings are either poached or baked before being dressed with the yoghurt sauce, whereas in the Lebanese version they are cooked in the yoghurt. *Shish barak* is a rather elaborate dish and my mother always reserved it for special occasions. That said, it freezes very well and you can make the dumplings ahead of time and keep them in the freezer until you are ready to serve, at which point all you will have left to do is to prepare the yoghurt sauce.

Serves 4–6

For the dough
175g (6oz) unbleached plain flour, plus extra
  for dusting
Sea salt

cont.

59

For the stuffing

1 small onion, peeled and very finely chopped

Pinch of ground cinnamon

¼ tsp ground allspice or Lebanese seven-spice mixture
(see page 331)

⅛ tsp finely ground black pepper

150g (5oz) freshly minced lean lamb, from the shoulder or
shanks (either ask your butcher to mince the lamb or do
it yourself using the fine attachment on a meat grinder)

For the yoghurt sauce

25g (1oz) unsalted butter

100g (3½oz) fresh coriander (about ½ bunch), most of the
stalk discarded, finely chopped

7 large garlic cloves, peeled and crushed

1kg (2lb 2oz) plain yoghurt (preferably goat's)

1 medium-sized organic egg, whisked

5cm (2in) diameter pastry cutter

Tip the flour into a mixing bowl, add 100ml (3½fl oz) of water
and a pinch of salt and knead with your hands for 3 minutes or
until you have a rather firm dough. Invert the bowl over the dough
and let it rest for 15 minutes. Then knead the dough for another
3 minutes or until it is smooth and malleable. Cover with a clean,
damp tea towel and let it rest for another 15 minutes.

Next make the stuffing. Put the chopped onion in another mixing
bowl, sprinkle with the spices and a little salt and firmly rub the
seasonings in with your fingers to soften the onion. Add the minced
meat and mix with your hands until the meat and onion are well
blended. Pinch off a little of the mixture and sear in a hot pan to
taste, then adjust the seasoning if necessary. Cover the mixture in
the bowl with a clean tea towel.

Sprinkle a large freezerproof platter with a little flour and have it
ready to put the dumplings on. Divide the dough into two, rolling
each piece into a ball and putting one back under the damp tea
towel. Flatten the other slightly, dip both surfaces in flour, shake
the excess off and roll out into a large circle, about 2mm (¹⁄₁₆in)
thick. Using the pastry cutter, cut the dough into as many circles as
you can, starting from the very edge and working your way

inwards. Knead the excess dough into a small ball and slip under the damp tea towel to let it rest.

Turn the circles over, then take one and lay it across the fingers of one hand. Place ¼ teaspoon of stuffing in the middle. Fold the dough over the filling, aligning the edges together to make a half circle. With your free thumb and index finger pinch the edges tightly together into a thin flat wedge. Fold the dumpling until the two ends meet. Pinch them well together and set the curled dumpling on the flour-dusted platter, with the fat part facing down – the finished dumpling should look like a mini tortellini but with a narrower uncurled rim. Continue making the dumplings and arranging them neatly on the platter until you have used up both dough – including the remaining balls of dough under the tea towel – and filling.

Put the dumplings in the freezer while you make the yoghurt sauce. This will firm them up and stop them becoming misshapen as you drop them into the sauce. If you are freezing them for later use, wait until they have frozen before covering them with cling film or slipping them into a freezer bag to avoid squashing them.

To make the yoghurt sauce, melt the butter in a frying pan over a medium heat. Add the chopped coriander and crushed garlic and sauté for 1 minute or until the mixture becomes aromatic, then remove from the heat, cover with a clean tea towel and set aside.

Put the yoghurt in a large heavy-based saucepan. Add the whisked egg and a little salt. Mix well and place over a medium heat. Bring to the boil, stirring constantly to help prevent the yoghurt from curdling. When the yoghurt has come to the boil, reduce the heat to low and simmer for 3 minutes, still stirring.

Take the dumplings out of the freezer and carefully drop them into the simmering yoghurt. Bring back to a simmer and stir in the sautéd coriander and garlic. Simmer for another 5 minutes or until the dumplings are cooked. Serve hot with vermicelli rice (see page 40) or good bread.

Aubergine and Rice Cake

MAQLUBEH

You need to cook *maqlubeh* in a pan with straight sides that are not too high. This will allow you to turn it over (*maqlubeh* means 'turned over' in Arabic) into a beautiful cake. You'll also need to select aubergines that are all the same size to give uniform slices for an attractive presentation. If you feel daunted by the turning-over trick, simply bake the *maqlubeh* in a baking dish – ideally Pyrex so you can see the layers – in the oven (preheated to 180°C/350°F/gas mark 4) for 45 minutes and serve straight from the dish. The presentation will not be as spectacular but the taste will be the same. The Palestinians have an interesting variation on this dish using carrots – sliced lengthwise then blanched to soften them – instead of the fried aubergines.

Serves 4

4 large aubergines (about 1kg/2lb 2oz total weight)
Sea salt
200g (7oz) short-grain white rice (bomba, Calasparra
    or Egyptian), rinsed under cold water and drained
60g (2oz) pine nuts
60g (2oz) blanched almond halves
50g (2oz) butter
500g (1lb 1oz) freshly minced lean lamb, from the
    shoulder or shanks (either ask your butcher to mince
    the lamb or do it yourself using the fine attachment
    on a meat grinder)
1 tsp ground cinnamon, plus extra for seasoning
1 tsp ground allspice or Lebanese seven-spice mixture
    (see page 331)
Finely ground black pepper
Vegetable oil for frying

Straight-sided saucepan about 22cm (8½in) in diameter
    and 20cm (8in) deep

Cut off and discard the stem ends of the aubergines. Peel away most of the skin, lengthways, to create a striped effect with thin strips of skin left on the vegetable. Next cut the aubergines lengthways in thin slices about 1cm (½in) thick. Arrange these in layers in a colander, sprinkling each layer with a little salt to let them sweat; in principle this should make them absorb less oil when you fry them.

Put the rice in a bowl and pour 300ml (½ pint) of boiling water over it. Add ½ teaspoon of salt and let it soak while you prepare the remaining ingredients. The rice will absorb some of the water and swell, and so will need less cooking water, which will help the cake stay firm.

Preheat the oven to 220°C (425°F), gas mark 7.

Spread the pine nuts and almonds on separate baking sheets and toast in the oven, 5–6 minutes for the pine nuts and 7–8 minutes for the almonds, until they turn golden brown. Remove from the oven and set aside.

Melt the butter in a frying pan and cook the minced meat, stirring and mashing it with a spoon or fork to break the lumps, until the meat has lost all traces of pink. Take off the heat, season with the spices, ¼ teaspoon of black pepper and a little salt and mix in most of the toasted nuts, holding back a tablespoonful for garnishing. Pinch off a little of the mixture and sear in a hot pan to taste, then adjust the seasoning if necessary.

Rinse the aubergine slices under cold water and pat them dry with kitchen paper. Pour enough vegetable oil into a large, deep-sided frying pan to deep-fry the aubergines, and place over a medium heat. To test whether the oil is hot enough, dip the end of an aubergine slice into it; if the oil bubbles around it, it is ready. Fry the aubergines until golden on both sides, then remove with a slotted spoon and leave to drain on several layers of kitchen paper.

Spread half of the minced meat in an even layer on the bottom of the 22cm (8½in) diameter saucepan. Arrange two-thirds of the aubergines in a layer over the meat, right up to the sides of the pan, using the best slices for the sides of the dish as these are the ones that will show. Drain the rice, spread it over the aubergines, then cover with the remaining meat and finish off with a layer of aubergines.

Season 350ml (12fl oz) of boiling water with a little cinnamon, salt and pepper – bearing in mind that the meat is already seasoned. Gently pour the seasoned water into the pan, cover with a tight-fitting lid and place over a medium heat. Bring to the boil then reduce the heat to low and simmer for 15–20 minutes or until the rice is cooked and the water fully absorbed.

Take off the heat, wrap the lid of the pan in a clean tea towel, put it back on the pan and let it sit like this for about 10 minutes.

The traditional way of serving this dish is by turning it over onto a round flat serving platter as if it were a cake. First place the plate upside down on top of the pan. Wearing heatproof gloves, hold the plate down firmly with one hand and, with the other, slide the pan slowly over the edge of the work surface. Put your free hand underneath the pan, pick it up and quickly turn it upside down. Slide the platter back onto your worktop and slowly lift the pan off to uncover the rice and aubergine cake. Sprinkle the reserved nuts on top and serve immediately with some plain yoghurt.

Courgette Omelettes
'Ejjet Kussa

These omelettes are a perfect example of the ingeniousness of Lebanese cooks, who never waste any food. My mother always made them when she prepared stuffed courgettes (see page 30) so that she didn't waste the pulp, but I often make them with whole courgettes because I really like them this way and it is simpler to prepare courgettes from scratch than to spend hours coring and stuffing them! You can vary this dish by using aubergine pulp from the recipe on page 30, or simply make parsley omelettes (*cejjet baqdunes*) by leaving out both courgette pulp and garlic. Follow the instructions below for either variation, the only difference being that you need to sauté the aubergine pulp in a little vegetable oil to soften it before adding to the eggs.

Serves 4

Pulp from 400g (14oz) pale green courgettes (about 175g/6oz pulp), very finely chopped, or 200g (7oz) pale green courgettes, coarsely grated
Sea salt
3 medium-sized organic eggs
50g (2oz) spring onions (about ½ bunch), trimmed and thinly sliced
50g (2oz) flat-leaf parsley (about ¼ bunch), most of the stalk discarded, finely chopped
2 garlic cloves, peeled and crushed
1 tbsp unbleached plain flour
¼ tsp ground cinnamon
¼ tsp ground allspice or Lebanese seven-spice mixture (see page 331)
⅛ tsp finely ground black pepper
Vegetable oil for frying

Sprinkle the chopped courgette pulp (or the grated courgettes) with a teaspoon of salt and rub firmly with your hands until soft and mushy. Squeeze between the palm of your hands to extract the excess liquid and set aside.

Break the eggs into a mixing bowl and beat well. Add the chopped spring onions and parsley and the crushed garlic. Mix well then add the courgette pulp (or grated courgettes), flour, spices and 2 tablespoons of water. Season with salt and mix well.

Put enough vegetable oil in a large frying pan to shallow-fry the omelettes and place over a medium heat. When the oil is hot, drop in 2 tablespoons of the egg mixture and spread into a medium-thin circle, about 8cm (3in) in diameter. You should be able to make 5–6 small omelettes per batch. Fry until golden on both sides, then remove with a slotted spatula and leave to drain on several layers of kitchen paper.

Continue making the omelettes – you might have to top up the oil between every other batch – until you finish the egg mixture. You should end up with 14 small omelettes. Alternatively, you can make four large omelettes by using a quarter of the egg mixture for each one. Serve tepid or at room temperature.

Fried Eggs with Sumac

BEYD MEQLI BIL-SUMMAQ

You can vary these very simple, lemony fried eggs by replacing the sumac with pomegranate syrup (see page 327). Use 1 tablespoon of pomegranate syrup diluted with 2 tablespoons of water and pour over the eggs just before they are cooked. The taste will change from lemony to an intriguing sweet-savoury flavour. We often had fried eggs for breakfast at the weekend, but I tend to have them for lunch these days.

Serves 4

4 tbsp extra-virgin olive oil
8 medium-sized organic eggs
1 tbsp ground sumac (see page 331)
Sea salt
100g (3½oz) spring onions (about 1 bunch),
    trimmed, to serve

Put the olive oil in a frying pan large enough to take all eight eggs and place over a medium heat.

Break each egg into a shallow bowl, making sure it stays whole, and when the oil is hot, carefully slide the eggs into the pan. This way the eggs go in all at once and will cook evenly. Gently shake the pan back and forth to spread the eggs evenly across the bottom.

Sprinkle the sumac all over. Season with salt, bearing in mind that some brands of sumac may have been mixed with salt to bulk it up. Cook until the whites are done and the yolks are still soft. Serve immediately with the trimmed spring onions and good bread.

Burghul with Chickpeas and Pork Belly

BURGHUL BI-DFINEH

Burghul bi-dfineh is a classic dish that seems to have gone out of fashion, which is a shame as it is both healthy and delicious. My mother used to make it with both pork meat and skin, which we loved. The closest I have come to her version here is by using pork belly. I also make it with lamb shanks, with equally good results. You can use *frikeh* ('burnt' cracked wheat – see page 4) instead of burghul for a more interesting smoky flavour. If you do, I suggest you make the dish with lamb, however. Follow the instructions as below, bearing in mind that you may need to use a little more water with *frikeh*.

Serves 4

50g (2oz) unsalted butter
2–3 pork or lamb bones (optional)
500g (1lb 1oz) pork belly, cut into 4 chunks, or
    4 lamb shanks
1 medium-sized onion, peeled and finely chopped
125g (4½oz) dried chickpeas, soaked overnight in cold
    water (enough to cover the chickpeas by 2–3 fingers)
    and ½ tsp bicarbonate of soda
2 cinnamon sticks
250g (9oz) coarse burghul, rinsed under cold water
    and drained
½ tsp ground cinnamon
1 tsp ground allspice or Lebanese seven-spice
    mixture (see page 331)   *cont.*   67

¼ tsp finely ground black pepper
Sea salt
450g (1lb) plain yoghurt, to serve

Melt the butter in a large saucepan over a medium heat and brown the bones (if using), then transfer to a large plate. Add the pork (or lamb) to the pan and brown on all sides. Remove to the same plate as the bones, then add the chopped onion to the pan, plus a little more butter if needed, and sauté until the onion is soft and transparent. Return both meat and bones to the pan.

Drain and rinse the chickpeas and add to the pan. Stir for a few minutes until they are well coated in butter, then add 1.5 litres (2½ pints) of water and the cinnamon sticks. Cover the pan with a lid, then bring to the boil, reduce the heat and let the mixture bubble gently for 1 hour or until the chickpeas and meat are tender.

Remove and discard both bones (if using) and cinnamon sticks. Add the burghul and season with the spices and some salt. Reduce the heat to low and simmer for about 25 minutes or until the burghul is done and the liquid completely absorbed. Wrap the lid in a clean tea towel, then replace over the pan and leave to sit for a few minutes. Serve hot with the yoghurt.

Sumac Chicken Wraps

MUSSAKHKHAN

Here is another recipe from Reem Kelani, my Palestinian singer friend (see also page 90), which I have adapted by reducing the generous quantities so typical of Palestinian cooking. *Mussakhkhan* ('heated' in Arabic) is probably the best known of all traditional Palestinian dishes. It was found throughout Palestine before 1948, with some regional variations. In Nazareth and the Galilee it is called *muhammar* (meaning 'baked', 'grilled' or 'reddened'). You can prepare it as below, to serve as a starter or snack, or you can make the dough and prepare it more like a pizza to serve as a main course. The recipe here is far simpler and quicker to prepare than if you were to make the main course version. The taste remains the same, with the sumac imparting a lovely tart flavour and giving the meat a pretty reddish colour. As for the Palestinian spice blend, it is made with allspice, cinnamon, dried garlic, cardamom and cloves. The proportions vary depending on who is making the mix. You cannot buy it here but you can buy the Lebanese seven-spice mixture (see page 331), which is close enough. If not, simply use allspice – its complex flavour with hints of cinnamon and cloves goes well with this dish.

Serves 8

500g (1lb 1oz) skinned and boneless chicken, cut into
   long strips
35g (1¼oz) pine nuts
4 medium-sized onions, peeled and finely chopped
125ml (4½fl oz) extra-virgin olive oil, plus extra for
   greasing and brushing
1 tbsp ground sumac (see page 331), plus extra for
   seasoning
Bouquet garni made with 1 drop of mastic (see page 322),
   2 cardamom pods, 2 cloves, ½ tsp coriander seeds,
   3 black peppercorns, ½ tsp cumin seeds, 1 dried chilli,
   1 bay leaf and a cinnamon stick, all wrapped in
   cheesecloth
1 large *shraak* or *marqûq* bread (see 'bread' on page 315)

For the marinade
2 tbsp extra-virgin olive oil
Juice of ½ lemon
¼ tsp finely ground black pepper
½ tbsp Palestinian mixed spices or Lebanese seven-spice
   mixture (see page 331) or allspice
Sea salt

Mix the ingredients for the marinade in a large mixing bowl, seasoning with salt. Add the chicken strips to the marinade, turning them in the mixture so that they are well coated in it, and leave to sit for 2 hours.

When the chicken has nearly finished marinating, preheat the oven to 220°C (425°F), gas mark 7.

Spread the pine nuts on a non-stick baking sheet and toast in the oven for 5–7 minutes or until golden brown. Remove from the oven and set aside. Leave the oven switched on, with the heat lowered to 180°C (350°F), gas mark 4.

Put the chopped onions and olive oil in a large frying pan and place over a medium heat. Cook for a few minutes until they start softening, then lower the heat to medium-low. Add the sumac and continue cooking the onions, over a low heat and adding a little water if necessary, until they are completely done but not browned. Add the toasted pine nuts and cook for a few more minutes.

Sauté the chicken in a separate pan, then add 250ml (9fl oz) of boiling water and the bouquet garni and cook, covered with a lid, until the water evaporates and the chicken is done.

Spread out the bread and cut into long pieces, each wide enough to wrap around the chicken and onions in the shape of a long cigar. Then spread a little onion on each slice of bread, and top with chicken. Sprinkle with a little more sumac and roll the bread tightly around the filling. Place in a lightly oiled baking dish and brush the roll with a little olive oil. Finish making the remaining wraps, arranging them in the baking dish and brushing them with oil as you go.

Bake in the oven for about 5 minutes and serve hot or warm.

Yellow Cake
Sfuf

Most Levantine meals end with fruit rather than a sweet dessert.
And sweets are the reserve of professional sweet-makers, bought to
serve with coffee when we have guests or family visiting, or simply
as an indulgence between meals. A few are made at home, however,
such as this cake which my mother often baked when we were
children. In fact, most Lebanese families would serve this on a
regular basis. It is one of the rare sweets that is almost exclusively
made at home; when made by a sweet-maker, it is never as good.
The classic recipe calls for only turmeric, but I love saffron and
have adapted my mother's recipe to produce a rather luxurious
version using this spice.

Serves 4

1 tbsp tahini
250g (9oz) plain white flour
125g (4½oz) fine semolina
½ tsp baking powder
75g (2½oz) unsalted butter (or 75ml (2½fl oz) extra
    virgin olive oil)
250g (9oz) golden caster sugar
good pinch of saffron threads
½ tsp turmeric
30g (1oz) pine nuts (or blanched almonds)

Baking disk measuring 21cm (8in) square and
    about 4cm (1½in) deep

Preheat the oven to 180°C (350°F), gas mark 4 and grease a deep
baking dish 21cm square with the tahini.

Mix the flour, semolina and baking powder in a mixing bowl.
Add the butter (or olive oil) and rub the fat in with your fingers
until it is well absorbed. Put the sugar in another mixing bowl. Add
150ml (5fl oz) water and the saffron and turmeric to the sugar and
stir until the sugar is completely diluted. Let the saffron/turmeric

infuse for 15 minutes then add the sweetened water to the flour and semolina mixture and blend well together. Pour the mixture into the baking dish, scatter the pine nuts (or almonds) on top and bake in the preheated oven for 35 minutes or until the cake has risen and it is cooked through.

Remove the cake from the oven and let cool before cutting it into medium squares or diamonds. Serve at room temperature. The cakes will keep for a week if stored in a sealed container and kept in a cool place.

Sticky Sponge Cake

NAMMURAH

This cake is as much a family sweet as it is a street one, the latter being more common in Egypt, where it is known as *bassbuma*, than elsewhere in the Levant. It may shock you initially to see the cake swimming in sugar syrup, but don't let this worry you. You can rest assured that the sponge will soak up all the syrup. All you need worry about is the number of calories you will be consuming with each slice. Not quite 1,000 calories a bite, but not far off!

Makes 24 squares

425g (15oz) semolina
75g (2½oz) golden caster sugar
100g (3½oz) unsalted butter, softened
300g (11oz) plain yoghurt
¼ tsp bicarbonate of soda
1 tsp tahini for greasing
50g (2oz) blanched almonds

For the sugar syrup
525g (1lb 2oz) golden caster sugar
1½ tsp lemon juice
1½ tbsp rose water
1½ tbsp orange blossom water

Baking dish measuring 20 × 30cm (8 × 12in) and about
4cm (1½in) deep

Put the semolina, sugar and softened butter in a mixing bowl and
work together with your hands until well blended. Add the yoghurt
and bicarbonate of soda and mix well together until you have a
firm batter.

Grease the baking dish with the tahini, then add the batter and
spread it evenly over the dish. Flatten it gently with the back of a
spoon, to form an even layer, then cover with a clean tea towel
and leave to rest for 3 hours.

Meanwhile, make the syrup. Put the sugar and 225ml (8fl oz) of
water in a saucepan. Add the lemon juice and place over a medium
heat. Bring to the boil, occasionally stirring the mixture. Boil for
3 minutes then add the rose and orange blossom water and boil for
a few seconds more. Take off the heat and set aside to cool.

Thirty minutes before the batter is ready, preheat the oven to
200°C (400°F), gas mark 6.

Divide the uncooked cake into 24 × 5cm (2in) squares and press
one blanched almond in the middle of each square. Bake in the
oven for 20–30 minutes or until golden.

Remove from the oven and pour the cooled syrup all over the
cake. Let it rest for 30 minutes at least so that it soaks up the syrup.
Serve at room temperature. You may find the traditional amount
of syrup excessive. If so, reduce the quantity to your liking, bearing
in mind that the sponge needs time to absorb the syrup and that
although it may look at first as if the cake is swimming in syrup,
it will eventually be fully absorbed.

Rice Pudding
REZZ BIL-HALIB

Another typical family sweet, rice pudding is comfort food par
excellence – soft and creamy, and lusciously sweet and fragrant
with the addition of rose and orange blossom water. I prefer to
use good-quality short-grain rice to regular pudding rice, which
contains broken-up pieces, but it is your choice. You can decorate
with slivered pistachios, as here, or give it a Turkish twist by
adding saffron. It will be all the more luxurious.

Serves 4–6

200g (7oz) short-grain white rice (bomba, Calasparra
  or Egyptian), rinsed under cold water and drained
300ml (½ pint) full-cream organic milk
100g (3½oz) golden caster sugar
1 tbsp rose water
1 tbsp orange blossom water
Slivered pistachios, to garnish

Put the rice in a saucepan with 500ml (18fl oz) of water. Place
over a medium heat and bring to the boil, then reduce the heat to
low and cook the rice for 20 minutes, stirring occasionally.

Once the rice has absorbed all the water, pour in the milk. Bring
to the boil then add the sugar and simmer for another 20 minutes.
At this stage you will need to stir the rice very regularly so that it
doesn't stick or dry up. You want the texture to be like that of a
custard, so add a little milk if you think it is becoming too dry.

When the rice has become very soft and very creamy, remove
the pan from the heat. Add the rose and orange blossom water,
mixing them in quickly, then pour into one big serving dish or
4–6 individual ones. Allow to cool before placing in the fridge.
Serve chilled or at room temperature, garnished with slivered
pistachios.

Sweet Walnut Coil

'Ammto Zahiyeh's Borma

This is my Syrian aunt's recipe for homemade baklava, which she formed into one big coil – hence the name *borma*, meaning 'rolled' or 'turned' in Arabic. She used to make her own dough, but to save time I substitute with a good-quality filo pastry, usually a Greek or Turkish brand.

Serves 6

275g (10oz) golden caster sugar
1 tsp lemon juice
1½ tbsp rose water
1½ tbsp orange blossom water
200g (7oz) shelled walnuts, finely ground
¾ tsp ground cinnamon
75g (2½oz) unsalted butter, melted, plus extra for greasing
6 sheets of Greek or Turkish filo pastry (measuring 31 × 46cm/12½ × 18in)

Baking dish measuring 25cm (10in) in diameter

Put 175g (6oz) of the sugar in a saucepan, add 75ml (2½fl oz) of water and place the pan over a medium heat. Bring to the boil and let the syrup bubble for 3 minutes, then add the lemon juice and ½ tablespoon each of the rose and orange blossom water. Remove the pan from the heat and set aside to cool.

Mix the ground walnuts with the remaining sugar, rose and orange blossom water and the cinnamon.

Preheat the oven to 220°C (425°F), gas mark 7, and brush the baking dish with a little melted butter. If using a non-stick dish or pan, you won't need to grease it.

Spread one sheet of filo on your work surface with the long side facing you – keep the other sheets covered so that they don't dry up and become brittle. Brush with some of the melted butter. Arrange one-sixth of the walnut filling in a thin line lengthways across the sheet, about 1cm (½in) from the edge nearest to you. Fold the pastry over the walnuts and roll tightly into a thin sausage. Coil up the roll and place in the centre of the baking dish or tin. Make the remaining walnut rolls and coil them around the initial coil until the dish is completely covered.

Brush the top with melted butter and bake in the oven for 20–25 minutes or until golden brown. Remove from the oven, pour the sugar syrup all over the *borma* and allow to cool. Serve at room temperature.

Halva

Where I grew up in Lebanon and Syria, halva meant a very sweet crumbly confection made with sesame seeds, or at least this is what I thought at the time. It wasn't until many years later when I saw it being made in the souks of Aleppo (see page 137) that I realised it was made with tahini, sugar syrup and a foamy substance extracted from the roots of soapwort (see page 330). I never ate any other kind of halva, nor knew it existed, until I started travelling. In Kuwait I tasted halva made with toasted flour, butter and sugar. It was dry and brittle and not particularly delicious, whereas the one I tried in Turkey, made with the same ingredients plus pine nuts, was smooth and luxurious. The same with Iranian halva, which has saffron and cardamom added to it. There are other variations, including one made with semolina, but it is the Turkish and Iranian versions that I like best. In both countries it is served at big family meals where there might be guests, as well as on special occasions such as a birth or death.

Serves 6

Turkish halva
150g (5oz) unsalted butter
150g (5oz) unbleached plain flour
50g (2oz) pine nuts
225g (8oz) golden caster sugar

Put the butter in a large deep-sided frying pan and place over a low heat. When the butter has melted, add the flour and pine nuts and toast, stirring all the time, until both flour and nuts are golden.

Put the sugar in a saucepan and add 400ml (14fl oz) of water. Place over a medium heat and bring to the boil. Let it bubble for 2–3 minutes, then add to the flour and nut mixture over a low heat. Quickly stir the syrup into the flour and continue stirring until you have a smooth well-blended mixture.

Cover with a clean tea towel and let it sit for 15 minutes. Then either make small quenelles with the mixture, using two spoons, or spread over a serving platter, shaping the halva the way you prefer.

Iranian halva
150g (5oz) unbleached plain flour
150g (5oz) unsalted butter
Vegetable oil for greasing
1 tbsp slivered pistachios, to garnish

For the sugar syrup
150g (5oz) golden caster sugar
½ tsp ground cardamom
Good pinch of saffron threads, soaked in 3 tbsp rose
    water

Cooking ring measuring 20 cm (8 in) in diameter, and tiny
    fluted or star-shaped pastry cutters (optional)

First make the sugar syrup. Put the sugar, cardamom and 125ml (4½fl oz) of water in a small saucepan and place over a medium heat. Bring to the boil, stirring regularly, then lower the heat and simmer for 3–4 minutes. Remove the pan from the heat and stir in the saffron-infused rose water, then set aside.

Put the flour in a large deep-sided frying pan and place over a medium-low heat. Cook, stirring constantly, for about 10 minutes or until the flour is golden. Add the butter and continue stirring until the flour has turned a darker colour, being careful not to let it burn. This should take about another 10 minutes.

Slowly add the sugar syrup, again stirring all the time to avoid making lumps. Stir over the heat for a few more minutes until there are no white streaks and the mixture has formed into a smooth mass. Put a shallow ring on a lightly oiled marble or glass chopping board or a tray. Spread the mixture inside the ring and leave to cool.

Cut the cooled mixture into tiny pieces using the smallest-sized fluted or star-shaped pastry cutters you have, or simply cut into wedges. You can also make individual quenelles using two spoons, like they do in Turkey. Garnish with the slivered pistachios and serve at room temperature.

Spiced Turkish Wheat Pudding
KESME BULAMACI

This interesting and relatively healthy dish is a speciality of south-eastern Turkey. It is often eaten as a sweet snack rather than a dessert.

Serves 4–6
50g (2oz) fine burghul, rinsed under cold water and
   drained
150ml (5fl oz) *pekmez* (see page 325)
1 small cinnamon stick, 1 whole dried allspice berry and
   5 cloves tied in cheesecloth
1 tsp cornflour
1 tsp unbleached plain flour
2 tbsp toasted sesame seeds (to toast them yourself,
   see page 330)
2 tbsp chopped walnuts

Put the burghul in a medium-sized saucepan and add 500ml (18fl oz) of water. Place over a medium heat and bring to the boil, then lower the heat to medium-low and leave to bubble gently for 10 minutes. Add the *pekmez* and sachet of spices, cover the pan with a lid and simmer over a low heat for 15 minutes, stirring regularly.

While the burghul is simmering, mix the cornflour and flour with 3 tablespoons of water. When the 15 minutes are up, add the flour mixture to the pan, together with the toasted sesame seeds and walnuts. Cook, uncovered, for another 10 minutes, stirring regularly, until the pudding has thickened. Take off the heat and remove the sachet of spices. Pour into one big serving bowl or individual bowls and serve at room temperature.

Turkish Coffee

There isn't a family meal in Lebanon that doesn't finish with a cup of Turkish coffee. In fact, I can't think of an occasion that doesn't call for it. People make Turkish coffee to offer visitors or simply to have when they want to sit and relax. It was lucky we didn't get many visitors when I was young because I was the one tasked with grinding the coffee beans whenever my mother made coffee. In those days we ground the beans for every brew and we did it in a beautiful narrow cylindrical brass grinder that had geometric patterns etched all over. I carefully poured the roasted beans into the top part of the grinder, then fitted the domed lid on top and slotted the articulated handle (which folded to fit inside the grinder when it was not in use) onto the grinding pole. I then slipped the bottom part, into which the ground coffee would fall, beneath the top one and started turning the handle to grind the coffee beans. It wasn't much of an exertion but I resented being the one who was always asked to do it rather than my sisters. I would protest, but only a little, before complying, mainly because I loved the grinder. I then stood by the stove to watch my mother 'cook' the coffee – Turkish coffee is boiled several times before it is served. I never lost the feeling of suspense, wondering whether my mother would be able to stop the coffee from boiling over or whether she'd be quick enough to remove the *rakweh* (the pot in which we made the coffee) in time before it spilled.

We always asked our guests how they liked their coffee. *Sadah* meant without sugar, *wassat* medium-sweet, and *helou* (like our name) sweet. In the recipe below, I give measurements for medium-sweet coffee. Simply adjust the amount of sugar if you want it less or more sweet and of course, omit the sugar altogether if you want it without any. Ideally you should use a *rakweh*, which is like a mini kettle with a long handle and wider at the bottom than the top, with a protruding flat spout. If you don't have one, just use a small saucepan, preferably with a lip to make pouring the coffee easier.

Serves 4

4 heaped tsp finely ground coffee
2 tsp golden granulated sugar

Rakweh, or small saucepan with a lip, and four
    demitasses

Put the coffee and sugar in the *rakweh* or saucepan with 250ml (9fl oz) of water and place over a medium heat. Stir the coffee and sugar into the water and bring to the boil. As the coffee is coming to the boil, it will foam up like milk. Immediately remove from the heat and allow it to settle down. Return to the heat and repeat a couple more times if you want your Turkish coffee to be foamy on top, or repeat several times if you prefer it smooth. Pour into the coffee cups and serve immediately.

On the Farm

I was a quiet and introverted child with an aversion to any
activity that could lead to physical injury. I never rode a bicycle
or climbed a tree or did any physical activity that most children
did. Instead, I spent most of my time in the kitchen with my
mother, grandmother or aunt, watching them cook or preserve
our seasonal bounty (the preserved foodstuffs are called *muneh*
in Arabic) for the winter months.

Spending time in my mother's or grandmother's kitchen in
Beirut was exciting but it was nothing compared to being in my
aunt's kitchen in Mashta el-Helou, my father's ancestral home in
the Syrian mountains. 'Ammto Zahiyeh ('*ammto* means aunt in
Arabic) made everything at home. There were no shops in Mashta
in those days – just one tiny counter that my cousin had set up in
his home where he had pens, paper and other necessities that
couldn't be made at home. He also kept the gigantic scales on
which everyone weighed the grain and other produce grown
on the family's farms before storing or selling them.

My aunt lived in a lovely nineteenth-century stone house at
the bottom of a rocky lane below the big family house. The latter
looked like a caravanserail, with a series of beautiful vaulted
rooms built around a large courtyard with a marble fountain in the
middle. It was known as al-Dar (house in Arabic) and was older
than my aunt's house. Each brother or sister occupied one or more
rooms depending on their share of the inheritance. My father had
two rooms but we preferred to stay with my aunt who had married
a cousin who built the house for her. We only went up to al-Dar
to play with our cousins or for family gatherings.

I loved walking up and down the rocky lane and always felt a
frisson as I entered or left the courtyard through a dark stone
archway. It wasn't the darkness that scared me but rather the
room that lay abandoned to one side behind a large padlocked
iron grill that was once the family prison. No one ever explained
who had been locked in there, whether they were villainous
members of the family or just outside aggressors, but the
menace of their memory haunted me every time I walked
through.

My aunt's home was arranged slightly differently from the
family compound. The courtyard was at the front of the house,

with outbuildings to one side where she kept two milking cows and chickens. And just behind the house was her husband's mausoleum, he had died quite young. The roof of the house was flat and we often went up there through the outside stone staircase, carrying fruit or vegetables to let them dry in the sun.

'Ammto Zahiyeh was totally self-sufficient. Her farmers grew everything for her and she prepared all her staples. Her cows provided all the milk she needed, both to drink and to make butter, yoghurt and cheese. I can still see her and my mother, each sitting on a low stool on either side of a canvas cushion where they had placed a lovely earthenware jar in which they made the butter. They took it in turns shaking the jar, back and forth, again and again, until my aunt made a sign to stop. She just knew when the time had come for her to plunge her hand into the jar to bring out the dripping mass of butter. As soon as she did this, I would jump from my chair to ask her for some to eat with her home-baked bread and some of her fabulous fig jam.

My aunt also dried vegetables but these took more preparation. Aubergines had to be cored, green beans topped and tailed, and okra peeled at the stalk end to produce a smooth pointed end. Every year, she would unfailingly explain how important it was not to puncture the okra so as not to let the mucilaginous substance seep out during cooking. She and my mother threaded the vegetable onto cotton string, which they hung between trees in the courtyard. When the vegetables were dry, they tied the strings into long necklaces, and hung them in the *qabu* (meaning cave in Arabic but really describing the dark room where my aunt kept her *muneh*).

In many parts of the Levant, life on the farm has remained pretty much the same. Of course, some rural people have abandoned the tradition of making their preserves and places like Mashta el-Helou have been developed beyond recognition. Still, even in the developed areas and in those many rural areas that are left untouched by modern life, the tradition of preserving, drying and making various confections out of seasonal bounty is very much alive. And every time I come across people growing and preserving their own produce, I immediately become nostalgic for those long past days when I helped my aunt, mother and grandmother do the same. The fact that most of the recipes in this chapter are for preserving, pickling, drying or making jam does not mean that people on the farm didn't eat fresh food. They did, and I have included recipes for typical rural dishes, but apart from these, the dishes served on the farm would be more or less the same as those served *en famille* in the city – albeit prepared with produce that came directly from the fields.

Meat and Grain Porridge

H'RISSEH

Made with either chicken or lamb and traditionally cooked to distribute to the poor, *h'risseh* goes back to the times of the Abbassid caliphs who reigned over a large empire, from their capital, Baghdad, from the eighth to the thirteenth century with only a short half century interlude in the ninth century when they moved their capital to Samarra. You can make an interesting and smoky variation of this dish by replacing the wheat with an equivalent amount of *frikeh* ('burned' green cracked wheat – see page 4). If you use *frikeh*, you don't need to break up the cooked chicken meat quite as finely as you do with the wheat. You can also substitute the chicken in this recipe with a shoulder of lamb (as in the recipe for the similar dish, *halim*, on page 134), making sure you trim away as much fat and skin as you can before cooking the meat. Whether you use chicken or lamb, the preparation is the same.

Serves 4

1 medium-sized chicken (about 1.5kg/3lb 5oz)
300g (11oz) whole wheat or barley
3 cinnamon sticks
½ tsp allspice or Lebanese seven-spice mixture
   (see page 331)
¼ tsp finely ground white pepper
Sea salt
100g (3½oz) unsalted butter

Put the chicken in a large saucepan and add 2 litres (3½ pints) of water. Place over a high heat and bring to the boil, skimming away any scum that rises to the surface. Reduce the heat to medium and add the wheat (or barley) together with the cinnamon sticks, then cover the pan with a lid and cook for 1¼ hours or until the chicken is done.

Lift the chicken and cinnamon sticks out of the pan, reduce the heat to low and let the wheat simmer while you bone the chicken. Discard the skin and tear or cut the meat in small pieces.

Return the meat to the pan, cover with the lid and continue
simmering for about 20 minutes or until the wheat is cooked.
Stir occasionally so that the mixture does not stick to the bottom
of the pan. If you find it is getting too dry, add a little water,
but not too much because the end result should be like a thick-
textured porridge.

Season the chicken and wheat with the allspice (or seven-spice
mixture), pepper and a little salt and reduce the heat to very low.
Then start stirring the mixture vigorously with a wooden spoon,
cutting into the chicken pieces to shred them. You want the meat
to disintegrate into the wheat. Turn off the heat beneath the
pan and keep covered.

Melt the butter in a small frying pan over a medium heat.
Cook until browned but making sure you don't let it burn. Stir
the browned butter into the chicken and wheat mixture. Taste,
adjusting the seasoning if needed, and serve hot.

Chicken with Frikeh

I had a wonderful moment in Syria a few years ago just outside
Apamea, a stunning Roman site south of Aleppo, where I spotted
a group of farmers by the roadside burning *frikeh*, 'burned' green
cracked wheat (see page 4). The last time I had seen farmers doing
this was back in 1982, near Qalb Lozeh, a fabulous Byzantine
church now surrounded by ugly concrete modern houses. Nearly
30 years later, the scene near Apamea was the same, although the
setting had changed from being totally magical and ancient to
rather modern and charmless. The building where the farmers
lived was modern and unfinished, like so many in the Syrian
countryside, with bulky and rusty farm equipment scattered
everywhere. The farmers were lovely, though, dressed in a funny
mix of traditional garb with modern accessories like baseball caps.
The green wheat had been gathered into large piles on the ground
while, nearby, a metal trestle table with a grill top had been set up

over a large plastic sheet. The farmers were scooping each pile of wheat onto the grill and setting fire to it. As the stalks burn, the ears of wheat fall through the metal bars onto the sheet. When the flames have subsided and all the wheat has fallen onto the sheet, the farmers then push the table to the side and start to fork the burned wheat, tossing it high up in the air. As it falls back, the burned chaff blows away. The farmers then gather the burned wheat into baskets and pour the grains onto another sheet, from high up once again, to get rid of more chaff. Once they have burned all the wheat, they spread it out on more plastic sheets and leave it to dry in the sun before cracking and storing it for the year.

In Lebanon, Syria, Jordan and Turkey, *frikeh* is cooked the same way as rice or burghul, using the broth from the boiled lamb or chicken that it is served with. Some add a little rice to the *frikeh* to make it lighter. I prefer it without as I love the distinctive smoky flavour. The cooking time I've given below is for *frikeh* that is cracked and well roasted. If the grains are whole and not very green, you'll need to increase the amount of stock reserved from cooking the chicken by 200ml (7fl oz) and cook for 45 minutes.

Serves 4

1 medium-sized chicken (about 1.5kg/3lb 5oz)
1 medium-sized onion, peeled
2 cinnamon sticks
Sea salt
25g (1oz) unsalted butter
200g (7oz) *frikeh*
½ tsp ground cinnamon
½ tsp ground allspice or Lebanese seven-spice
    mixture (see page 331)
⅛ tsp finely ground black pepper

Put the chicken in a large saucepan and add 1.5 litres (2½ pints) of water. Place over a high heat and bring to the boil, skimming away any scum that rises to the surface. Add the onion, cinnamon sticks and some salt, then reduce the heat to medium, cover the pan with a lid and simmer for 45 minutes.

Remove the chicken and cut into either four or eight joints. Strain the stock and measure out 600ml (1 pint) to cook the *frikeh*. Pour the remaining stock into a clean saucepan, add the chicken joints and place over a very low heat to keep the chicken hot.

Melt the butter in a saucepan over a medium heat. Add the *frikeh* and stir until it is well coated with the butter. Pour in the reserved stock, season with the spices and some salt and bring to the boil. Reduce the heat to low and simmer for 30 minutes or until the *frikeh* is cooked to your liking and the stock is absorbed. Take off the heat, wrap the lid in a clean tea towel, replace over the pan and leave to steam for a few minutes.

Spoon the *frikeh* into a shallow serving bowl. Arrange the chicken pieces (having first removed the skin, if you prefer) over the *frikeh* and serve hot. Traditionally *frikeh* is served with yoghurt but you can also serve it with steamed or sautéed vegetables.

Mansaf

Mansaf, lamb cooked in rehydrated dried yoghurt (see page 89) and served on a bed of rice laid over paper-thin bread, is the national dish of Jordan although it originates from Hebron in the West Bank. A typical Bedouin dish served at large family gatherings, celebrations or to honour special guests, it was traditionally made with a whole lamb with the head proudly placed in the middle of the dish to indicate that the animal had been slaughtered for the occasion. Nowadays it is often made with a shoulder, a leg or shanks. The dried yoghurt used for the dish is how Bedouins would preserve the milk from their goat herds; it is known as *jamid* in Jordan. Here the yoghurt is placed in cotton sacks and salted every day until it thickens. The sacks are left to drain – rinsed regularly on the outside to get rid of the whey – until the yoghurt is solid enough to shape into balls. These are then put out to dry (in the shade to keep their white colour) until they become rock hard, after which they are stored away. They are mixed with water to reconstitute them before being used in such dishes as *mansaf*.

You can make *mansaf* with fresh yoghurt instead, although the flavour will not be the same: as the yoghurt dries, it also ferments giving *jamid* a particular flavour that imparts a faintly sour taste to the lamb as it cooks. I use a mixture of both types – *jamid* for the sour flavour and fresh yoghurt for creaminess. The recipe below is adapted from one I found in a small Arabic cookbook, *The Palestinian Kitchen*, which my friend the singer Reem Kelani gave me. In the original recipe, the lamb is cooked in the yoghurt/ *jamid* mixture from the outset, but the yoghurt can curdle with such long cooking and I prefer to boil the lamb separately, then finish it in the yoghurt sauce. While the flavour of the meat may not be quite as intense, the consistency of the sauce is much better. You can use chicken instead of lamb, although the dish will not be as celebratory.

Serves 6

4 lamb shanks (about 1kg/2lb 2oz total weight)
1 medium-sized onion, peeled
1 cinnamon stick
Sea salt
2 balls of *jamid* (about the size of tennis balls), soaked
    overnight in 750ml (1⅓ pints) of water
1kg (2lb 2oz) Greek-style plain yoghurt
1 tsp finely ground black pepper
1 tsp ground allspice
1 tsp ground cinnamon
Good pinch of saffron threads
100g (3½oz) unsalted butter
500g (1lb 1oz) short-grain white rice (bomba,
    Calasparra or Egyptian), rinsed under cold water
    and drained

To serve
100g (3½oz) pine nuts
100g (3½oz) blanched almonds
2 loaves of *marqûq* bread (see 'bread' on page 315)
Handful of flat-leaf parsley sprigs, finely chopped

Put the shanks in a large saucepan and cover with water. Add the onion and cinnamon stick and place over a medium-high heat. Bring to the boil, skimming away any scum that rises to the surface, then reduce the heat to medium-low. Season with salt, cover the pan with a lid and let it simmer for 1 hour or until the lamb is done.

While the lamb is cooking, knead the *jamid* in its soaking water water to help it dissolve completely. Strain the liquid and put in another large saucepan, add the Greek-style yoghurt and place over a medium heat. Bring to the boil while stirring constantly to prevent the yoghurt from curdling. Add the spices, mix well and turn the heat off as soon as the yoghurt comes to the boil. Cover the pan and keep warm.

Preheat the oven to 220°C (425°F), gas mark 7.

Spread the pine nuts and almonds on separate non-stick baking sheets and toast in the oven, 5–6 minutes for the pine nuts and 7–8 minutes for the almonds, until they turn golden brown. Remove from the oven and set aside to use later.

Melt the butter in a saucepan and add the rice, stirring it in the butter until well coated, then pour in 1 litre (1¾) pints of water. Add some salt and bring to the boil, then lower the heat and cover the pan with a lid. Simmer for 10–15 minutes or until the rice is done and the water fully absorbed. Wrap the lid in a clean tea towel and replace the lid over the rice to keep warm.

Remove the cooked lamb from the stock and take the meat off the bone. Drop the boiled lamb into the yoghurt sauce and place the pan over a low heat. Bring to a simmer, stirring all the time and adding a ladle or two of stock until you have a sauce the consistency of single cream. Taste and adjust the seasoning if necessary.

To serve, lay the bread over a large round serving platter. Spread the rice over the bread then arrange the meat over the rice. Ladle as much sauce as you would like over the meat and rice without making the dish soupy. Whatever sauce is left over, pour into a sauceboat. Garnish with the toasted nuts and chopped parsley and serve immediately.

Turkish Wheat, Pulses, Dried Fruit and Nut Pudding

Aşure

Prepared for the feast day in the Muslim calendar that commemorates Noah's escape from the flood, this is a typically rural dish made with whatever people have growing in their fields or their neighbours' fields, which they will have picked and dried themselves. The pudding is also prepared to commemorate the martyrdom of the Prophet's grandsons, Hassan and Hussein, and is called after the occasion's name, Ashura (in Arabic) or Aşure (in Turkish). Lebanese Christians have a simpler version of this dish, using only wheat and nuts, which they make for the feast day of St Barbara. People from the Lebanese mountains, like those in rural Turkey, would use their own home-grown wheat to prepare *aşure*.

Serves 8

For soaking overnight
100g (3½oz) wheat, rinsed
2 tbsp dried chickpeas
2 tbsp dried cannellini beans
2 tbsp dried broad beans
¾ tsp bicarbonate of soda
50g (2oz) pudding rice or short-grain white rice
   (bomba, Calasparra or Egyptian), rinsed under
   cold water and drained
4 dried figs
6 dried apricots
2 tbsp sultanas

For cooking the pudding
25g (1oz) unsalted butter
200g (7oz) golden caster sugar
3 tbsp shelled hazelnuts, coarsely chopped
1 tbsp cornflour
125ml (4½fl oz) full-cream organic milk
100ml (3½fl oz) rose water

To garnish
1 tsp ground cinnamon
1 tsp sesame seeds
1 tsp nigella seeds
50g (2oz) shelled walnuts
Pomegranate seeds

Put the wheat in a saucepan and add 2 litres (3½ pints) of water. Place over a medium heat and bring to the boil, then take off the heat and leave to soak overnight. Put the chickpeas, cannellini beans and broad beans in separate bowls and cover well with water. Add ¼ teaspoon of bicarbonate of soda to each bowl and leave to soak overnight. Place the rice in another bowl and the dried fruit in another, and leave these to soak overnight as well.

The next day, return the pan of soaked wheat to the heat, bring to the boil and simmer, covered with a lid, for about 1 hour or until tender. Drain and rinse the chickpeas, cannellini beans and broad beans and cook in separate pans until done, then peel them.

Drain the dried fruit and chop both figs and apricots into small pieces the size of the plumped-up sultanas.

Drain the rice and add to the cooked wheat, together with the drained sultanas and chopped figs and apricots. Add the butter and bring back to the boil. Add the chickpeas, beans and broad beans and simmer for 10 minutes.

Meanwhile, preheat the oven to 220°C (425°F), gas mark 7.

Spread the walnuts for the garnish on a non-stick baking sheet and toast in the oven for 6–8 minutes or until golden brown. Remove from the oven, then chop up coarsely and set aside.

Next add the sugar in 3–4 batches to the *aşure*, stirring well between each addition. (According to Nevin Halıcı, whose recipe I have adapted here, the wheat will harden if you add the sugar all at once.) Add the hazelnuts and simmer for another 15 minutes, stirring all the time so that the mixture does not stick to the bottom of the pan, until the *aşure* thickens and becomes like a textured porridge. Quickly whisk the cornflour and milk together and add

to the pan. Stir until the *aşure* starts bubbling again, then remove
from the heat and add the rose water.

Pour the *aşure* into a serving bowl and sprinkle with the ground
cinnamon, sesame and nigella seeds, then scatter the toasted
walnuts and pomegranate seeds all over and serve hot or at room
temperature.

Pickling Solution

The two main traditional methods of preserving seasonal produce
are drying and pickling. My mother and grandmother would start
making their pickles as the summer drew to a close, filling large jars
with cucumbers or *meqteh* (see page 323), green tomatoes and
aubergines, which they stuffed with garlic (see page 100). They also
stuffed bell peppers with shredded cabbage before pickling them;
and they added beetroot to pickled turnips to colour them bright
pink (see page 103). My aunt Zahiyeh didn't pickle in quite the
same way. She made *makduss* (see page 97) by stuffing aubergines
with walnuts, garlic and cayenne or chilli pepper and preserving
them in olive oil. We liked to wrap her *makduss* in bread to eat
as a sandwich.

Pickles were ever present at our table, served with everything
from the simplest fare to precious seasonal one such as roasted
wild birds. Towards the end of summer I would abandon the
kitchen to accompany my uncles on their bird-shooting expeditions.
I loved watching them in action; and I loved eating the little birds
they caught even more. My uncles were excellent shots and by the
end of the day we had dozens of the furry little creatures, all strung
together on a cord suspended from a wing mirror of the car to
take back home. The birds that feed on figs, in particular, are
considered a great delicacy, both in Lebanon and Syria. I would
help to pluck and gut them, and once they were all prepared, my
grandmother would season them with sea salt before threading
them onto skewers. While we were getting the birds ready, my
uncles lit a charcoal fire to grill them. As she grilled the birds, my

grandmother pressed them every now and then between two layers of pita bread to soak up the fatty juices. My siblings and I always fought over who would get the juiciest pieces of bread to wrap around our little birds. And despite the fact that eating them is now seen as completely non-PC, they remain one of my favourite foods. My grandmother always served them with a plate of her homemade pickles.

There are several basic requirements for making pickles so that they last you through the year. The first is to select both vegetables and vinegar very carefully. The vegetables need to be very fresh, without blemishes or rot spots, and the smaller the better. You should also pay special attention to the variety of vinegar if it is not homemade. Buy the very best red wine vinegar you can afford as it will make a difference to both the taste and degree of sourness of your pickles. The cheaper the vinegar the nastier the taste, especially as the pickles age! Cleanliness is also very important. Hands and utensils must be thoroughly cleaned and the jars (screw-top jars or clip-top ones with a rubber seal) need to be sterilised, which you can do in the oven. Wash the jars well in soapy water, rinse and dry them (or wash them in the dishwasher), then stand them on a baking tray and heat them in the oven (preheated to 140°C/275°F/gas mark 1) for 30 minutes. Turn off the heat and let the jars cool inside the oven before using them. Once sealed in a jar, the pickles need to be stored in a cool dark place. If you are in a hot country, refrigerate them as soon as they are ready to eat and try to keep them in the coolest place outside that you can find. A layer of mould may sometimes develop on the surface, in which case simply skim it off and rinse the pickles before serving.

The way produce is pickled in the Levant varies from one country to another. In Lebanon, for instance, the brine is a mixture of salted vinegar and water that changes in proportion from half vinegar/half water to one-third vinegar/two-thirds water, depending on how sour you like your pickles. Some people add peeled garlic and/or hot chillies, although many keep their pickles plain, which is how I like mine. If you decide to use chillies (quantity depending on personal preference), cut into the bottom of each chilli to open the flesh and release some of the heat into the brine, but make sure you remove the chillies as soon as the pickles have reached the right degree of piquancy, otherwise they may become too hot.

Below are the different pickling solutions typically used in the Levant:

Makes a 1 litre (1¾ pint) jar

Lebanese pickling solution
300ml (½ pint) water
150ml (5fl oz) red wine vinegar
2 tbsp sea salt
1 tsp golden granulated sugar

Turkish pickling solution
1 litre (1¾ pints) white vinegar
2 tbsp sea salt

or

1 litre (1¾ pints) water
500ml (18fl oz) white wine or champagne vinegar
1 tbsp sea salt

Iranian pickling solution
500ml (18fl oz) cider vinegar
2 tbsp sea salt

Pickled Aubergines Four Ways

Aubergines are a very versatile vegetable, particularly when it comes to pickling them. In each of the four recipes below, small aubergines are used, blanched and drained of any excess liquid before being preserved. Serving all four aubergine pickles would make quite an impressive spread, offering an interesting contrast in flavours. They are the perfect way to beef up a homemade mezze, for instance, without going to too much trouble on the day.

For each recipe, you will need one or two 1 litre (1¾ pint) sterilised glass jars (see page 95). To get rid of the excess liquid once you have boiled or steamed the aubergines, and hence stop them from spoiling in the jar, place in a colander with a weighted bowl on top. Leave to drain for 24 hours then spread on kitchen paper before stuffing and pickling them.

Syrian Makduss

Syrians are the only people in the Levant to preserve aubergines in olive oil. Even though *makduss* is a pickle, it is often served as a dish on its own rather than as a condiment.

Makes two 1 litre (1¾ pint) jars

1.5kg (3lb 5oz) small aubergines (about 30 in total)
2 tbsp coarse sea salt
Extra-virgin olive oil

For the stuffing
Cloves from 4 garlic heads (about 200g/7oz total weight),
   peeled
2 tsp fine sea salt
200g (7oz) shelled walnuts
½ tsp cayenne pepper or 2 fresh green chilli peppers,
   trimmed and deseeded

Peel and discard the husk and stalk of each aubergine, leaving a rounded, uncut top. Put the aubergines in a saucepan and cover with water. Add the coarse sea salt and place over a high heat. Bring to the boil then reduce the heat to medium, cover the pan with a lid and let it bubble gently for 5 minutes or until the aubergines are half cooked. Drain the aubergines, ideally for 24 hours (see page 96).

Next make the stuffing. Put the peeled garlic cloves in a blender with the fine sea salt and process until nearly smooth. Add the walnuts and cayenne pepper (or fresh chilli peppers) and blend until the walnuts are ground medium-fine. The stuffing should have a fine crunch to it.

Take one aubergine and make a slit down the middle, lengthways, cutting halfway into the flesh and making sure you don't slice through the other side. Prise the flesh open to create a pocket for the filling and press a teaspoon of walnut and garlic mixture into the aubergine. Smooth the stuffing with the spoon or your finger so that it's level with the aubergine skin. Put on a plate and fill the remaining aubergines in the same way.

Pack the aubergines in layers, with the filled side facing up, in two sterilised glass jars, fitting the aubergines quite snugly together but without crushing them. Cover with extra-virgin olive oil, seal the jars shut and store in a cool, dark place. The pickles will be ready after about one month.

IRANIAN *TORSHI-YE BÂDENJÂN*

The following recipe, which I have adapted from one in Margaret Shaida's wonderful book *The Legendary Cuisine of Persia*, includes a rather unusual filling that is quite different from the Lebanese, Syrian and Turkish ones. As in the other recipes, be sure to buy the aubergines very fresh, with a smooth skin and firm flesh. It is only after boiling or steaming them that they should look old and shrivelled!

Makes a 1 litre (1¾ pint) jar

750g (1lb 10oz) small aubergines (about
    15 in total)
2 tbsp coarse sea salt
1 tbsp nigella seeds
1 tsp coriander seeds
4 small green bell peppers
500ml (18fl oz) cider vinegar

For the stuffing
250g (9oz) flat-leaf parsley, most of the stalk
    discarded, finely chopped
250g (9oz) fresh coriander, most of the stalk
    discarded, finely chopped
1½ tbsp dried mint
1½ tbsp dried basil
10 garlic cloves, peeled and crushed
2 tsp fine sea salt

Remove the peel and stalk from the aubergines but without cutting into the top, then steam for about 10 minutes or until soft. Drain the aubergines, ideally for 24 hours (see page 96).

To make the stuffing, put the chopped fresh and dried herbs in a bowl. Add the crushed garlic and 2 teaspoons of salt and mix well.

Take one cooked aubergine and make a slit down the middle, lengthways, cutting halfway into the flesh and making sure you don't slice through the other side. Gently prise the slit open and stuff with a little of the herb mixture. Close the filled pocket and wipe the aubergine clean. Repeat with the remaining aubergines.

Stand or lay a third of the stuffed aubergines in the sterilised pickling jar. When you have made one layer, sprinkle with half the coarse sea salt, nigella and coriander seeds. Then lay two green peppers over this first layer of aubergines and repeat to make another layer, sprinkling with the remaining salt, nigella and coriander seeds and using the remaining peppers. Finish with a layer of aubergines on top.

Pack the jar tightly then pour the cider vinegar over the aubergines to cover completely. Add any remaining salt, then seal shut and gently shake back and forth to distribute the salt. Leave to sit in a cool dark place for two weeks at least before serving.

Lebanese *Kabiss Batinjen*

Here the filling is a simple mixture of crushed garlic flavoured with either cayenne pepper or fresh chilli peppers, while the pickling solution is subtler than that the one used in either the Turkish or Iranian recipes. As soon as I arrived home from school I'd tuck into these, simply wrapped with pita bread, as my *merenda*. I found it frustrating watching my mother or grandmother prepare the pickles as I could not try them until much later when they were ready to eat. The garlic paste was too sharp to even taste and the blanched aubergines were simply inedible even when sprinkled with salt. Luckily, there was always the option of dipping into one of the previous year's jars to fish out a few pickled aubergines for me to nibble on while my mother and grandmother were busy making the new lot.

Makes two 1 litre (1¾ pint) jars

1.5kg (3lb 5oz) small aubergines (about 30 in total)
1 tbsp coarse sea salt
450ml (16fl oz) Lebanese pickling solution (see page 96)

For the stuffing
Cloves from 4 garlic heads (about 200g/7oz total weight),
    peeled
2 tsp fine sea salt
½ tsp cayenne pepper or 2 fresh green chilli peppers,
    topped and deseeded

Peel and discard the husk and stalk of each aubergine, leaving a
rounded, uncut top. Put the aubergines in a saucepan and cover
with water. Add the coarse sea salt and place over a high heat.
Bring to the boil then reduce the heat to medium, cover the pan
with a lid and let it bubble gently for 5 minutes or until the
aubergines are half cooked. Drain the aubergines, ideally for
24 hours (see page 96).

Put the garlic in a blender with the fine sea salt and cayenne pepper
(or fresh chilli peppers) and process until nearly smooth. The garlic
paste should have a fine crunch.

Take one aubergine and make a slit down the middle, lengthways,
cutting halfway into the flesh and making sure you don't slice
through the other side. Prise the flesh open to create a pocket for
the stuffing and press half a teaspoon of garlic paste into each
aubergine. Smooth the stuffing with the spoon or your finger so
that it's level with the aubergine skin. Put on a plate and fill the
remaining aubergines in the same way.

Arrange the aubergines in layers in two sterilised glass jars, with the
filled side facing upwards and packing them quite snugly together
but without crushing them. Pour in the pickling solution, dividing it
evenly between each jar to cover the aubergines. Seal the jars shut
and store in a cool, dark place. The pickled aubergines should be
ready after two weeks or a little longer.

Turkish *Patlican Turşusu*

The Turkish word for pickles, *turşusu*, is basically the same as the Iranian *torshi*. These pickles are interesting because the aubergines are filled with blanched cabbage and sealed with slices of red bell pepper. It is a good idea to choose fatter aubergines here because the cabbage is bulkier than the garlic or herb pastes used in the previous recipes.

For a 1 litre (1¾ pint) jar

750g (1lb 10oz) small aubergines (about 15 in total)
Juice of 2 lemons
1 quantity of Turkish water and vinegar pickling solution
   (see page 96)
3 tbsp sunflower oil

For the stuffing
200g (7oz) white cabbage, finely shredded
50g (2oz) dill, chopped
6 garlic cloves, peeled and crushed
2 tbsp Aleppo pepper or *pul biber* (see page 313)
1 red bell pepper, sliced lengthways and deseeded
Handful of chives

Peel and discard the husk and stalk of each aubergine, leaving a rounded, uncut top. Fill a medium-sized saucepan with water, add the lemon juice and place over a medium-high heat. Bring to the boil, add the aubergines and boil for 3 minutes. Remove the aubergines with a slotted spoon and put in a colander to drain. Blanch the shredded cabbage in the same water and drain. (Drain both ideally for 24 hours – see page 96.)

Put the drained cabbage in a mixing bowl, add the chopped dill, crushed garlic and Aleppo pepper (or *pul biber*) and mix well.

Take one aubergine and make a slit lengthways down the middle, cutting halfway into the flesh and making sure you don't slice through the other side. Gently prise the flesh open to create a pocket, then fill this with as much cabbage stuffing as you can. Cover the filling with a slice of red pepper, tying this in place with one or two chives. Place the stuffed aubergine in the sterilised glass jar and fill the remaining aubergines in the same way, stacking them neatly into the jar.

Pour the water and vinegar solution into a saucepan and bring to the boil. Boil for 2 minutes then add the sunflower oil. Allow to cool and then pour over the aubergines. Seal the jar shut and store in a cool place. The aubergines will be ready in about one month.

Various Vegetable Pickles

There really is no need to give separate recipes for each type of pickle (unless you're stuffing them, that is, like the aubergines in the recipes on pages 96–102) when the method is the same for almost every kind of vegetable. The recipe below is for cabbage leaves, but quantities are also more or less the same for every vegetable, bearing in mind that some are smaller or larger than others and as a result you will need to increase or decrease the weight slightly. The most common pickling vegetables in Lebanon are cucumbers or *meqteh* (see page 323). Aside from cabbage leaves, you can also pickle long, thin green chilli peppers (although you may need to increase the weight by 100g/3½oz as they are smaller than other vegetables and you can fit more in the same-sized jar); green tomatoes; and cauliflower, which is larger and denser and as a result you will need to use a little less (about 300g/11oz, trimming the bottom stalks to have only the top leaves). Some vegetables are ready before others and my suggestion is that you taste whichever vegetable you are pickling after two weeks to check if it is ready.

Makes a 1 litre (1¾ pint) jar

500g (1lb 1oz) cabbage leaves
4 garlic cloves (optional), peeled
1 fresh red chilli pepper (optional)
1 quantity of Lebanese or Turkish pickling solution (see
    page 96)

Roll up the cabbage leaves or cut them into medium-sized pieces
– you will be able to fit more cabbage in the jar if you do this.
Pack the leaves in a sterilised glass jar (see page 95). You can
add peeled garlic cloves and one chilli pepper to pep up the taste,
if you wish.

Pour the pickling solution over the cabbage leaves to cover
them, then close the jar and store in a cool, dark place. Eat after
2–3 weeks.

Pickled Turnips

LIFT

The method here is the same as for pickling other vegetables except
for the addition of beetroot to colour the pale turnips a shocking
pink, which never fails to surprise diners who are unfamiliar with
these pickles. Be sure to keep the jar away from the light and heat,
though, or the colour will fade.

Makes a 1 litre (1¾ pint) jar

500g (1lb 1oz) small turnips
1 small beetroot, unpeeled and cut in quarters
1 fresh red chilli pepper (optional)
1 quantity of Lebanese pickling solution (see page 96)

Trim the stalk and root ends of the turnips, pulling out any thin
roots on the skin. If the turnips are very small, cut them almost in
half by making one deep vertical incision in the middle from the tip
and stopping about 5mm (¼in) short of the stalk end; if they are
small to medium in size, cut them in thin slices by making several

deep vertical incisions every 1cm (½in), again making sure you do not slice through the other side.

Pack them in a sterilised jar (see page 95), interspersing with the beetroot quarters and adding the chilli pepper (if using). Pour over the pickling solution to cover the turnips, then close the jar and store in a cool, dark place. Eat after 2–3 weeks.

Strained Yoghurt

LABNEH

Labneh is often described as a cheese, but it isn't: it is simply yoghurt that has been strained, with no rennet added to aid coagulation. The type of yoghurt you choose will obviously influence how good your *labneh* is. I often make mine using goat's yoghurt, but sheep's or cow's yoghurt will do just as well. Just make sure you buy an organic or live-culture variety.

Makes 500g (1lb 1oz)

1kg (2lb 2oz) plain yoghurt

Lay a double layer of cheesecloth over a colander and pour the yoghurt into it. Gather up the edges of the cloth and tie the opposite ends together to make a pouch. Leave a space between the knots and the yoghurt so that you can hang up the pouch. Hang on the taps over the sink or suspend elsewhere over a large bowl to let the liquid drain off. Leave to drain overnight and serve with olive oil and *za'tar* (see page 333) or preserve as in the recipe on page 89.

Strained Yoghurt Balls

KABISS LABNEH

A great way of preserving *labneh*, or strained yoghurt (see page 104), this is tastiest when made with goat's or sheep's yoghurt. If you add a chilli pepper and/or sprigs of dried thyme or another dried herb to the oil, you will make the *labneh* balls even more interesting. It is important to mix enough salt with the strained yoghurt before shaping it into balls so that it does not spoil.

Makes a 1 litre (1¾ pint) jar

1 tsp sea salt
1 quantity of *labneh* (see page 104)
Extra-virgin olive oil
1 fresh red chilli pepper (optional)
2 sprigs of dried thyme (optional)

Lay a clean piece of cotton or linen cloth over a tray, then sprinkle the salt over the strained yoghurt. Pinch off a little of the yoghurt and shape it into a ball the size of a small walnut. Place on the cloth and shape the rest of the yoghurt in the same way, spreading the balls on the cloth. Leave them to dry in a cool place for a day or two.

Carefully pack them in a sterilised glass jar (see page 95) and cover with extra-virgin olive oil. Add the chilli pepper and sprigs of thyme (if using) and close the jar. Store in a cool, dark place and eat after 1–2 months.

Drying Fruit, Nuts and Vegetables

In the Levant, drying is as important a method of preserving produce as pickling. Normally carried out at the end of the summer, it is applied not only to fruits and vegetables but to nuts as well – pistachios (see page 326) in particular.

Gaziantep in south-eastern Turkey is famous both for its dried vegetables and for its pistachios, and I love visiting it during the drying season. Pistachios are mostly planted on red clay soil in the surrounding countryside, which creates a wonderful backdrop to the distinctive trees with their slender trunks and wide branches that fan out gracefully, each branch carrying beautiful clusters of pink and red nuts. When fresh, the nuts are covered with a thick pink or red skin, and the combination of the pinks and greens, the red earth and the brilliant blue sky – the weather is always perfect at this time of the year – makes for a stunning scene, the traditional floral prints worn by the women who do the harvest adding yet more colour.

The pistachio harvest happens once every two years. The harvesters start the day early, with the women cooking a large pot of *beyran*, lamb soup, for breakfast, which they eat with flatbread and tea, sitting in the shade of the pistachio trees on blankets that they will later use for collecting the pistachios. After they have eaten their breakfast, the harvesters shake the blankets and get ready to pick the pistachios. The men lean wooden stepladders against the trees while the women lay the blankets around the base of the trunks to catch the nuts. Then some of the men climb into the trees to pick clusters of nuts from the top branches, letting them drop onto the blankets, while others stay on the ground to strip the lower branches. As the nut clusters fall, the women sort the ripe nuts from the unripe ones and the leaves that fall with them. They throw any unripe nuts and leaves off the blankets before gathering the blankets around the nuts and carrying them to a pickup truck where a couple of men unload the nuts straight into the back of the truck. I had never seen such huge piles of fresh pistachios – a symphony of red and pink. Some of the nuts are delivered to market traders to be sold fresh – they are considered a great delicacy when in season – while the rest are dried to be used in baklava (see page 279) and other preparations.

Another spectacular scene at this time of the year is the red peppers drying in the middle of parched fields – a truly eye-catching sight. The last time I had seen this was 30 years ago, on my way from Izmir to Istanbul. Along one stretch of the road women were spreading the peppers on long white cotton sheets to dry in the sun. I didn't stop at the time, however, and have always regretted it. During a recent visit to the area, the scene was quite different. The sheets – much larger and made of plastic instead of cotton – were heaped with mounds of fresh peppers that were about to be spread to dry in the sun. Right next to the fresh peppers were sheets covered with already dried peppers that a group of men were packing into white sacks exactly like the original hessian ones except that they were woven out of plastic – no one seems to use natural materials any more. A big truck was parked in the middle of the field with some of the sacks already loaded onto it. The operation was enormous, more like a factory than a smallholding, although traditional drying methods were still being used.

Not far from all this activity was a small encampment where I found a lovely family – a middle-aged mother, her two young daughters and their father, a rugged countryman. They had migrated for the summer – a common practice among Turkish rural folk, who move either to find new pasture for their flocks or to help with the harvest as paid hands. They had set up a tent where they slept and a raised wooden terrace with a straw roof where they ate and relaxed. The father had even planted a miniature garden at the entrance of their little domain with a tiny fountain to provide freshness. I loved how he had made their temporary encampment as agreeable and cool as he could in the middle of the parched countryside. I reached them as they were finishing lunch, and with customary hospitality they immediately invited me and my companion, Filiz, to share their modest fare. The mother had just baked the most delicious flatbread, which she offered us together with some of her own homemade cheese.

After we had eaten, we drove up into the mountains where Filiz – a great friend and my guru on all culinary matters in Gaziantep – had been to visit families who had moved their sheep to graze and who made cheese with their milk. The mountains were bare, rocky and starkly beautiful, and the encampment when we came upon it was almost biblical: no vehicle in sight, just a couple of donkeys and a horse, with children running around. The scene appeared timeless, until we got closer, that is, and saw the plastic sheeting covering the walls of the tents. All the adults were toothless but this did not stop them from smiling broadly as they invited us to sit on the stone benches they had built outside their tents. After the customary greetings and exchange of niceties, we followed one of the women into the tent, where she was making cheese. She had already shaped one batch into small squares and was putting it to soak in brine. Everything was incredibly primitive. No electricity, no running water, and no gas fire – nothing that could indicate that the year was 2010. It reminded me of my early years in Mashta el-Helou when my aunt had no electricity or running water, but our life in her stone house was luxurious in comparison!

They must have had a television back in their permanent home because while we were sitting with the women, drinking tea and eating cheese, I watched one of the young and rather beautiful teenage girls get on the horse and start brandishing a toy gun, which she proceeded to shoot at her siblings and cousins as if she were a heroine in a Western. She even pretended to shoot the horse! It was a magical afternoon and all the more unexpected given how close we were to the city.

The families also had vegetables drying in the sun, more or less the way my aunt and mother had theirs. But their vegetables were nowhere near as pretty as those we saw the following day driving to another small town. On one side of the road, a young couple was stringing cored aubergines, courgettes and peppers on long cotton strings that they then suspended on a triangular structure. They had hung row upon row until they'd filled the entire frame, creating the most glorious pyramid of different shades of purple, green and yellow. As we drew closer, we saw that they had also filled the inside of the frame; laying sheets on the ground where they had spread diced aubergines to dry – to be used in a lovely risotto-like dish made with either rice or coarse burghul.

All this said, you can actually dry your own vegetables at home, in your own kitchen – you don't need a sunny Levantine terrace, roof or field. You can dry vegetables either using a food dehydrator – they are fairly reasonable to buy – or simply in the oven, preheated to the lowest setting. Lay the vegetables on non-corrosive trays and place them in the oven, switching the trays every 30 minutes so that the vegetables dry evenly. You will need to keep an eye on them towards the end to make sure they don't scorch. It is better to turn off the oven a little before they are completely dry and let the vegetables continue drying in the cooling oven than to risk spoiling the batch. To cook with the dried vegetables, first soak them in water until they are rehydrated, then use as you would fresh vegetables.

Here is how to prepare various kinds of vegetables for drying:

Aubergines and Courgettes

Cut the tops off and core the vegetables using a narrow apple corer or special corer that you can buy in Lebanese shops, leaving a shell that is just a few millimetres thick.

Peppers

I suggest you dry only red or yellow peppers as the green ones don't have a nice colour when they are dried. Cut the tops off and remove the seeds and as much of the white ribs inside as you can without piercing the peppers or misshaping them.

Okra

Use a very sharp knife to peel the top off, leaving a smooth pointed end.

Green Beans

These need to be topped and tailed and stringed if the strings are tough. You can leave them whole or cut them into 5–6cm (2–2½in) pieces.

Butter, Cannellini or Other Beans

These are left to dry on the plant then spread on straw trays outdoors to dry further.

Herbs

Bunch these up and hang upside down somewhere dry. They will take quite a while to dry completely, about two weeks at least. I only dry mint, which is used extensively both as an ingredient and as a garnish, but you can dry basil or thyme (specifically *Thymus vulgaris*) to make your own *za'tar* (see page 333. Or you can

109

spread the herbs on sheets or straw trays. In either case, they need to be kept away from the sun in order to retain their colour.

Grape Leather and Sweet Walnut 'Sausages'

BASTIK AND CEVIZ SUCUĞU

My father loved investing his hard-earned money in land and whenever he finished a contract (he was a civil engineer specialising in building roads and bridges), he would add to his property portfolio by buying a piece of land, either in the city or in the mountains. I make him sound like a tycoon, which he was not. Just a landowner at heart, like his ancestors. One year we all got very excited because he bought a mini vineyard in B'hamdun, a famous summer resort and my maternal grandfather's place of birth. The vineyard was on a hill with the vines planted in terraces. The grapes were white, very small and very sweet and every summer we had baskets and baskets of fruit that we couldn't eat. My mother had to find ways to use this abundance. She made sweet wine similar to that served in the Greek Orthodox church we belonged to and she also tried her hand at making *malban* (grape 'leather') like my aunt's, with varying degrees of success. When I visited a place near Gaziantep, in south-eastern Turkey, where they were making *bastik* (Turkish for *malban*) and sweet walnut 'sausages', I was flooded with memories of picking grapes in our own little vineyard at B'hamdun and making *malban* at Mashta el-Helou, even though the location was very different.

The action was happening in a large hangar filled with the sweet walnut 'sausages' hanging from hundreds of cast-iron rings. On one side, set over wood fires, were huge, shallow copper cauldrons in which men were stirring the bubbling grape juice that they thickened with cornflour for it to set around the walnuts into 'sausages'. The sunlight streamed through high narrow windows and bounced against the copper, bathing the whole room in a magical golden light that made me feel as if we had stepped back

110

in time. And in a way I had, to my Mashta days, because what they were preparing in this big hangar was the same as my aunt's grape 'leather'; and when they started spreading some of it over the sheets with wooden trowels, I could just imagine my aunt, mother and cousins doing the same, if on a much smaller scale. They made theirs with the juice of grapes that the farmers brought up in huge baskets and tipped into a big tub set up in the courtyard of our big family house. My mother and aunt then washed my feet, as well as my siblings' and my young cousins', and lifted us, one by one, into the tub to trample the grapes. It was the most fun I ever had as a child. We jumped up and down on the fruit, splashing the juice all over our clothes, and with each big splash, we screeched with laughter and splashed even more.

That day, together with the times my aunt killed a chicken for our meal, were the best part of my Syrian summers. I never tired of running after the headless chicken, trying to avoid the trail of blood, tickled by how it stayed alive despite having lost its head. I may have been a quiet child but I was definitely not squeamish. After we finished crushing the grapes, we were lifted out of the vat and cleaned up before my aunt and mother strained the grape juice into large pots, which they placed over wood fires. They boiled the juice down until it became thick, then poured it over white sheets, laid all over the courtyard, spreading the hot concentrated juice very thinly over the sheets, which they left to dry in the sun. 'Ammto Zahiyeh always reserved a little of the sweet grape 'soup', as I liked to call it, to give each of us in a bowl. Many years later, on a visit to Regaleali Winery in Sicily, I tasted a by-product of their wine making, a kind of fermented grape juice, which reminded me of the Syrian grape 'soup' that I so loved as a child.

The next day, my mother and aunt gently peeled the grape 'leather' off the sheets. They cut it into squares, then folded the squares like handkerchiefs and stored them in large tin boxes. We always took a few of these tins back home and we ate the *malban* wrapped around walnut halves as a sweet snack after school. I occasionally see *malban* in the souks in Aleppo; it is also very common in the bazaars of Gaziantep although sometimes the Turkish version has one side dusted in cornflour, which makes it less silky than the Syrian variety. But I don't remember anyone in Mashta making the sweet walnut 'sausages' and it was the first time I had seen them being made.

At the entrance of the hangar was a young man whose sole job was to string the walnut halves onto the cotton threads. We watched him do this, leaving a space between each, before tying the walnut threads onto the metal rings so that they looked a little like wind chimes. When the grape juice reached the right consistency, a couple of men took these rings from him and started dipping the walnut threads into the thickened boiling juice with a deft circular motion, several times, until the nuts were encased in the grape jelly, forming long sausage shapes that were slender except where they bulged around the nuts. The men then hung the rings over the cauldron to let the excess jelly drip back into it before removing them to hang on the beams to let them dry completely. The best of these sweet 'sausages' are made with real grape juice, as is *bastik*, although much of both types of confectionery are now made with *pekmez* (see page 325.

Makes 1 large sheet of grape leather

1.6kg (3lbs 7oz) seedless grapes, taken off
   the stems
Lemon juice to taste
100g (3½oz) golden caster sugar

Put the grapes in a large saucepan and crush them as much as you can with a potato masher. Add 120ml (4fl oz) water and place over a medium heat. Cook for about 15 minutes or until the grapes soften. Mash them more using the potato masher and add the juice of half a lemon (about 1 tablespoon) and the caster sugar. Stir until completely diluted and taste for sweetness. It should be sweet although not cloyingly so and the lemon should liven up the taste but not make it tart. After that, adjust both sugar and lemon to your taste and cook for another 30 minutes. Strain through a very fine sieve into a clean pan, pressing on the pulp to extract. Stir 1 tablespoon cornflour in 60ml (2fl oz) water and whisk it into the grape juice, then continue whisking for another 5 to 10 minutes until the juice has thickened.

   Preheat the oven to 60°C (140°F), gas mark ¼. Line a large baking sheet with cling film that you can use in a microwave or a large silicone pastry mat. Pour the grape juice onto it and if necessary spread it evenly to have a thickness of about 1 or 2mm (just under ¹⁄₁₀in). Place in the oven making sure you don't let the cling film touch the sides of the oven or the rack. Also be sure not to let it flap over the grape juice which will interfere with the drying. It will be quite a few hours before the mixture becomes grape leather, so it is best to leave it in the oven overnight and check after 8 hours to see if it has dried. Once done, peel off the cling film or the non-stick baking sheet and roll or cut into squares and fold like a handkerchief. Wrap in cellophane and store in a sealed container where it should last for quite some time.

Curing Olives

Throughout the Levant, olives are as much of a staple as bread. They are served for breakfast, lunch and dinner, and most Lebanese people finish their main meal with an olive or two, the way the French do with a piece of cheese. Olives are probably one of the earliest exports of Phoenician traders who established city-states along the Lebanese coast. My uncle owned olive groves in the Chouf Mountains, south-east of Beirut, and I still remember the hive of activity during olive harvest, when the olives were both taken to the press and brought in basketfuls to the house for my grandmother to preserve. She and my mother prepared the green olives in three different ways. They either left them whole, slit each olive lengthways with a sharp knife or crushed it with a clean stone or pestle to burst the flesh open but without breaking the olive pit. The preserving method was the same, although the taste differed depending on the initial preparation.

Once they had prepared the olives, they put them in a bowl and covered them with water, letting them soak for two days but changing the water twice a day. They then cut a few lemons into thin wedges and washed some fresh chilli peppers to have ready before they drained the olives and started layering them in large sterilised glass jars, arranging a few lemon wedges and a chilli or two in between the layers. The olives were then covered with water in which a large amount of salt had been dissolved. I still remember how my mother and grandmother would float an egg in the salted water to make sure they had added enough salt – a method known in Arabic as *fowshet el-baydah* ('floating of the egg'). The uncut olives took longest to cure, about six months, while the slit ones became edible after two months and the crushed ones after three weeks.

Black olives were preserved in olive oil rather than brine, after first being washed in several changes of water then placed in a large crock and sprinkled liberally with sea salt. The olives were turned over twice a day for about four days to make sure they absorbed the salt uniformly. They were then covered with extra-virgin olive oil, plus a little wine vinegar, and turned over for two more days before being packed in sterilised glass jars. Depending on how ripe they were to start with – black olives are basically ripe green olives – they were ready to eat almost immediately or after 1–2 weeks.

The olives lasted us all year until the next harvest. During that time my mother would vary the flavour by dressing the olives with a little garlic and lemon juice or with orange peel and thyme. In Iran, they have a particularly famous dressing called *parvardeh* in which the cured olives are mixed with a thick sauce made by mixing pomegranate syrup with chopped walnuts, garlic and herbs, as in the recipe below.

Olives Marinated with Walnuts, Herbs and Pomegranate Syrup

ZEYTUN PARVARDEH

    60g (2oz) shelled walnuts
    4 garlic cloves, peeled
    60ml (2fl oz) pomegranate syrup (see page 327)
    ½ tbsp dried mint
    ½ tbsp dried coriander
    1 tsp ground angelica (see page 314)
    150g (5oz) green olives
    Sea salt
    Finely ground black pepper

Put the walnuts and garlic in a food processor and process until finely chopped. Transfer to a mixing bowl that is large enough to also take the olives. Add the pomegranate syrup, dried herbs and ground angelica and mix well. Add the olives and taste before

you season with a little sea salt and freshly ground pepper.
Serve immediately or store in a sealed jar in the fridge to serve
later.

Making Qawarma

We usually spent the first part of our summers in Syria with
'Ammto Zahiyeh and the latter part with my Lebanese
grandmother, in Rechmaya, a lovely village perched above a
dramatic valley in the Chouf Mountains. By the time we got to
my grandmother, she and her sister, Tante Marie, who lived there
all year round, were in full flow preparing their winter preserves,
together with my mother's sister, Tante Jeannot, who never
married.

Everything about Rechmaya was different from Mashta
el-Helou. The houses were on the road with balconies at the front
and lush orchards at the back. Some houses were old while others
had been built more recently but none had vaulted rooms like those
at my aunt's house. Amenities were more modern: there was no
electricity or running water at first in Mashta whereas these were
always available in Rechmaya, at least from what I can remember.
But the rhythm of life was fairly similar in each place. My
grandmother's family grew most of their produce and they made
everything at home, including their *qawarma*, a lamb 'confit'
consumed during the winter months when sheep are too thin to
slaughter; it is one of the staples of Lebanese mountain people.
The preparation of *qawarma* started long before we arrived for
the summer, from the moment Tante Marie bought the lamb and
started fattening it. She, my grandmother and Tante Jeannot
treated it like a precious child, hand-feeding it on mulberry leaves
and visiting it between feeds to make sure it was happy. They
even gave it a name. But the lamb's life as a pet was brief and its
pampered existence came to a brutal end at the end of the summer
when it had grown plump enough to be killed.

The slaughter may have been bad news for the poor lamb, but it
was an occasion for great feasting in the family. Once it had been

115

butchered by one of my uncles, my grandmother, mother and aunts set about preparing the meat. And not one scrap of that animal was wasted. The principle of no waste is an established rule in Lebanese culinary tradition and throughout the Levant, and the making of *qawarma* is a perfect example of this wise approach to food.

The first thing they did was to prepare the offal, which otherwise spoiled quickly. My grandmother cut up the liver, still warm, into small pieces and placed it on a plate, together with a little mound of diced fat from the tail, for the family's breakfast. I would sit next to her while she prepared some liver bites for me. She'd tear off a piece of pita bread and placed a cube or two of liver on it. She'd then add a cube of fat, season the meat with salt and different spices, wrap the bread around the meat and pop the whole thing into my mouth. For some reason, I don't quite remember the slaughter (perhaps I was not allowed to watch it), but I can still taste the exquisite freshness of the raw liver. People may baulk at the thought of eating raw liver for breakfast, but in Lebanon it is considered one of the ultimate delicacies.

With breakfast over, the hard work would begin. My grandmother and mother took charge of singeing the head and feet of the lamb. They then washed them, in several changes of water and soap, before scrubbing the stomach and intestines, which they also washed many times, until they were so clean you could hardly smell them. Then one would cut the tripe in pieces, which she sewed into pouches, while the other turned the intestines inside out. They stuffed the pouches and intestines with a mixture of rice, meat and chickpeas and put them to simmer in a large pot together with the head and feet.

While my mother and grandmother were making the *ghammeh* (see page 158), my aunts, using razor-sharp knives, chopped most of the meat and tail fat into very small pieces. They melted the fat and cooked the meat in it to make *qawarma*. The leg meat was reserved for *kibbeh* (see page 42) and I still remember how they pounded it in a large marble mortar with a wooden pestle. The fillet was reserved for grilled kebabs while the bones, with whatever meat that was left on them, were cooked with wheat to make *h'risseh* (see page 86).

The proportions for making *qawarma* is twice as much meat as fat. You won't find sheep-tail fat in the West, but the fat from around the kidneys is a good substitute and I recommend you use it with meat from the neck or the shoulder. First melt the fat, then cook the hand-chopped meat in it, adding enough sea salt for the qawarma to taste almost too salty – this will preserve it better – and cook, uncovered, stirring the meat very regularly until the meat is well browned. Pour into sterilised glass jars (see page 95) and allow to cool completely before covering the jars with the lids. Qawarma should last the whole year if kept in the fridge.

Tomato Paste

Another favourite moment of my Lebanese mountain summers was when my grandmother and mother joined forces to make tomato paste for both households. They would squeeze mountains of tomatoes with their hands into a large fine sieve that they had set over a very large pot. My grandmother then salted the strained tomato juice and boiled it down until it turned into a thick dark paste. They didn't leave the pot for long, taking it in turns to stir the tomatoes regularly, and whenever my grandmother stirred the juice, I would be there with my spoon asking for a taste – my mother would have told me to go away. I loved trying the paste as it reduced, the flavour becoming more and more intense. And I still love nibbling on tomato paste when I use it, although none of the commercial ones have the same intense flavour, except for the Sicilian estrattu, which they dry in the sun, stirring the tomatoes regularly until the paste is so thick you can cut it with a knife. It is the only tomato paste that gives me a madeleine moment when I taste it because the intense flavour and thick texture is so close to the paste my mother and grandmother made. You really need to wait till high summer to make your own and you need to choose tomatoes that are very ripe but without any rot spots.

Makes three 500g (1lb 1oz) jars

4kg (8¾lb) ripe tomatoes, peeled, deseeded and finely
    chopped
1 tbsp sea salt
Juice of 1 lemon

Put the chopped tomatoes and salt in a very large saucepan and place over a low heat. Cook, stirring regularly – less so at the beginning than towards the end when the mixture becomes very thick – until the tomatoes have reduced by a little more than 50 per cent.

Add the salt and mix well, then pour into three sterilised jars (see page 95) and add a teaspoon or so of lemon juice to each jar. This will help preserve the paste and keep its colour. Wait until the paste is completely cool before sealing the jars shut. Kept in the fridge or a very cool larder, it will last for at least a year.

Pepper Paste

It was in a remarkably ugly setting in Gaziantep that I finally got to see how pepper paste is made. Gaziantep is a bustling, sprawling city in south-eastern Turkey with a small historic centre that is the only part worth visiting. However, during the month of September it is just as interesting to walk through the modern neighbourhoods because wherever you go, you will see families busy preserving food as if they were still living in the middle of the countryside, using the pavements or narrow lanes outside their homes as if they were gardens or courtyards.

Pepper paste is an essential ingredient in Turkish cuisine, and when I asked my friend Filiz (who is the person to go to for all things culinary in Gaziantep) where would be the best place to see it being made, she asked a shop owner who sold it and we were directed to a shabby modern building in a busy part of the town. One of the families residing in the building had hired a massive bright red metal pepper crusher, which had just been delivered in a truck. The driver unloaded it onto the pavement where sacks of trimmed peppers were waiting. The men of the family dumped sack after sack into the machine and put bucket after bucket under the spout to collect the minced peppers. They then formed a chain to take the buckets up onto the roof where the women were waiting, having laid plastic sheets all over the ground. The women poured the contents of the buckets over the sheets, spreading the paste so that it would dry evenly.

They were also drying aubergines, which they had strung all around the parapet, and dyed lamb's wool, which they had hung on ropes in between the sheets on which they had spread the pepper paste. That week, it was this family's turn to take over the roof space in order to make their year's preserves. The following week was the turn of the family on the floor above them and the week before it had been the turn of the family living below. It may not have been such a pretty scene as my Lebanese grandmother and her sister at work during the summer in Rechmaya, but the results were essentially the same.

Even though you cannot get the same peppers as the large mild ones growing in that part of Turkey or northern Syria, you can make your own pepper paste by mixing a few hot chilli peppers with regular red bell or Romano peppers to get the subtle heat that is so typical of Turkish pepper paste. You can also make the paste using dried peppers (mostly guajillos, with a tiny percentage of arbol for the heat), which you need to trim, deseed and soak before processing with salt, as below.

Makes about 750g (1lb 10oz)

2kg (4lb 4oz) red peppers (either bell or Romano),
    trimmed and deseeded
50g (2oz) red chilli peppers, trimmed and deseeded
2 tbsp sea salt

Chop up the peppers in a food processor until completely pulverised. Transfer to a saucepan and add 125ml (4½fl oz) of water. Place over a medium heat and simmer, stirring regularly, for about 15 minutes. Take off the heat and add the salt, mixing it in well.

Pour the pepper purée into a large, shallow non-stick or Pyrex baking dish – you do not want to use a material that may corrode. Cover with cheesecloth and put to dry in a sunny place – inside if you do not have a terrace or garden, or outside if you do. Stir every day and leave to dry in the sun until you have a thick paste. Alternatively, you can spread the purée on a baking tray and place in the oven, on a low heat, stirring the paste every few hours until it has baked to a very thick paste.

Once dried, transfer to sterilised glass jars with tight-fitting lids (see page 95) and cover with olive oil before sealing shut. Store in a cool dark place.

Kishk

Kishk is made by fermenting burghul with yoghurt, drying it, then crumbling and sifting it to get a fine powder resembling white wholewheat flour. An important winter staple in the Lebanese mountains, it is prepared at the very end of summer. Watching the process was another highlight of my childhood summers and I often put my hands and arms into the big tub as my grandmother or aunt stirred more yoghurt into the wheat, which they did every day for about a week until the mixture thickened and soured. I pretended I wanted to help, but I was really after the cool feel of the yoghurt against my skin. When the mixture had thickened and fermented to the level they required, they picked it up in handfuls, laying it out on white sheets spread in the shade to let it dry. This took a few days and when the *kishk* was dry, my grandmother brought out a large fine metal sieve and she, my mother and my aunts sat around the sieve to crush the hardened chunks between the palms of their hands for my grandmother to sift the crumble into a fine powder that is used with *qawarma* (see page 115) to make a hearty breakfast soup. *Kishk* is also mixed with tomatoes, onion, walnuts and olive oil to make a topping for the Arabic equivalent of pizza, *manaqish* (see page 240).

Tarhana is the Turkish equivalent of *kishk*. The base is the same – burghul and fermented yoghurt – but the dish otherwise varies from region to region or even family to family. In some regions, they add vegetables while in others they make it with wholewheat. It can also be made into a coarse powder speckled with green and red bits from the various vegetables that have been added, ground up finely or left in jagged chunks that look like pieces of modern sculpture. There are many more variations of *tarhana* than *kishk* but the end result is the same. All are reconstituted with water to make a thick soup, or in some cases a thick topping or filling for savoury pastries. The taste is rather sour due to the fermentation process and the soup is always served blistering hot. You can omit the meat or *qawarma* and simply make the soup with butter and garlic for a vegetarian option.

Serves 2

60g (2oz) *qawarma* (see page 115) or 30g (1oz) butter and
    30g (1oz) freshly minced lamb, from the shoulder or
    shanks (either ask your butcher to mince the lamb or do
    it yourself using the fine attachment on a meat grinder)
4 large garlic cloves, peeled
125g (4½oz) *kishk*
Sea salt

Put the *qawarma* and garlic in a saucepan, place over a medium heat and cook until the garlic is softened. If you are using minced lamb, first melt the butter over a medium heat, add the garlic and sauté until soft, then add the meat and cook until browned.

Add the *kishk* and 500ml (18fl oz) of water, stirring these in gradually, a little at a time, so that the mixture does not become lumpy. Depending on the brand of *kishk*, you may need a little more or less water to achieve the right consistency.

Bring to the boil, stirring constantly, then reduce the heat to low and simmer for 3 minutes. Taste before adding any salt as the *kishk* is already salted. The soup should be thick but not too thick – more like a thin porridge. Serve very hot with pita or crusty bread.

Shanklish

Even today, nearly 50 years later, I can still picture my wonderful aunt Zahiyeh making *shanklish*, the Syrian equivalent to Roquefort, bending over a big enamel tub to knead the *qarisheh* (curd). She produced the curd by boiling yoghurt with a little lemon juice until it curdled and then draining it overnight. The next morning she tipped the curd into the tub and seasoned it with salt and chilli flakes before kneading it. She would then ask my mother to help her make cheese balls the size of oranges which they set to dry over straw before packing them into earthenware jars and placing them in the *qabu* (cool room where my aunt kept her preserves) to let the cheese ferment. The balls were left for a few weeks until they developed a coat of mould, at which stage my mother and grandmother took them out of the jars to rinse off the mould. They then rolled the cleaned cheese balls in dried thyme and stored them again but this time in glass jars. I always wanted to lend a hand, and my aunt was very sweet, letting me shape a few cheese balls, which she inevitably had to reshape after I'd finished.

To make the cheese you need to boil yoghurt with a little lemon juice (about half a lemon to 3kg (6lbs 6oz) yoghurt and make sure your yoghurt is live culture. The yoghurt will curdle as soon as it comes to the boil, at which point you will take it off the heat and put to strain in cheesecloth. The excess liquid should drain within a few hours. Then you knead the curds with enough salt to make the cheese salty but not so much to make it inedible and add as much Aleppo pepper as you need for your cheese to be as spicy as you'd like. After that, roll the cheese into balls the size of a small orange and spread on a clean kitchen towel to dry (outside if you have space or somewhere away from the heat and draughts in your kitchen. Leave to dry for a couple of days then put in clean jars and leave for another few days until mould develops on the cheese – traditionally this was done in earthenware jars that were only used to ferment the cheese and the right bacteria was inside the jars, but I doubt very many people do this now. Anyhow, you need to rinse off the mould then roll the cheeses in dried thyme and store again in clean jars where they will start ageing – although the cheese is so good, it is difficult to leave it to age too long. Store the jars in a cool place or the refrigerator.

Fig Jam

I don't think I have ever had a better fig jam than my aunt Zahiyeh's. She used pale green figs from the tree on the other side of the lane from her house, which she referred to as my father's tree because he ate all the figs from it when he was a child. They were his favourite fruit. Like him, I love figs and I always helped to pick them for the jam, often annoying my mother by eating more than I put in the basket. My aunt was much more relaxed about my greed. In fact, she nearly killed me when I was six months old by weaning me on figs. Before she made the jam, she first dried the figs. We would take baskets and baskets of them up onto the flat roof of her house together with white sheets that we spread out and anchored with stones at each corner and along the edges. We then pressed the figs open and spread them, open side up, on the sheets to let them dry in the sun. When they were dry, my aunt set about making the jam, cooking the figs with a little sugar, mastic, bay leaves and aniseed. She would spread the thick jam in layers inside empty baklava tins, sprinkling toasted sesame seeds in between each layer, and always gave us a few tins to take back home with us. I guess there isn't much chance of getting home-dried figs like hers in the West to make this jam. The best you can do is to buy the highest-quality dried figs you can find.

Makes two 500g (1lb 1oz) jars

1kg (2lb 2oz) dried figs
900g (2lb) golden granulated sugar
Juice of ½ lemon
1½ tsp ground aniseed
115g (4oz) toasted sesame seeds (to toast them
   yourself, see page 329)
1 tsp orange blossom water
¼ tsp ground mastic (see page 322)

Put the figs and sugar in a large saucepan and add 750ml (1⅓ pints) of water. Place over a medium heat and cook, stirring all the time, until the sugar is dissolved. Add the lemon juice and the aniseed and continue stirring until the figs have softened and the syrup thickened. This will take about 30 minutes.

Take the pan off the heat and add the sesame seeds and orange blossom water and mix well. Let the figs cool a little, then add the mastic and quickly mix it in. Cover the pan with a clean tea towel and let the jam cool before transferring it to two sterilised jars (see page 95). Seal the jars shut and store in a cool dark place.

Apricot Jam

My mother always made our jams when we were children. Depending on the season and what the ambulant vendors had piled high in their carts, she would buy kilos and kilos of fruit to turn into jam. My two favourites were apricot and quince (see page 125). You can vary the recipe below, substituting the apricots with the same quantity of hulled strawberries or pitted plums or cherries, or whatever fruit you feel like using, simply adjusting the quantity of sugar slightly, depending on how sweet or sour the fruit is.

Makes two 500g (1lb 1oz) jars

1kg (2lb 2oz) fresh apricots, pitted and halved
500g (1lb 1oz) golden caster sugar

Put the apricots and sugar in a large saucepan, ideally a copper jam-making one, and place over a medium-high heat. Bring to the boil and boil for 5 minutes, stirring constantly. Then reduce the heat to medium and leave to bubble gently for a further 25 minutes, still stirring regularly.

Make sure the jam has thickened properly or it will not last as long, nor be as good. Test by placing a drop on a chilled saucer and leaving for a few seconds. If the surface of the jam wrinkles when you push it with a finger, it is ready. If not, the jam will need to boil for a few more minutes.

Let the jam cool a little in the pan before transferring to two sterilised jars (see page 95). Allow it to cool down completely before sealing the jars.

Quince Jam

I love quince jam, both for its pretty pink colour and for the texture of the fruit, which doesn't seem to soften too much. And I was always mesmerised by the sight of my mother patiently slicing quinces into a mountain of tiny triangular pieces, which turned from pale when raw into a gorgeous pink as they started cooking. You can substitute the quince in this recipe with apples, if you prefer, which may take a little less time to cook.

Makes two 500g (1lb 1oz) jars

1.25kg (2¾lb) quinces, peeled and cored (making 1kg/2lb 2oz of prepared quince)
750g (1lb 10oz) golden caster sugar
1 tsp lemon juice
2 cloves (optional)

Cut the peeled quinces into quarters, slice each in half lengthways and then cut these into small thin triangular pieces.

Put the quince pieces in a large saucepan, preferably a copper jam-making one, add 250ml (9fl oz) of water and place over a medium heat. Bring to the boil and allow to bubble for 3–4 minutes, stirring constantly. Add the sugar and boil for a further 5 minutes, continuing to stir, then reduce the heat to medium-low and leave to bubble for 15–20 minutes or until the water has evaporated and the jam thickened. Make sure you stir the mixture all the time so that it doesn't stick. By the time the jam is ready, the colour should have changed to pink or reddish depending on the type of quince.

In the Souk

I don't like shopping much but I love wandering in the souks, both to soak up the hectic atmosphere when they're open and to enjoy the near emptiness and eerie silence when they're closed, when all the doors to the stalls are shuttered, and stray cats and the occasional street food cart are the only sign of life.

In fact, street food is one of the reasons I like souks, from when I was very young. I still remember nagging my mother to take me along whenever she went to the old souks of Beirut. In those days, most of the city centre was taken up by souks, each specialising in a type or class of merchandise. If my mother wanted to buy ready-to-wear clothes, we went to souk el-Tawileh, the Bond Street of pre-civil war Beirut. If, on the other hand, she wanted to sew casual clothes, we would head to souk el W'qiyeh (in Arabic the souk of 200 grams) where fabrics were sold by the weight; and for my father's new suits, we went to souk el-Joukh (the souk of woollens) to buy fabrics to give his tailor.

As for food shopping, we had two options. For exotic, early or out-of-season produce, we went to souk el-Franj (the souk of the French or foreigners). Such produce was too expensive for ambulant sellers to have on their carts and my mother, like most Lebanese people then, considered it very chic to serve out-of-season fruit and vegetables – it showed sophistication and wealth, hence the trip to the souk instead of stepping out onto the balcony or up to the window to call to street vendors for seasonal, local produce from their carts. And unlike the street vendors who had piled the produce high on their carts, as if they had just tipped it out of the harvesting baskets without any semblance of order or sense of display except for the abundance, I was convinced that the shop-holders in souk el-Franj spent their days picking their fruit or vegetables one by one, polishing them then arranging them in neat displays.

If my mother wanted to make stuffed tripe, a great Lebanese delicacy, we would head to a rather humble, ramshackle market, souk el-Nuriyeh (the gypsy souk), to a butcher whom she trusted to clean the innards well. We always had to be careful with our shoes as we entered his shop. The water ran constantly through the shop and out onto the pavement as his boys washed the innards. In fact, we had to be careful wherever we stepped. The vendors trimmed

129

their produce and just chucked the skins, trimmings, or any other rejects right onto the road outside their shops or stalls.

I really didn't mind the dirt. I loved Souk el-Nuriyeh because of the street food vendors even if all I could do was to look longingly at their carts, knowing that no amount of pleading was going to sway my mother to let me buy anything to eat, neither grilled corn, nor roasted nuts, nor sesame galettes. I was simply not allowed to eat on the street. Just not what well brought-up girls did, as she kept repeating to my great frustration. I am sure that my fascination with street food dates back to those maddening shopping trips when I hoped that my mother would one day relent and let me buy something. But no, her resolve that I should behave like a proper young girl never wavered. As a result, it is almost impossible for me now to pass a street vendor without wanting to buy something. Unless, that is, I am in Cairo where the lack of hygiene brings my mother's exhortations right back and I find myself thinking like her!

There was one place, though, where my mother did allow me to eat on the street, and that was at the Birkeh (fountain), a small stall right by a lovely nineteenth-century marble fountain (hence the name) where they made the most luscious Lebanese puddings. One was thickened with rice flour and spiced with caraway and cinnamon (*meghli*) and the other was made with milk and flavoured with rose water (*muhallabiyeh*). They also sold wonderfully refreshing drinks such as *jellab*, a smoked drink made with date syrup and packed with crushed ice, plump pine nuts and raisins – soaking the nuts rehydrates them and makes them taste as if they are fresh.

The Birkeh was in Souk Ayass, which was neither chic nor downmarket; and we always made a detour to go there. I am still not sure why my mother relented and broke her strict rule of no street food at the Birkeh. Perhaps because it felt more like a café, with the fountain's edge serving as both seats and tables. Or perhaps because it was spotless and there were elegant ladies amongst the customers – there were none at the carts.

Still, when I think back to those days, I wonder why I never paid attention to the lovely Ottoman buildings that lined the souks' busy streets instead of concentrating on street food. Admittedly, the buildings were grimy and run down, but the arched windows, the iron work and the graceful proportions were beautiful. It was only when the whole area was devastated during the civil war that I, and many others, realised what lovely architecture had been lost.

The war is long over now and much of downtown Beirut has been rebuilt, although more like an Ottoman theme park for luxury brands, fancy restaurants and cafés rather than the way it was.
I guess it would be unrealistic to expect the magical, bustling souks of my youth to come back to life; although there is at present an attempt at rebuilding the souks of Beirut, the contemporary version is a huge, modern shopping complex that could be anywhere in the world from Los Angeles to Singapore, with the same brands, rather non-descript architecture (except for isolated gems such as Zaha Hadid's design for Aishti, the Lebanese Bergdorf Goodman) and that same soulless quality that they all share.

Fortunately, Beirut is the only city in Lebanon to have lost its old souks. Sidon to the south and Tripoli to the north have kept theirs, fairly intact, despite the encroachment of modern life.

Whenever I walk through the vaulted stone alleyways of the souks in Sidon, I feel as if I have been transported back in time, especially if it is after dark when muscular moustachioed bakers in shirtsleeves throw menacing shadows as they remove baked loaves from their wood-fired ovens while street vendors peddle boiled giant fava beans and other specialities on carts fitted with flickering lights, adding to the nostalgic atmosphere and mystery.

As for the souks of Tripoli, they are less fascinating, later in date and without much architectural merit. Still, they are organised like proper souks, with each trade grouped in its own section. The coppersmiths in one corner, beating trays or shaping large cooking pots, which they then line with tin, while a little further on, woodworkers carve spoons and cookie moulds and a little further still, I can revel in a world of alternative fashion stopping at stalls crammed with glittery little girls' clothes right next to others selling sober veils and coats for when they become women and need to hide their charms from any male that is not family, right next to cobblers making men's pointy shoes – Arab men love these shoes regardless of them having gone out of fashion.

The bazaars of Turkey and Iran as well as the souks of Syria are all organised in the same way as the souks that I describe above, a labyrinth of narrow alleyways where the trades are grouped in speciality with the spices in one corner, the meat in another, the vegetables and fruits in another, the nuts and sweets in another and so on. And throughout you will find street food vendors. People go to the souks both to sell their produce to the traders and to buy what they need.

Noodle Soup

ASH-E RESHTEH

Tajrish is my favourite market in Tehran, not only because of the hustle and bustle of the narrow alleyways bursting with seasonal produce (both familiar and unusual) and local specialities, but also because of the cafés – like the one where they serve only *ash-e reshteh* soup and *halim* (see page 134). I went there with the late Minou Saberi, a lovely woman whom I took to immediately when we cooked together for an article on Iranian food that I was writing, but who sadly died only a few days later.

Persian noodles are made with just flour and water and you can buy them from any specialist shop selling Middle Eastern foodstuffs. If you don't have one near you, however, you can replace them with linguine or other similar pasta. As for *kashk*, it is basically dried buttermilk (see 'dried yoghurt' on page 89), sold in the shape of tennis balls, which you mix with a little water to reconstitute, or in jars already reconstituted into a creamy paste. You can use sour cream as a substitute but it is not the same thing and its taste is nowhere near as sour as that of *kashk*. The texture is also different – *kashk* thickens the soup differently. My suggestion would be to try to find some *kashk* with a very long shelf life.

Serves 4–6

3 tbsp vegetable oil

1 medium-sized onion, peeled and thinly sliced

½ tsp turmeric

¼ tsp finely ground black pepper

60g (2oz) dried kidney beans, soaked overnight in cold water (enough to cover the beans by 2–3 fingers) and ½ tsp bicarbonate of soda

60g (2oz) dried chickpeas, soaked overnight in cold water (enough to cover the chickpeas by 2–3 fingers) and ½ tsp bicarbonate of soda

60g (2oz) dried mung beans, soaked in cold water for 30 minutes (enough to cover the beans by 2–3 fingers)

60g (2oz) brown lentils, soaked in cold water for 30
   minutes (enough to cover the lentils by 2–3 fingers)
Juice of 1 lemon
½ tsp dried dill or a few sprigs of dill, coarsely chopped
½ tsp dried oregano
150g (5oz) flat-leaf parsley, most of the stalk discarded,
   coarsely chopped
150g (5oz) fresh coriander, most of the stalk discarded,
   coarsely chopped
60g (2oz) spring onions, trimmed and thinly sliced
60g (2oz) spinach, shredded
Pinch of dried chilli flakes
Sea salt
100g (3½oz) Persian noodles or linguine or tagliatelle
1–2 tbsp *kashk* or sour cream, plus extra to serve

To garnish
2 tsp dried mint fried in 2 tbsp vegetable oil (*na'nâ dâgh*)
Pinch of saffron threads

Put the oil and onions in a large saucepan and place over a medium
heat. Fry the onions until golden brown, then add the turmeric and
pepper.

Drain and rinse the kidney beans and chickpeas and add to the
onions. Add 1.5 litres (2½ pints) of water and bring to the boil.
Reduce the heat to medium-low, cover the pan with a lid and
simmer for 45 minutes.

Drain and rinse the mung beans and lentils, and add to the soup
with the lemon juice, dill and oregano. Simmer for another 45
minutes, stirring every now and then and checking on the water –
adding a little more if the soup becomes too thick.

Add the fresh herbs, spring onions, spinach, chilli flakes and some
salt, and simmer for another 20 minutes. Then add the noodles
(or linguine or tagliatelle), which you can break in half or in smaller
pieces, and simmer for 5 minutes or until the noodles are soft but
not mushy. Stir in the *kashk* (or sour cream), then taste and adjust
the seasoning if necessary.

133

Transfer to a soup tureen, making swirls with more creamy *kashk* (or sour cream) and drizzling the fried dried mint and its oil all over. Sprinkle the saffron threads over the white tracks of *kashk* and serve immediately.

Wheat and Meat Porridge

HALIM

I had this for breakfast in a lovely café by the market of Rasht in Gilan Province in northern Iran. The café was painted pink with pink tablecloths and plastic pink tulips; and it was on the ground floor of a 1920s building with very high ceilings and large windows giving onto a courtyard where one of the cooks was using a big wooden mallet to beat the *halim* in a large cauldron. He must have been at it for hours but the resulting porridge was all the better for his exertions, with a smooth, stretchy texture. Much nicer than the *halim* I had in the *ash-e reshteh* restaurant in Tajrish, which was rather watery. You find the same porridge with slight variations and under different names (*h'riss*, *harisa* or *h'risseh* – see page 86) throughout the Arab world, but it is only in Iran that I had it for breakfast, and as street food. Everywhere else, it is served as an alms dish or to commemorate Ramadan or other religious occasions. The other difference is that Iranians cook the meat and wheat separately, whereas elsewhere they cook both ingredients together. You can make your life easier by using a hand-held blender to pulverise the wheat, instead of stirring it all the time and eventually beating it. The texture will not be quite the same – probably something to do with how the gluten is broken up – but the taste will be just as good.

Serves 4–6

250g (9oz) wheat, soaked overnight in cold water (enough to cover the wheat by 2–3 fingers)
Sea salt

500g (1lb 1oz) lean lamb, from the shoulder or neck
1 medium-sized onion, peeled and coarsely chopped
½ tsp turmeric
¼ tsp finely ground black pepper

To serve
90g (3oz) ghee or clarified butter (see page 318), melted
Ground cinnamon
Golden caster sugar

Drain the wheat and rinse it under cold water, then put in a large saucepan. Pour in enough water to cover by about two fingers, add some salt and place over a medium heat. Bring to the boil then reduce the heat to low and simmer for 2 hours. As the wheat begins to soften, start stirring it and cook for another hour, stirring more or less all the time.

Put the meat, onion and spices in another pan. Cover with water and place over a medium heat. As the water comes to the boil, skim away any scum that rises to the surface, then lower the heat to medium-low and simmer until the meat is very tender. Strain, reserving the stock, and place the meat in a food processor. Process until finely shredded.

Add some of the wheat to the meat and process until well blended. Add this mixture to the remaining wheat and simmer, stirring constantly, until you have a homogeneous porridge with a somewhat stretchy texture.

Pour the porridge into a soup tureen, drizzle the melted ghee (or clarified butter) all over, then sprinkle with cinnamon and sugar. Serve immediately with extra cinnamon and sugar for those who want it.

Omelette Sandwiches

SANDWICH EJJEH

There is a marvellous old man in the souk of Aleppo who spends his days making nothing but omelette sandwiches. Though he's pretty old, his movements are those of an agile young man and the way he beats the eggs, which he does for each omelette, is quite mesmerising as he works with great speed. Once he's beaten them, he adds a little chopped parsley and spring onion, then he throws the mixture into a large pan full of very hot oil and, unlike any omelette I have seen made before, the egg mixture puffs up as it cooks. As the bubbles form, he presses on them with a spoon. The omelette cooks in minutes and when he takes it out, he holds it over the pan for a while to drain away the excess oil, then he lays it on pita bread and sprinkles it with a little more parsley and onion before rolling the bread around it. But as much as I love the idea of a herb omelette, and enjoy seeing the old man in action, I can never bring myself to sample his sandwiches. His stall is filthy, as are his clothes and the bowls in which he beats the eggs and keeps the chopped herbs and onion. But I often remember him when I recreate his omelette sandwiches in my kitchen, even more so now with the souks having been destroyed wondering where he is making his omelettes, that is if he is still alive. Mine never puffs up like his, but it is delicious all the same.

Makes 4 sandwiches

6 medium-sized organic eggs
50g (2oz) spring onions (about ½ bunch), trimmed
    and thinly sliced, plus extra to garnish
50g (2oz) flat-leaf parsley (about ¼ bunch), most of
    the stalk discarded, finely chopped, plus extra to
    garnish
2 garlic cloves, peeled and crushed
1 tbsp unbleached plain flour
¼ tsp ground cinnamon
¼ tsp ground allspice
⅛ tsp finely ground black pepper
Sea salt

Vegetable oil for frying
2 medium-sized round pita breads (see page 234)

Break the eggs into a mixing bowl and beat well before stirring
in the chopped spring onion and parsley and crushed garlic. Add
2 tablespoons of water along with the flour, spices and some salt,
and mix well.

Pour enough vegetable oil into a large frying pan to shallow-fry
the omelettes, and place over a medium heat. When the oil is hot,
drop in one-quarter of the egg mixture and spread into a medium-
thin circle. Fry until golden on both sides, remove with a slotted
spatula and put to drain on several layers of kitchen paper. Make
the remaining omelettes in the same way.

Open the pita breads at the seams and break apart to make four
discs. Lay an omelette over the rough side of each disc of bread.
Sprinkle with a little spring onion and parsley and roll the pita
around the omelette. Wrap the lower half of each sandwich in
a paper napkin and serve immediately.

Kibbeh Sandwiches

The souks of Aleppo were the best preserved and most enchanting
of the Levant, until the regime saw fit to bomb the rebels hiding
in its narrow alleyways, resulting in a good section burning down.
These souks form an extensive labyrinth where traders have their
stalls in medieval vaulted alleyways not far from where residents
live in narrow streets lined with beautiful stone walls which hide
lush courtyards and in some cases palatial homes. I used to love
getting lost in the less familiar parts before finding my way back to
the main artery between Bab Antaki (Antioch Gate) and the ancient
citadel, where Souk el-'Attarine ('attarine means 'perfumers' in
Arabic, although the souk also sells spices) and the street food
vendors are. Across the road from Bab Antaki was a lively open-
air market where seasonal vegetables and fruit are piled high,

137

sometimes right on the pavement on rough pieces of cloth. I often checked out what was in season there before entering the souk through Bab Antaki and stopping at a *kibbeh* stall just outside the ancient gate.

Kibbeh, covered in detail in the first chapter, 'En Famille', is an elegant dish and not normally sold on the street. It comes in all shapes and sizes and can be fried, grilled or baked, or cooked in a variety of sauces, not to mention eaten raw. I am not sure why this vendor has chosen to sell it on the street. His are shaped into flat discs, filled with spiced tail fat (see page 332) and fried. He gives them a street-food twist by rolling them inside pita bread, together with fresh herbs, tomatoes and onion. Rather unusual but very popular, judging by the crowds around his cart who grab at the fabulous mound of fresh mint he has on his table, picking it up by the handful and stuffing it into their mouths with each bite of their sandwich – no other stall I have seen has fresh mint on offer like this. I like to think of these sandwiches as a somewhat more stylish and healthier version of a standard hamburger.

Makes 4 sandwiches

1 quantity of uncooked *kibbeh* (see page 42)

For the kibbeh filling
100g (3½oz) unsalted butter, softened, plus melted
   butter for brushing
1 tsp Aleppo pepper (see page 313)

For the sandwiches
4 medium-sized round pita breads (see page 234)
2 medium-sized tomatoes, cut in half and thinly sliced
1 small onion, peeled and thinly sliced
Fresh mint leaves

Divide the *kibbeh* into eight equal-sized balls. Lightly moisten your hands in salted water (dipping them in the bowl of water used during the preparation of the *kibbeh*) and flatten each meatball between the palms of your hands until you have a thin disc measuring about 15cm (6in) in diameter.

Preheat the oven to 220°C (425°F), gas mark 7.

To make the *kibbeh* filling, place the softened butter and Aleppo pepper in a bowl and mix together until they are well blended.

Spread a quarter of the spiced butter over one disc of *kibbeh* and cover with another disc. Press on the edges to seal and lay on a non-stick baking sheet. Fill and mould together the remaining discs in the same way, then brush with melted butter and bake in the oven for 10–15 minutes or until done to your liking.

Open the pita breads along the seams and lay one half over another, rough side up. Place one filled *kibbeh* disc over each double layer of bread. Divide the tomato and onion slices equally between the sandwiches, arranging them down the middle of each. Scatter the mint leaves over the tomatoes and onions if you want them in your sandwich (unless you prefer to serve them on the side) and roll the bread around the *kibbeh* to create a fat wrap. Serve immediately.

Camel Kebabs

Kabab Jamal

There is one stall in the souks of Aleppo that I return to again and again, transfixed by the furry camel's head the butcher hangs up as a shop sign. One day the head will be covered with dark fur and another day it will be honey coloured, depending on the camel he has slaughtered on the day. Even the expression of the head changes, as does the length of the neck. The hanging head indicates that the butcher specialises in camel meat. The place holds a terrifying appeal for me, from the camel's head that looks very much alive despite being severed from its body, to the upper part of the skeleton on display, with its enormous ribcage. I have been inside to taste the meat, which the butcher minced for me, saying that it was too tough to eat grilled in pieces. It was not too bad – closer to beef than lamb and drier than both. The butcher also told me that all good Muslim men had to eat camel at least once a year. The reason? They are among the few animals that are monogamous. As a result their meat is desirable, again only for men. Women's liberation has yet to arrive in the souks of Aleppo.

The recipe below can be made with camel meat, if you can find it, lamb or beef, although I never use beef myself – I find lamb juicier and more flavoursome. As for the name, the Syrians have a strange habit of switching the names of dishes. Kabab in Syria means minced meat, while in Lebanon it means diced grilled meat and minced meat is known as *kafta*. The Syrians also prepare their minced-meat brochettes differently, simply seasoning the minced meat with salt, pepper and allspice, while the Lebanese add onions and herbs to the mince. I am giving the Lebanese version below. To make it Syrian, all you have to do is omit the onions, herbs and cinnamon, and use allspice rather than the seven-spice mixture.

Serves 4

2 medium-sized onions, peeled and quartered
100g (3½oz) flat-leaf parsley (about ½ bunch), most of the stalk discarded
600g (1lb 5oz) freshly minced lean lamb, from the shoulder or leg (either ask your butcher to mince the lamb or do it yourself using the fine attachment on a meat grinder)
½ tsp ground cinnamon
½ tsp ground allspice or Lebanese seven-spice mixture (see page 331)
¼ tsp finely ground black pepper
Sea salt
4 medium-sized round pita breads (see page 234)

For the garnish
2 medium-sized onions, peeled and thinly sliced
Few sprigs of flat-leaf parsley, coarsely chopped
2 tbsp ground sumac (see page 331)
1 tbsp lemon juice
1 tbsp extra-virgin olive oil

12 metal skewers (preferably flat)

Put the onions and parsley in a food processor and process until finely chopped. Transfer to a mixing bowl, add the minced lamb, spices and some salt and mix with your hand until well blended.

Pinch off a little of the mixture and sear in a hot pan to taste, adjusting the seasoning if necessary. Then divide the meat into 12 equal-sized portions.

Preheat the grill to high or start a charcoal fire on a barbecue.

Roll each portion of meat into a ball. Put one in the palm of your hand, take a long skewer, preferably a flat one to help the meat stay on better, and start wrapping the meat around it, squeezing the mixture upwards, then downwards to bind it around the skewer in the shape of a long sausage. Taper the ends and place on a rack ready to grill or barbecue. Shape the remaining balls of meat around the skewers in the same way.

Quickly prepare the onion and parsley garnish by tossing all the ingredients together, seasoning with salt and pepper. Spread the mixture on the pita breads.

Cook the meat for 2–3 minutes on each side or until the meat is done to your liking. Slide onto the pita breads, on top of the onion and parsley garnish, and serve hot.

Iranian Minced Meat Kebabs

KABAB KOUBIDEH

Here is the Iranian take on a hamburger, and like the *kibbeh* sandwiches (see page 42), it is healthier and fresher. It is always served with *sangak* (a flatbread baked over pebbles that is quite exceptional) together with sharp pickles (see page 99), sumac and fresh herbs. Iranians have marvellous flat metal skewers, which they keep in their own round metal case as if they were fishing rods. Flat skewers make it easier to wrap minced meat around them as the minced meat does not hold very well on normal round thin skewers. If you can't find flat skewers, just make patties and cook as if they were hamburgers.

500g (1lb 1oz) freshly minced lamb, from the shoulder
  that has been skinned and trimmed of most of the
  fat (either ask your butcher to mince the lamb or do
  it yourself using the fine attachment on a meat
  grinder)
1 medium-sized onion, peeled and finely grated
1 tsp breadcrumbs
¼ tsp turmeric
¼ tsp baking powder
Sea salt
Finely ground black pepper
2 *sangak* or other Iranian flatbread (see 'bread' on
  page 315)

For the garnish
Iranian pickles (see page 98 and 102)
Selection of fresh herbs (mint, tarragon, dill or coriander),
  coarsely chopped

4 metal skewers (preferably flat)

Put the minced meat and grated onion in a large mixing bowl.
Add the breadcrumbs, turmeric and baking powder and season
with salt and pepper. With your hand, mix all the ingredients
together until well blended. Then knead the meat mixture for a
few minutes to bind the meat and make it easier to wrap around
the skewers.

Preheat the grill to high or start a charcoal fire on a barbecue.

Fill a small bowl with cold, lightly salted water and wet your
hand before pinching off a quarter of the meat to wrap around a
skewer, pressing the mixture up then down to cover two-thirds of
the skewer. Squeeze lightly with your fingers to make indentations
at regular intervals along the mixture. Repeat with the remaining
skewers, then grill or barbecue the kebabs for 2–3 minutes on
each side or until done to your liking.

Slip the meat off each skewer onto half a flatbread, the meat
running along the length of the bread. Scatter a few pickles and

fresh herbs on top, then roll the bread tightly over the meat and garnish. Wrap the lower half of each sandwich in a paper napkin and serve immediately with more pickles and fresh herbs for those who would like them.

Couscous Sandwiches

SANDWICH MOGHRABBIYEH

It seems rather odd to think of pasta as a filling for a sandwich but in one stall, on the edge of the spice section in the souks of Tripoli in northern Lebanon, they serve just that. The stall belongs to a burly man with the bushiest beard I have ever seen. He never seems to change position, always standing behind a big hot plate on which he has a mound of fresh *moghrabbiyeh* (a large-grain couscous – see page 323) mixed with boiled chickpeas and caramelised onion. Whenever a customer arrives, the Hajj, as everyone calls him because he went on pilgrimage to Mecca, tears open a large pita bread, arranges the two layers one on top of the other and spoons a generous amount of the couscous mixture onto the bread, arranging it in a line down the middle. He then rolls the bread tightly around the filling to make a fat wrap that is surprisingly tasty despite it being starch on starch. It is definitely not a sandwich for those watching their figures. In Lebanon, you can buy the pasta freshly made, but it is only available dried in the West.

Serves 4–6

75g (2½oz) unsalted butter
16 baby onions, peeled
150g (5oz) dried chickpeas, soaked overnight in cold
    water (enough to cover the chickpeas by 2–3 fingers)
    and ½ tsp bicarbonate of soda
500ml (18fl oz) chicken stock
1 cinnamon stick
½ tsp ground caraway

cont.   143

1 tsp ground allspice or Lebanese seven-spice mixture
  (see page 331)
¼ tsp finely ground black pepper
250g (9oz) dried *moghrabbiyeh*
Sea salt
¼ tsp ground cinnamon
4–6 medium-sized round pita breads (see page 234)

Melt 2 tablespoons of the butter in a large saucepan and sauté the
onions until lightly golden. Remove to a plate and set aside.

Drain and rinse the chickpeas and add them to the pan with the
chicken stock. Bring to the boil, skimming away any scum that
rises to the surface, then add the cinnamon stick, ground caraway,
allspice (or seven-spice mixture) and black pepper. Reduce the heat
to medium-low and simmer, covered with a lid, for 45–60 minutes
or until the chickpeas are tender. Add the fried onions and simmer
for another 10–15 minutes.

While the chickpeas are cooking, put the *moghrabbiyeh* in a bowl,
cover it with boiling water, stirring well so that the pellets do not
stick together, and let it sit for 15 minutes. Drain and stir in the rest
of the butter, then put the *moghrabbiyeh* in a steamer and steam,
covered, for 20 minutes.

When the chickpeas are ready, add salt to taste. Then tip the
moghrabbiyeh into a large frying pan. Using a slotted spoon,
remove the onions and chickpeas from the stock and add them to
the *moghrabbiyeh*. Add the ground cinnamon and about 250ml
(9fl oz) of the stock and place over a medium-high heat. Sauté for
about 5 minutes, adding more stock if the mixture seems too dry.
Taste and adjust the seasoning if necessary.

Open out a pita bread at the seams, breaking it into two and
putting the two layers one on top of the other, rough side up, then
arrange as much *moghrabbiyeh* as you like down the middle. Roll
the bread tightly around the filling, wrap the lower half of the
sandwich with a paper napkin and serve immediately.

Falafel Sandwiches

Falafel, together with tabbuleh (see page 22) and hommus, are now part of the global menu, but they are originally from Egypt where they are known as *ta'miyah*. Egyptian *ta'miyah* is rather different from Lebanese/Syrian falafel – softer and starchier. The sandwiches are also made differently. Egyptian pita is smaller and thicker and when made with wholewheat, it is called *aysh baladi*. The bread is cut in half across the middle and the pocket opened and filled with the *ta'miyah* and garnish. Lebanese/Syrian pita is large, round and very thin. It is opened at the seam and the two layers placed one on top of the other, rough side up. The filling is then arranged down the middle and the bread rolled around it. As for the garnish, in Egypt you might have crisps or French fries, shredded lettuce or tomatoes, radishes or pickles. In Lebanon and Syria the choice is generally herbs, tomatoes and pickles. Only the tahini sauce is a constant in all three countries, although its name differs – *tahina* in Egypt and *tarator* in Lebanon and Syria.

Serves 4–6

110g (4oz) dried chickpeas, soaked overnight in cold
    water (enough to cover the chickpeas by 2–3 fingers)
    and ½ tsp bicarbonate of soda
175g (6oz) peeled split dried fava beans, soaked overnight
    in cold water (enough to cover the beans by 2–3
    fingers) and ½ tsp bicarbonate of soda
5 large garlic cloves, peeled
1 medium onion, peeled and quartered
1 small leek, trimmed and cut into 2–3 pieces
Large handful of coriander leaves
1 tsp ground cumin
1 tsp ground allspice or Lebanese seven-spice mixture
    (see page 331)
¼ tsp finely ground black pepper
⅛ tsp cayenne pepper
Sea salt
½ tsp bicarbonate of soda

cont.

Vegetable oil for frying
4–6 medium-sized round or oval pita breads
  (see page 234)

For the tahini sauce
125ml (4½fl oz) tahini
Juice of 1 lemon or to taste
2 garlic cloves, peeled and crushed

For the garnish
1–2 firm ripe tomatoes, diced
2–3 pickled cucumbers, quartered lengthways
4–6 sweet chilli pickles, cut in half lengthways
2 pickled turnips (see page 103), thinly sliced

Drain the chickpeas and fava beans and rinse under cold water. Put
in a blender together with the garlic, onion, leek, coriander, spices
and a little salt, and process into a smooth paste. If your blender is
too small, process in batches. Transfer to a mixing bowl and taste,
adjusting the seasoning if necessary. Add the bicarbonate of soda
and mix well. Cover and leave to rest for 30 minutes in the fridge.

Meanwhile, make the tahini sauce. Put the tahini in a mixing bowl
and gradually whisk in the lemon juice, alternating it with 90ml
(3fl oz) of water. Taste from time to time to make sure that you
get the right balance of tartness while keeping the consistency like
that of creamy yoghurt. The tahini will first thicken to a purée-like
consistency before starting to dilute again. If you decide to use less
lemon juice, make up for the loss of liquid by adding a little more
water or vice versa. Add the crushed garlic and a little salt. Taste
and adjust the seasoning if necessary.

Pinch off a handful of the falafel mixture and shape between the
palms of your hands into a fat round patty with tapering sides,
about 5cm (2in) in diameter. Place on a plate and continue making
the patties until you have finished the mixture. You should end up
with about 16 falafel, depending on how fat you have made them.

Heat enough vegetable oil in a large, deep-sided frying pan to
deep-fry the falafel. To test whether the oil is hot enough, add a
small piece of bread; if the oil bubbles around it, it is ready. Drop
in as many falafel as will fit comfortably in the pan, and fry until

golden – about 2 minutes on each side. Remove with a slotted spoon and drain on several layers of kitchen paper. Lay another wad of kitchen paper on top and pat the falafel to absorb as much oil as you can. Continue frying and draining until all the falafel are cooked.

If using round pita bread, open each one at the seams and break it apart, laying the two pieces one on top of the other, rough side up. Spread 3–4 falafel down the middle and crush them open a little. Divide the garnish ingredients equally between the sandwiches and drizzle over as much tahini sauce as you would like, bearing in mind that too much will make the bread soggy and hence eating the sandwiches rather messy. Better to dip the sandwich into the sauce than have it seep out of the wrap. Roll up the bread tightly and wrap the lower half of each sandwich in a paper napkin to serve immediately.

If using oval pita breads, open each along one seam to create a large pocket, and fill with the falafel and equal amounts of garnish. Drizzle with tahini sauce to taste and serve at once.

Lamb Shawarma

SHAWARMA LAHMEH

You find *shawarma* (derived from the Turkish word çevirme, which means to turn or rotate) on every street corner in Lebanon and Syria as well as in many Western countries. *Shawarma* is a very large, fat kebab, once made only with lamb but now also with chicken. The meat is sliced into wide, thin pieces, marinated overnight and threaded onto a long skewer. Interspersed between the layers of meat are slices of fat, or skin if chicken has been used. The skewer is fixed in front of a vertical grill and left to rotate over a moderate heat for 2–3 hours or until the meat is cooked through. During cooking, the fat melts down the whole length of the kebab, basting it and keeping it moist. A *souvlaki* is the Greek version, made with pork. The Turkish version, made with lamb or beef, is

147

called *doner kebab*. Even before the meat is cooked all the way through, the *shawarma* seller starts slicing the outer, cooked layer to order and piles the thin slivers of meat onto pita bread. On top of the meat go sliced tomatoes, onions, pickles, herbs and tahini sauce if the meat is lamb or garlic sauce if it is chicken. The bread is rolled tightly over the filling, half wrapped in paper and handed to the customer for him/her to eat on the go. *Shawarma* is not usually prepared at home, but here is a delectable adaptation taught to me by my Lebanese butcher in London who has now returned to Lebanon, to my great sadness, although he is delighted to be back home.

Serves 4–6

800g (1¾lb) lamb meat, from the shoulder, skinned and
   most of the fat removed, thinly sliced
2 medium-sized onions, peeled and thinly sliced
Juice of 1 lemon or to taste
4 tbsp extra-virgin olive oil
½ tsp ground cinnamon
½ tsp ground allspice or Lebanese seven-spice mixture
   (see page 331)
Leaves from a few sprigs of fresh thyme
Sea salt
Finely ground black pepper
2–3 medium-sized round pita breads or 4–6 oval ones
   (see page 234)

For the tahini sauce
125ml (4½fl oz) tahini
Juice of 1 lemon or to taste
2 garlic cloves, peeled and crushed

For the garnish
4–6 small tomatoes, thinly sliced
½ medium-sized red onion, peeled and very thinly sliced
4–6 gherkins, thinly sliced lengthways
½ tsp finely chopped mint
½ tsp finely chopped flat-leaf parsley

Put the meat in a large mixing bowl, add the onions, lemon juice, olive oil, spices, and thyme, then season with salt and pepper and mix well. Place in the fridge and leave to marinate for 2–4 hours, stirring occasionally.

Meanwhile, make the tahini sauce. Put the tahini in a mixing bowl and gradually whisk in the lemon juice, alternating it with 90ml (3fl oz) of water. Taste from time to time to make sure that you get the right balance of tartness while keeping the consistency like that of creamy yoghurt. The tahini will first thicken to a purée-like consistency before starting to dilute again. If you decide to use less lemon juice, make up for the loss of liquid by adding a little more water or vice versa. Add the crushed garlic and a little salt. Taste and adjust the seasoning if necessary.

After the meat has finished marinating, place a large frying pan over a medium-high heat. When it is very hot, add the meat and sauté for a couple of minutes or until done to your liking.

If you are using round pita breads, tear them open at the seams to make 4–6 circles of bread. Laying these rough side up, arrange equal quantities of meat down the middle of each. Divide the garnish ingredients between the pita pieces and drizzle over as much tahini sauce as you would like, bearing in mind that too much could make the bread soggy. Roll each sandwich tightly, wrap the bottom half in a paper napkin and serve immediately.

If you are using oval pita breads, open at one seam to create a large pocket. Spread one side of the bread inside with tahini sauce, then fill each pita with equal amounts of sandwich ingredients before serving immediately.

Chicken Shawarma

SHAWARMA DJAJ

Often the *shawarma* stalls have one lamb and one chicken version grilling side by side. The main difference is not so much in the seasoning, nor in the garnish, but in the sauce. Lamb *shawarma* is moistened with tahini sauce (see page 147) while chicken *shawarma* is flavoured with an eggless garlic mayonnaise or *tûm* as it is known in Arabic. Before the Syrian revolution, Midan was a popular street food area in Damascus, particularly fun to visit during Ramadan. It was there that I had chicken *shawarma* with a difference – the chicken sandwiched inside *kibbeh* balls (see page 42) instead of bread. Even the marinade used for the chicken was different: a blend of tomato paste and crushed garlic, seasoned with cayenne pepper, Syrian seven-spice mixture and salt. The vendor rolled the *kibbeh* balls into the fat dripping from the *shawarma* and stood them against the bottom part of the grill to heat up while he spread garlic mayonnaise and pomegranate syrup (see page 327) over a paper platter. He then arranged a few slices of pickles, tomato and cucumber along one half and lined the halved *kibbeh* balls on the other. Into these, he stuffed a generous amount of chicken *shawarma*. But he never gave me his recipe for the marinade, so I've included the Lebanese version here.

Serves 4

3 medium-sized organic or free-range chicken breasts
  (about 500g/1lb 2oz in total), with the skin left on
1 medium-sized onion, peeled and thinly sliced
Juice of 1 lemon
115ml (3½fl oz) extra-virgin olive oil
¼ tsp ground cinnamon
¼ tsp ground allspice or Lebanese seven-spice mixture
  (see page 331)
¼ tsp finely ground black pepper
Leaves from a few sprigs of thyme
Sea salt
2 medium-sized round pita breads or 4 oval ones (see
  page 234)

For the garlic sauce

10 large garlic cloves, peeled
170ml (6fl oz) extra-virgin olive oil
Juice of ¼ lemon
3–4 tbsp *labneh* (see page 104) (optional)

For the garnish

2 small tomatoes, thinly sliced
1 small red onion, peeled and very thinly sliced
4 gherkins, thinly sliced lengthways
Handful of fresh mint leaves, coarsely chopped
Few sprigs of flat-leaf parsley, most of the stalk
    discarded, coarsely chopped

Put the chicken breasts in a mixing bowl with the onion, lemon
juice, olive oil, spices and thyme, season with salt and mix well.
Place in the fridge and leave to marinate for 2–4 hours.

Meanwhile, make the garlic sauce. Put the garlic cloves and a little
salt in a mortar and pound with a pestle until reduced to a very fine
paste. Drizzle in the olive oil very slowly, stirring constantly as if
you were making mayonnaise. Stir in the lemon juice and *labneh*
(if using) to take the edge off the garlic flavour.

Preheat the oven to 180°C (350°F), gas mark 4.

Transfer the chicken to a roasting tin and roast in the oven for
25–30 minutes or until cooked through. Remove from the oven,
then discard the skin from the chicken pieces and shred the meat
into thin slivers.

If you are using round pita breads, tear the bread open at the
seams and break apart to make four circles of bread. Laying the
pieces rough side up, spread as much garlic sauce as you like down
the middle of each without making the bread too soggy and arrange
equal quantities of chicken on top. Divide the garnish ingredients
between the pita pieces and roll each tightly around the filling.
Wrap the lower half of each sandwich in a paper napkin to serve
immediately.

If you are using oval pita bread, open at one seam to create a large
pocket. Spread one side of the bread inside with garlic sauce, then

151

fill each pita with equal amounts of sandwich ingredients and serve immediately.

Turkish 'Andouillette'

KOKOREÇ

I was fascinated by the bazaars of Eminönü, at the heart of Istanbul, on my first trip to Turkey back in the 1970s and again when I returned in the 1980s, but I hardly ever go there now. They have become a little too touristy. Instead, I prefer to walk through the narrow lanes behind, looking at kitchen equipment, or clothes or plastic jewellery, and I naturally stop whenever I come across a cart selling street food. Many have a glass box mounted on them with the food dumped inside. I rarely buy anything to eat, but I like to watch the action. One vendor could be touting a pile of Albanian liver (cut into cubes and fried with different spices, a dish probably brought into Turkey by Albanians – hence the name), while another may extol the tastiness of his bland chickpea pilaf, topped with two or three pieces of chicken to indicate that the rice has been cooked in chicken stock. And if the vendor is touting *çiğ köfte*, a mass of raw meat mixed with fine burghul and reddened with pepper paste, he will make sure to tell his clients that he mixed the *köfte* that morning with meat from a freshly slaughtered lamb. I am not sure I would believe these assurances, but I've never suffered any ill-effects the few times I have had *çiğ köfte* as a street food.

Every now and then, I buy a portion of pilaf and watch the vendor cut the tiniest piece of chicken to put on the rice, wondering why he even bothers. I am also not sure why I bother either. Possibly in the hope that one day I will find one that tastes good. It never does. It looks bland and it tastes just as bland, which is not the case with *kokoreç*, a large fat sausage made of lamb intestines – a kind of Turkish andouillette. The sausage is threaded onto a skewer that is put to rotate horizontally in front of a fire, often charcoal, until it is cooked through. The vendor then slices a piece of the sausage, puts it on his wooden board and proceeds to chop it very finely. He places the minced *kokoreç* on a hot plate and stirs it for a minute or so, adding more seasonings, to crisp the meat further and heat it up before stuffing it into the ubiquitous fat baguette-like bread that the Turks seem to favour for their sandwiches. *Şampiyon* is the undisputed master of *kokoreç*, but they have now expanded everywhere and I much prefer to buy my *kokoreç* sandwich from individual stallholders like the one I discovered on my last visit to Istanbul, tucked away in a narrow lane not far from the spice bazaar, near the cheese sellers.

His stall is tiny, with just enough space for the charcoal rotisserie placed over a cabinet containing all he needs to make the sandwiches. He also has two low tables where customers can sit to eat their *kokoreç* and where he has jars of tiny pickled peppers. I didn't have the courage to try them. They looked pretty lethal, and as I spoke no Turkish and he no English, I couldn't find out if they were mild. So I decided not to take the risk.

I also decided against giving a recipe for *kokoreç* as it is very difficult to get hold of lamb intestines in the West. Even if you are lucky enough to know a farmer who would give you some, you will still need to clean them, which is no easy feat. You are better off trying this dish when you are in Turkey, and you will enjoy it all the more knowing how and with what it is made.

Stuffed Mussels

MIDYE DOLMASI

If there were one street food I could take with me to a desert island, it would have to be stuffed mussels. In the old days, before I was conscious of pollution or perhaps because it was not so widespread, I ate stuffed mussels anywhere. I remember the first time I visited Istanbul in the mid 1970s. I stayed at the Pera Palace, still in its faded glory, spending my mornings in mosques and museums – I worked in the art world in those days – and my afternoons and early evenings in the bazaars. Apart from enjoying the hustle and bustle of these markets, and being generally curious about all the unfamiliar foods, I was on a mission to find the ultimate stuffed mussels. I had never eaten them before and had

153

fallen in love with this elaborate delicacy that was sold so cheaply on the street when it could have been on the menu of a Michelin-starred restaurant. My hotel was just down the road from Çiçek Passajı (Flower Passage), a lovely small market leading into a maze of narrow streets full of charming restaurants. Every afternoon, I walked up to the market to sample stuffed mussels. At that time, there were many stalls selling them, while today only one remains. I went from one vendor to the next, tasting the mussels. If they were good, I would linger, gesturing to the vendor to give me one more, then another and another until I had eaten half a dozen extra mussels. Once I'd finished feasting on mussels, I would buy a fat slice of *kaymak* (very thick clotted cream that is rolled up like a Swiss roll), which I ate on my balcony drizzled with honey. I loved that first visit to Istanbul, and what is wonderful is that more than 30 years later I can still stroll up to Çiçek Passajı, albeit not from the Pera Palace (now fully restored and way beyond my budget), to find the same scene and some of the same shops. And fortunately the last remaining stuffed-mussels vendor is one of the best in town. He also sells *midye tava* – mussels that are threaded onto skewers and dipped in flour and then water several times to build up a coating which crisps up when fried. The fried mussels are stuffed into half a fat baguette-like loaf and drizzled with a walnut sauce to produce an irresistible sandwich (reproduced on page 156).

It is not that easy to find mussels that are large enough for stuffing. If you can't find any, simply change the dish to a pilaf by preparing 2–3 times the amount of rice stuffing and cooking it completely. Steam the mussels separately and arrange them, on the half shell, on top of the cooked rice.

Serves 4

4 tbsp extra-virgin olive oil
1 tbsp pine nuts
2 small onions, peeled and finely chopped
110g (4oz) paella or other white short-grain white rice
   (bomba, Calasparra or Egyptian), soaked in warm water
1 tbsp raisins
1½ tbsp tomato paste (see page 332)
¼ tsp ground cinnamon
¼ tsp ground allspice
¼ tsp paprika

Pinch of cayenne pepper
Pinch of ground cloves
Sea salt
Finely ground black pepper
About 40 medium-to-large mussels in their shells
1 tbsp chopped flat-leaf parsley
1 tbsp minced dill
Lemon wedges, to serve

Put the olive oil, pine nuts and onions in a saucepan and sauté, stirring regularly, until lightly golden. Drain the rice and add to the pan. Add the raisins, tomato paste and spices, and some salt and pepper, then pour in just enough water to cover – about 250ml (9fl oz). Bring to the boil, reduce the heat to low and simmer, covered with a lid, for 8–10 minutes or until the water is absorbed and the rice barely done. Take off the heat, wrap the lid in a clean tea towel and place back over the pan before setting it aside to cool down.

Preparing the mussels is a lengthy and rather difficult process, so allow time and be patient. First pull off and discard the beards, if there are any, and rinse the mussels under cold water – don't let them soak or they will die. Lay one mussel on a tea towel on your work surface and insert the tip of a small sharp knife in between the two shells at the slanted end. Slide the knife downward and all around the shell until you cut into the muscle – the mussel will open easily with the two halves remaining attached. Prepare the rest of the mussels in the same way. Take your time and don't rush this part of the preparation or you will either break the shells or hurt yourself with the knife.

Once you have opened all the mussels, stir the fresh herbs into the rice and fill each mussel with a teaspoon or more of the rice mixture, depending on how large it is. Close both halves of the shell together, wipe away any rice grains sticking to the outside and arrange in 2–3 layers in the top part of a steamer. Weigh down the filled mussels with a plate and steam for 20–25 minutes. Remove the steamer section and let the mussels cool. Serve at room temperature with the lemon wedges.

Fried Mussels

MIDYE TAVA

There are two ways of eating mussels on the street in Turkey:
stuffed and steamed (see page 153), or threaded onto skewers
and fried. In Anadolu Kavağı, a fishing village north of Istanbul
on the Asian side, I have seen them prepare fresh anchovies in
the same way. Frying skewered mussels or anchovies is not
so easily done at home unless you have a very large frying pan
to accommodate the skewers. But you can fry them individually,
which the Turks also do. I sometimes use batter instead of
caking them in flour and dipping them in water, as they do in
Turkey. The fritters end up much lighter. If you prefer to use
anchovies for this dish, make sure they are small and very fresh,
for which you'll need either a good fishmonger or a place by
the sea!

For the *tarator*, you can use walnuts, almonds or pine nuts
instead of hazelnuts. Ideally any unblanched nuts should be
peeled after being soaked. Though you can make the sauce
without going to the trouble of soaking and peeling the nuts, the
texture won't be as soft and the *tarator* will taste slightly different.
You can pound the ingredients using a pestle and mortar for an
even finer-textured sauce, but only if you have the patience and
energy.

Serves 6

45 large mussels in their shells or 36 fresh
   anchovies
Plain flour for dusting
Freshly ground black pepper
Vegetable oil for frying
3 baguettes, cut in half widthways, each half split
   open lengthways
Salad garnish (lettuce leaves, trimmed spring onions,
   sliced tomatoes, fresh flat-leaf parsley leaves)
Lemon wedges, to serve

For the Turkish tarator
300g (11oz) skinned hazelnuts
3–4 slices soft white bread, crusts removed
1 large garlic clove, peeled
170ml (6fl oz) extra-virgin olive oil
Juice of 1½ lemons or to taste
Sea salt

12 wooden skewers, soaked in water for at least
   30 minutes

First make the *tarator*. Put the hazelnuts in a deep bowl, cover
with boiling water and let them soak for 1 hour. Drain the nuts and
put in a food processor together with the bread, garlic clove and
1 tablespoon of water. Blend until smooth, then slowly add the
olive oil while still blending. When the oil is completely absorbed,
add the lemon juice and salt to taste. If the mixture seems too thick,
thin with a little more water or with lemon juice if the sauce could
do with being more tart. Taste and adjust the seasoning if
necessary.

If using mussels, first pull off and discard the beards, if there are
any, and rinse the mussels under cold water. Place in a steamer and
steam for 3 minutes or until all the shells have opened, discarding
any that remain shut. Remove the mussels from the shells and place
on a plate.

Pour some flour into a dish long enough to hold the skewers and
season with salt and pepper. Pour a little water into a similar-sized
dish. Thread equal amounts of the cooked mussels onto each
skewer.

Pour enough vegetable oil into a large, deep-sided frying pan to
deep-fry the mussels. To test whether the oil is hot enough, add a
small piece of bread; if the oil bubbles around it, it is ready.
Quickly dip one of the skewers in the flour, then in the water and
again in the flour, repeating a few times until the mussels have a
nice coating that will act like a batter. Drop the skewer in the hot
oil and do the same with the remaining skewers, frying them in
batches until crisp and golden all over.

Remove the skewers with a slotted spoon and leave to drain on several layers of kitchen paper, sprinkling with more salt if necessary. It is a good idea to skim the oil clean in between each batch so that you don't end up with burning bits of batter clinging to the mussels.

Make sandwiches by sliding the mussels off the skewers and into the split-open baguette halves, adding your choice of salad ingredients as a garnish and *tarator* to taste. Serve immediately with the lemon wedges and more *tarator* for those who want it.

Stuffed Tripe

GHAMMEH

One of my favourite stalls in the souks of Tripoli in northern Lebanon is one that is a little off the beaten track. I always have a hard time finding it but when I finally get there, I can never resist a giggle at how unappetising the stuffed tripe (*krûsh*) and intestines (*fawaregh*) look inside the steaming glass cabinet where they are displayed. I don't let this put me off, though, because they are almost as good as those made at home, with the advantage that the stallholders do all the hard work that I am about to describe in the recipe below. I have omitted the instructions for the intestines, usually included in this dish, because they are hard to find in the West, and even more time-consuming to make.

Serves 6–8

4 sheep's trotters
1 medium-sized sheep's stomach
2 cinnamon sticks

For the stuffing
100g (3½oz) dried chickpeas, soaked overnight in cold
    water (enough to cover the chickpeas by 2–3 fingers)
    and ½ tsp bicarbonate of soda

1 tsp bicarbonate of soda

200g (7oz) short-grain white rice (bomba, Calasparra or Egyptian), rinsed under cold water and drained

2 × 400g cans of Italian tomatoes, drained, deseeded and coarsely chopped

250g (9oz) peeled and chopped onion (about 1 large one)

250g (9oz) freshly minced lamb neck fillets (either ask your butcher to mince the lamb or do it yourself using the fine attachment on a meat grinder)

1 tsp ground allspice or Lebanese seven-spice mixture (see page 331)

¼ tsp finely ground black pepper

¼ tsp ground cinnamon

Sea salt

To serve (optional)

6–8 garlic cloves, peeled and crushed

Lemon juice to taste

Singe the sheep's trotters over a gas fire until there are no hairs left on them, then wash in soapy water a couple of times. Rinse well under cold water. Wash the sheep's stomach thoroughly in several changes of water, adding soap if necessary, and rinse well. Cut the cleaned stomach into 6–7 pieces, each measuring about 15 × 20cm (6 × 8in).

Next make the stuffing. Drain and rinse the chickpeas, then add the teaspoon of bicarbonate of soda and stir in well to coat the chickpeas. Leave for 15–20 minutes and rinse well. The purpose of this operation is to soften the chickpeas further and hence shorten their cooking time.

Put the rice in a large mixing bowl, add the remaining ingredients and some salt, and mix well.

Put the trotters in a large saucepan, pour in enough water to cover by 2–3 fingers and place over medium-high heat. Bring to the boil, skimming away any scum that rises to the surface. Add the cinnamon sticks, then reduce the heat, cover with a lid and simmer for 30 minutes.

Fold a piece of tripe in half and sew up the long side and one of the short sides. Repeat with the remaining pieces of tripe, then fill these with the stuffing, making sure they are only three-quarters full to allow space for the rice to expand during cooking. Sew the pouches shut.

Add the stuffed tripe to the trotters, pouring in more water to cover, if necessary, and seasoning with salt. Bring back up to the boil, then reduce the heat and simmer, with the lid on, for 1½– 2 hours or until tender. Serve very hot with some of the cooking liquid on the side. You can, if you want, season the accompanying broth with a little crushed garlic and lemon juice.

Sesame Galettes

Sesame galettes are a street staple throughout the Levant, although they vary in shape from one country to another. In Lebanon, for instance, they are made in the shape of handbags. The vendor tears the fat 'bag' part open to sprinkle the inside with a little *za'tar* (see page 333). In Tripoli, in the north of Lebanon, and in Syria the galettes are shaped into flat, round discs and are often sold filled with halloumi cheese seasoned with sumac. It would be too repetitive for me to supply recipes for all the variations, so I am giving just two recipes here – the one below for Turkish *simit* and the one on page 162 for Lebanese *ka'keh*.

Turkish Sesame Galettes

SIMIT

I don't think you can go through the bazaars of Turkey, or through any street for that matter, without coming across a *simit* (sesame galette) seller. The ones sold here, and in Egypt, are ring-shaped – as in the recipe below.

Makes 4 galettes

150g (5oz) unbleached plain flour, plus extra for dusting
1 tsp (½ × 7g sachet) fast-action yeast
¼ tsp sea salt
Unsalted butter for greasing
125ml (4½fl oz) *pekmez* (see page 325)
100g (3½oz) sesame seeds

Mix the flour, yeast and salt in a large mixing bowl and make a well in the centre. Add 125ml (4½fl oz) and 2 tablespoons of water and mix until you have a rough dough.

Transfer the dough onto a lightly floured work surface and knead for 3 minutes. Shape into a ball, then invert the bowl over the dough and leave to sit for 15 minutes. Remove the bowl and knead for 3 more minutes until you have a smooth dough, then shape into a ball once again. Grease a separate mixing bowl with a little butter and transfer the dough into it. Cover with cling film and leave in a warm, draught-free place for 1¾ hours to let it rise.

Lightly dust your work surface with flour and knead the dough again for a minute or so. Roll it into a thick sausage and divide into four equal-sized pieces. Roll each piece into a ball, cover with a clean damp tea towel and let it rest for another 30 minutes.

Roll each piece of dough into a long sausage measuring about 35cm (14in) long. Holding one end of the dough, twist it a few times. Bring the other end round to join the ends together and form a ring. Place on a lightly floured worktop and prepare the other pieces of dough in the same way.

161

Mix the *pekmez* with 125ml (4½fl oz) of water in a large bowl and spread the sesame seeds on a flat plate. Dip each galette in the *pekmez* water and then roll in the sesame seeds. Place on a non-stick baking sheet (or one lined with baking parchment or a silicone mat) and repeat the process with the three remaining galettes. Set aside for another 20–30 minutes to rise a little more.

Meanwhile, preheat the oven to its highest setting.

Bake the galettes for 20–25 minutes or until crisp and golden brown. Serve hot straight out of the oven or reheated later in the day. *Simit* do not keep but, like all bread, they freeze very well. All you will have to do is defrost them before reheating.

Lebanese Sesame Galettes

KA'KEH

I use a slightly different dough here from the classic one that I was given by the same baker who gave me the recipe for *mishtah* (see page 236). The dough is made with three different types of flour – plain, wholewheat and cornmeal – before being coated in sesame seeds, and makes a more interesting alternative to the pita bread dough.

Makes 6 galettes

500g (1lb 1oz) unbleached plain flour, plus extra for
   dusting
100g (3½oz) wholewheat flour
100g (3½oz) fine cornmeal
2¼ tsp (1 × 7g sachet) fast-action yeast
2 tsp fine sea salt
Toasted sesame seeds (to toast them yourself, see page
   329), for sprinkling

7.5cm (3in) diameter pastry cutter

Mix the flours, yeast and salt together in a large mixing bowl and make a well in the centre. Gradually add 400ml (14fl oz) of warm water, incorporating the flour as you go. Knead in the bowl until you have a rough ball of dough.

Transfer the dough onto a lightly floured work surface and knead for 3 minutes. Invert the bowl over the dough and leave to rest for 15 minutes. Remove the bowl and knead the dough for a further 3 minutes or until it is smooth and elastic. Roll into a ball and place in a clean, lightly floured bowl. Cover with cling film and let it rise in a warm, draught-free place for 2 hours.

Fold after the first hour to strengthen the dough and make it rise better. The best way to do this is to first dust your hands and work surface with flour, then invert the bowl over one hand to let the dough drop onto your palm. Gently slide it onto the work surface and pat it into a thick flat circle. Fold one-third of the dough over from your right. Fold the left third over, then fold the top third over and the bottom one over it. Return to the bowl, with the folded sides down, and leave to finish rising.

When it is ready, transfer the dough to your work surface. Divide into six equal-sized pieces and roll each piece into a ball. Place on a lightly floured tray, cover with a tea towel that is wet but not dripping and let the dough rise for 45 minutes.

Line a large baking sheet with baking parchment or a silicone mat, or use a non-stick baking sheet, and sprinkle over the sesame seeds in an even layer.

Roll out each ball of dough to a disc about 25cm (10in) in diameter. Using the pastry cutter, cut an opening near the top of each disc before gently stretching the opening to create a handbag-like shape. Transfer onto the baking sheet lined with sesame seeds. Cover with a floured baker's couche or tea towel and let the discs rest for about 15 minutes.

Preheat the oven to its highest setting.

Brush the galettes with water and sprinkle with sesame seeds to cover. Bake in the oven for 6–8 minutes or until puffed up and very lightly golden. The baking time may vary, depending on how hot your oven is. As with pita bread (see page 234), I suggest you check the galettes after 5 minutes. Like *simit* (see page 161),

these are best served immediately or still warm. Alternatively,
you can let them cool on a wire rack and freeze them for
later use.

Stuffed Pancakes

QATAYEF

If ice cream at Dimashq was one of my routine afternoon stops in
Damascus (see page 170), Ramadan Brothers who make *qatayef*
(stuffed pancakes) at the western end of Straight Street – a main
artery of the souks running parallel to Souk el-Hamidiyeh – was
where I went to for a sweet evening snack, and this almost daily
despite the calorie count. There are two Ramadan Bros stalls, right
next to each other, and both make *qatayef*. I prefer the first one as
you come from Souk Madhat Basha, where the *qatayef* are the
most scrumptious I have ever tasted. They use sheep's milk *qashtah*
(clotted cream – see page 318) to fill the pancakes, whereas most
other stallholders use cream made with powdered milk. I love
watching them make the pancakes, first stirring the batter by hand,
then putting it into a hand-held funnel and pouring the batter in
spurts onto a hot griddle. While one person makes the pancakes,
another fills them with walnuts or clotted cream and fries them.
They are then dropped into a large pot full of sugar syrup. You can
also have them unfried – topped with clotted cream, pinched into a
cone and drizzled with fragrant sugar syrup. I like the fried version
and always ask for mine to be fried on the spot so that they are
very crisp, with the soft cream inside (Arab clotted cream does not
melt during cooking), offering a luscious melting contrast. The
walnut pancakes, on the other hand, can sit for an hour or longer
after being fried without softening. Still, I prefer to have both types
of pancake fried on the spot and the Ramadan Brothers always
oblige. I have been going to them for over 20 years and as soon as
they see me, whether I have been there only the day before, or a
few months previously, one of the brothers immediately instructs
his young worker to fry some *qatayef* for me. It was during a visit
to Damascus that I finally managed to break my mother's resistance

to street food. I insisted that she tasted my cream *qatayef*; she gingerly took a bite, still unsure about eating on the street, but she had to agree that it was excellent and finally gave in and accepted a pancake of her own.

Makes 12 small pancakes to serve 4–6

125g (4½oz) unbleached plain flour
½ tsp (¼ × 7g sachet) fast-action yeast
Pinch of sea salt
Vegetable oil for frying
175g (6oz) *qashtah* (clotted cream – see page 318)

For the walnut filling
75g (2½oz) ground walnuts
1 tbsp golden granulated sugar
¼ tsp ground cinnamon
1 tbsp orange blossom water

For the sugar syrup
525g (1lb 2oz) golden caster sugar
1½ tsp lemon juice
1½ tbsp rose water
1½ tbsp orange blossom water

Mix the flour, yeast and salt in a mixing bowl and add 175ml (6fl oz) of water. Whisk together until you have a smooth batter, then cover with a clean tea towel and let the batter rest for 1 hour or until it has risen and its surface is bubbly.

Meanwhile, combine the ingredients for the walnut filling in a bowl and set aside.

Next make the syrup. Put the sugar and 225ml (8fl oz) of water in a saucepan. Add the lemon juice and place over a medium heat. Bring to the boil, occasionally stirring the mixture. Boil for 3 minutes then add the rose and orange blossom water and boil for a few seconds more. Take off the heat and set aside to cool.

Shortly before the batter is ready, grease a shallow frying pan with a little vegetable oil and place over a medium heat. When the pan is very hot, measure a heaped tablespoon of batter and pour it into

165

the pan, to make a disc 7cm (2¾in) in diameter and about 1cm (½in) thick. It is best to spread the batter as you are pouring it into the pan; the mixture is too thick to spread by tilting the pan.

Cook on one side for 2–3 minutes or until the bottom of the pancake is barely coloured and the top is dry and pockmarked all over with tiny holes. Remove to a plate lined with baking parchment and finish making the remaining pancakes in the same way. Allow the pancakes to cool.

Lay one pancake on your palm, smooth side down, and spread 1 tablespoon of either the walnut filling or the clotted cream in a line down the middle, leaving the edges clear. Fold the pancake in half, aligning the edges and pinching them tightly shut with your fingers – you don't want them to open during frying. Place each stuffed pancake on a plate and continue filling the rest so that you have six pancakes filled with cream and six with the walnut mixture.

Pour enough vegetable oil into a large, deep-sided frying pan to deep-fry the filled pancakes and place over a medium heat. To test whether the oil is hot enough, dip the corner of one pancake in it; if the oil bubbles around it, it is ready. Slide in as many pancakes as will fit comfortably in the pan and fry for 2–3 minutes on each side or until golden all over.

Remove each pancake with a slotted spoon and drop in the sugar syrup, turning in the syrup until well coated, then transfer to a serving platter. Serve tepid or at room temperature the same day. They are really best eaten soon after they are made as they quickly become soggy.

Milk Pudding

MUHALLABIYEH

Whenever I make this dish, I always remember the *birkeh* or stall where I used to stop with my mother, either for *muhallabiyeh* or *meghli* (see page 168). They never changed their recipe, but I like to experiment with the classic one and I often flavour my milk pudding with saffron to give it a beautiful yellow colour and an exotic taste of the *One Thousand and One Nights*. At other times, I might grind cardamom seeds and add them to the milk for an Arabian touch. You can make your own variation provided you keep the taste subtle so as not to overwhelm the rose and orange blossom water. On the other hand, some people don't find this flavour so appealing as it reminds them of perfume. If you belong to that camp, simply reduce the amounts given below or omit them altogether, although this will make the *muhallabiyeh* rather boring. As for the texture, I use cornflour to thicken the milk and not too much of it so that it stays soft and silky. You can use ground rice instead, but there will be a noticeable difference in texture, with the cornflour producing a finer dish.

Serves 4–6

1 litre (1¾ pints) full-cream organic milk
4½ tbsp cornflour
150g (5oz) golden caster sugar
¼ tsp ground mastic (see page 322)
2 tsp orange blossom water
2 tsp rose water
60g (2oz) raw shelled pistachios, soaked in cold water for
   about 1 hour and then peeled if you have the patience

Put the milk and cornflour in a saucepan. Place over a medium-high heat and bring to the boil, whisking all the time. Reduce the heat to low, add the sugar and ground mastic and continue whisking for 7–10 minutes or until the milk has thickened.

Add the orange blossom and rose water and simmer, still whisking, for a further 2 minutes. Take off the heat and pour into one large

167

shallow bowl or into 4–6 individual ones, depending on their size. Let the milk pudding cool, then garnish with the pistachios and serve at room temperature or slightly chilled.

Caraway and Cinnamon Pudding

MEGHLI

My mother had three girls before she finally produced the boy she, my father and the rest of the family really wanted, mainly because he would carry the family name to the next generation. And to celebrate his birth, she, like all other Lebanese mothers, made an industrial amount of *meghli*, keeping some at home to serve those who came to congratulate her on the happy occasion and sending out the rest to family and friends for them to share in the happiness. I doubt she made the *meghli* herself. She would have been too weak so soon after delivery to stir the pudding for the requisite amount of time. *Meghli* means 'boiled' in Arabic, and it does indeed need to boil, for a minimum of an hour, before it reaches the right consistency. Some people boil it for less time, but the resulting pudding is bland and watery. Ready-made *meghli* is an acceptable alternative, but it is well worth your while spending the time stirring the mixture until it thickens into the velvety fragrant custard-like mixture that is one of my favourite puddings. It's traditional to sprinkle shredded coconut over the pudding, although I'm not so fond of it myself. If you would like to include it, however, simply sprinkle a little over the pudding before adding the nuts.

Serves 4

100g (3½oz) ground rice
2½ tbsp ground caraway
1½ tbsp ground anise
1½ tsp ground cinnamon
200g (7oz) golden caster sugar

168

To garnish
60g (2oz) pine nuts
60g (2oz) shelled walnuts
60g (2oz) blanched almond halves

Place the nuts for garnishing in a deep bowl and cover with boiling water, letting them soak for 1 hour. Ideally the walnuts should be peeled after soaking, but only if you have the patience. If so, you may prefer to leave them to soak in a separate bowl.

Put the ground rice in a large saucepan with 2.5 litres (4⅓ pints) of water. Add the ground caraway and anise and place over a high heat. Bring to the boil, whisking constantly, and boil for 25 minutes, still whisking all the time. Reduce the heat to medium and cook for another 5 minutes, whisking as you go.

Add the cinnamon and whisk for another 20 minutes, then reduce the heat to medium-low, add the sugar and whisk for a further 10 minutes. Remove from the heat and pour into a single shallow serving bowl or into 4–6 individual ones, depending on their size. Let the pudding cool before garnishing with the drained nuts. Serve chilled or at room temperature.

Syrian Ice Cream
BUZA BIL-QASHTAH

Souk el-Hamidiyeh, in the heart of Damascus, is a long, wide, vaulted alley that starts at a busy main road and finishes by the Roman archway that leads to the Omayyad mosque. As you near the archway, you can stop at Bekdash, the most famous ice-cream shop in the whole Middle East. And if you happen to be there on a Friday or a holiday, you will not be able to move for the number of people. The souk will be deserted, with all the shops and stalls shut except for the throng outside and inside Bekdash, all clamouring for their celebrated ice cream. I do not share the general enthusiasm for Bekdash. The ice cream there has long ceased to be as good as its reputation. Instead, I prefer the cleaner and quieter Dimashq (Arabic for 'Damascus'), on the same side of the alley but higher up nearer the main road. The selection is the same but made with greater care. I always order their *qashtah* (clotted cream – see page 318) ice cream, which is creamier than the regular kind, with more body. Both have a surprising chewy texture because of the *salep* (see page 329) that thickens the ice cream when boiled with it while giving it its stretchy consistency. Because Dimashq is never mobbed, I can sit quietly and watch the clientele at leisure: a fascinating mix of regular Damascene shoppers and rural folk who are in the city to shop or visit relatives. Unfailingly, there will be a docile child-bride led by the hand by her husband. Sometimes he will be good-looking, other times not so. The sight of such a couple always fills me with sadness as I imagine how dreadful the young girl's life must be, unless of course the husband and his family are kind to her. Even then, having to bear children at such a tender age as well as having to cook and clean can't be much fun, however natural it seems to them. It is still fairly traditional in Syria, at least in rural areas, to marry soon after puberty.

A more cheerful sight is that of the strong men making the ice cream by the cashier's desk. Their method is totally different from that of any Western ice-cream maker and the entire process is manual. The mixture is poured into deep, round, metal containers that have been frozen. There are four in a line and depending on how busy the shop is, either all four are used or just one or two. The men use a large spatula to scoop up the ice-cream mixture and hold it against the walls of the container to freeze it. Once the mixture has frozen against the metal, they scrape it off and let it fall to the bottom. They then grab a massive wooden pestle and start pounding the frozen mixture into a smooth, homogeneous mass, which they sprinkle with coarsely ground pistachios on both sides before rolling it into a cylinder – the ice cream is served in slices as if it were a Swiss roll. Going to Dimashq for a *qashtah* ice cream is a daily routine when I am in the city. Here is a recipe that is pretty close to theirs but using crème fraîche instead of *qashtah*.

Makes 1.2 litres (2 pints)

1 litre (1¾ pints) full-cream organic milk
1 tbsp salep (see page 329)
200g (7oz) golden caster sugar

300g (11oz) crème fraîche
3 tbsp rose water
½ tsp ground mastic (see page 322)
2 tbsp coarsely chopped pistachios, to garnish (optional)

Put the milk in a saucepan, reserving a tablespoon or two to mix with the ground mastic, and place over a medium heat. Add the salep little by little while whisking the milk all the time until it boils. (If you add the powder too quickly, it will form lumps.) Add the sugar and carry on whisking the mixture for another 7–10 minutes or until it has thickened.

Remove from the heat and pour into a large jug. Add the crème fraîche and rose water. Stir the mastic into the reserved milk before adding it to the ice-cream mixture – because it is a resin, it will turn into a sticky gum if you add it to a very hot liquid, especially if you do it quickly. Whisk until the mastic is well blended into the mixture and let it cool.

Pour into an ice-cream maker and churn the mixture following the manufacturer's instructions. Transfer to a freezerproof container and freeze until you are ready to serve it. Serve sprinkled with pistachios, if you wish.

Iranian Saffron Ice Cream

BASTANI SA'LABI

One of the things I had to taste when I visited Iran was their famous saffron ice cream. But when I got to Tehran, I realised it was not so easy to track down the real thing, made with proper saffron and shavings of frozen cream inside the mix. Still, I persisted until I found a friend who knew a specialist ice-cream maker in Tajrish market where they made it the old-fashioned way. I have adapted the recipe below from one in Margaret Shaida's *Legendary Cuisine of Persia*. The interesting thing is that, unlike Syrian ice cream (see page 169), the milk isn't boiled with the salep.

171

As a result, the ice cream is thinner, without any of the stretchy texture of the Syrian one. It is also a lot sweeter.

Makes about 600ml (1 pint)

Good pinch of saffron threads
1 tbsp rose water
500ml (18fl oz) full-cream organic milk (preferably goat's)
250g (9oz) golden caster sugar
200ml (7fl oz) double cream, poured into a shallow dish
   and frozen
1 tsp salep (see page 329)
2 tbsp coarsely ground pistachios (optional)

Put the saffron to soak in the rose water and leave to infuse for 15 minutes at least, preferably half an hour.

Put the milk, sugar and saffron-infused rose water in a mixing bowl and whisk together until the sugar is completely dissolved. Slowly add the salep while whisking all the time. (If you add the powder too quickly, it will form lumps.)

When the salep is fully incorporated, pour the mixture into the ice-cream maker and churn following the manufacturer's instructions. Just before the churning has finished, chop up the frozen cream and add to the mixture. Transfer to a freezer-proof container and freeze until you are ready to serve it. Serve sprinkled with pistachios, if you wish.

Jellab

If you look up *jellab*, you will find many different recipes, all suggesting a different type of syrup or *dibs* (see page 325). Some say to make it with grape syrup, others suggest carob. However, traditional *jellab* is made with date molasses. Even more important than this, however, is the smoking of the ingredients (or the syrup) with essences (*bakhur* in Arabic). I have yet to understand the full process and even my friends Youmna and Leila, at Mymouné, who make the best commercial preserves in Lebanon, have not been able to produce a good *jellab*. In the recipe below I haven't attempted to make the drink from scratch, therefore, but use ready-made syrup – just make sure you read the ingredients list and buy one that has date syrup in it. The drink is not only very refreshing on account of the crushed ice but also interesting because it is packed with soaked pine nuts (rehydrating nuts makes them taste like fresh ones) and plumped-up sultanas. Simply remember to soak both raisins and pine nuts for a few hours, or preferably overnight, before you intend to serve the drink.

Serves 4

60ml (2fl oz) *jellab* syrup
Crushed ice
60g (2oz) pine nuts, soaked overnight in cold water
60g (2oz) sultanas, soaked overnight in cold water

Pour the syrup into a large jug. Add 750ml (1⅓ pints) of water and stir until well blended with the syrup. Pack the drink with crushed ice, then drain the pine nuts and sultanas and mix in with the *jellab* in the jug. Serve immediately, making sure you spoon equal amounts of nuts and sultanas into each glass.

Salep

SAHLAB

Salep is a warming winter drink made by boiling milk with powdered salep (see page 329) and sugar until the milk thickens. You can drink it from a cup or have it in a bowl as if it were a sweet soup. I still remember how in Beirut, as teenagers, we would stop at a salep stall with a few tables and chairs in the old souks not far from Ajami, the ultimate late-night restaurant that served hommus and other mezze dishes through the night both to flighty revellers like us and to souk traders or early shoppers. Our salep stall served the warming drink in thick ceramic soup plates. The stallholders sprinkled it with ground cinnamon and served it with croissants still warm from the oven of the nearby bakery. I didn't do this very often as my parents were very strict and didn't let me stay out late, but every now and then they would relax the rules, or more likely be away for a day or two, allowing me and my sisters to enjoy our short-lived freedom.

I like to make salep in London during the cold winters, not only to enjoy the sweet warming drink but also because it reminds me of those long-gone days. You find the same drink in Turkey, where it is usually served with *simit* (see page 161), Syria and Egypt. In Egypt, they garnish it with nuts, raisins and desiccated coconut, while in Syria they add a sprinkling of ground cinnamon, just as they do in Lebanon.

Serves 4

1 litre (1¾ pints) full-cream organic milk
½ tsp ground mastic (see page 322)
1 tbsp salep (see page 329)
6 tbsp golden granulated sugar or to taste
Ground cinnamon for sprinkling

Pour the milk into a large saucepan, reserving 1–2 tablespoons to mix with the mastic, and place over a medium heat. Gradually add the salep, in very small amounts so that it does not form lumps, as you whisk the milk. Bring to the boil, whisking the milk all the time, and keep whisking for about 5 minutes after the milk has boiled. Add the sugar and whisk for another 3 minutes, then whisk in the mastic and ladle into cups or soup bowls. Sprinkle with cinnamon and serve hot on its own or with croissants or *simit* (see page 161).

At the
Restaurant

My father spent much of his working life travelling for business. We were always sad to see him leave and forever impatient for his return, not only to have him home with us again, nor for the many gifts he brought back but because he took us out for long leisurely lunches to celebrate the family being together again.

One of his favourite restaurants was M'hanna in Zahleh, a town north east of Beirut, which was (still is) famous for its riverside mezze restaurants. He drove us there in his wonderful 1950's Buick, which he kept well into the 1960s. My two sisters, brother and I sat on the spacious banquette in the back while my mother sat in front, with my baby sister in her arms. The drive wasn't very long and as much as we loved being in the magnificent car, we repeatedly asked when we would arrive. The reason for our impatience was not so much lunch. Rather, it was the bridge leading to the restaurant which was lined with street vendors selling all kinds of nuts and candy. We knew we had to wait until after lunch to buy candy but this never stopped us from nagging our parents to get some as we crossed the bridge – my favourites were white candy floss (*ghazl el-banat*, see page 284) and a very white, rather hard, nougat flavoured with mastic (see page 322) which seems to have disappeared. My parents cheerfully ignored our pleas and hurried us past the vendors into the restaurant, promising to buy us whatever we wanted on the way back.

The headwaiter knew us well and he always gave us a table by the river. My father started discussing the menu as soon as we sat down. 'What do you have that is good today?' he asked. The question did not refer to any of the mainstays on the menu such as hommus, *baba ghannuge* or tabbuleh but rather to what was in season, or to any number of delicacies that needed to be extremely fresh such as raw lamb's liver, lambs' testicles (*beyd ghanam* in Arabic), tiny birds (*'asafir*, one of my all-time favourites, even if seriously non pc), and so on. My father nodded whenever the waiter named a dish we wanted, and by the time they had finished, our order stretched to more than 20 mezze dishes.

The waiters arrived soon after, carrying large trays laden with our mezze, which they served in stages. The dips, salads and cold vegetable dishes first, followed by the savoury pastries then the hot

177

dishes. The colours and textures on the table were gorgeous. The smooth, pale ivory of the dips was beautifully set off by the crisp, golden browns of the savoury pastries, *kibbeh* balls and falafel, while the herb salads and vegetable dishes added brilliant notes of greens and reds. We ate straight from the serving dishes, scooping our food with torn pieces of pita bread or lettuce leaves but even at our young age, we knew we had better keep our fingers clean!

Whenever we got bored, we left our parents to their conversation and went to play by the water. They didn't mind. It was accepted practice for people to come and go from a mezze table. Nor did they worry about us children coming to any harm. The waiters kept a watchful eye on us – in Lebanon, as in other Mediterranean countries like Italy, children are kings and queens and everyone feels protective towards them. When we had enough of playing and started to feel peckish again, we returned to find new dishes on the table.

My mother and father sipped milky *arak* (an alcoholic aniseed drink similar to Pernod) from small tumblers while we drank freshly squeezed fruit juices. In the winter, we had orange juice, in the summer watermelon or melon juice and in the autumn, we tried not to stain our lovely clothes with pomegranate juice.

The restaurant scene, at least for that kind of family or group mezze dining, hasn't changed much in Lebanon. The M'hanna of my childhood is still there, albeit much larger. It has spawned many other M'hannas across the country, while many more restaurants have opened alongside them in Zahleh. In fact, the town has become a sort of Disneyland for mezze restaurants. I don't go there any longer. The tranquil atmosphere of my childhood has been replaced by noisy crowds and bustling waiters. Instead, whenever I am back in Lebanon (or Syria or Turkey for that matter where the restaurant scene is pretty similar), I prefer to go to places that remind me of those lovely childhood outings, restaurants that have been there for years and where both atmosphere and menu remain largely unchanged. In Iran, the restaurant menus are limited to kebabs and rice with few side dishes like pickles, yoghurt and cucumber or wild garlic salad and some crudités. If they offer any appetisers and stews like those you would eat at home, the selection would be not only limited but often of inferior quality, while in Lebanon and Syria, restaurants are big on mezze and grilled meats or fish leaving the stews, stuffed vegetables and different kinds of *kibbeh* to home-cooks. It is only in Turkey, in the small *lokantasi* restaurants (see page 224) that you can enjoy home-cooked dishes. In some, the quality is excellent while in others it is rather mediocre. It really depends on the owner and who he/she chooses to prepare the food.

Levantine Bread Salad

FATTÛSH

I have been going to Chez Sami, a restaurant right on the beach north of Beirut and still one of my favourites in Lebanon, for a great many years. The entrance is through a beautiful vaulted hallway (once part of an Ottoman stone house) into a large glazed modern extension, which serves as the main seating area during the winter when it is too cold to sit outside on the beach terraces. Fortunately Lebanon is famous for its moderate weather and the terraces are shut for only a few months of the year.

The clientele at Chez Sami is an eclectic mix: prosperous families, trendy youngsters and important-looking men, either politicians and/or wealthy businessmen. It is where the high and mighty or simply well off go to eat fish. One night when I was dining there with my family, I noticed the maître d' moving some diners from the terrace opposite ours. I wondered why he was asking them to leave their tables. Then a swarm of strapping young men came out onto the beach below, apparently looking for someone or something. More and more peculiar, I thought, until it dawned on me that it had to be the prelude to the arrival of a political bigwig. And true enough, it wasn't long before a group of overdressed women and well-groomed men sauntered onto the emptied terrace, with no less than our president amongst them. It was astonishing to see them go to the trouble of giving him his own terrace and allowing his men to monopolise the beach, searching for a threatening object or person, but without anyone bothering to search the rest of the restaurant or any of the customers – some, like us, very close. It would have taken just a few steps from where I was sitting for me or anyone else for that matter to leap up and attack him or, worse, shoot him. But this is quite normal in Lebanon: the whole dramatic scene was enacted more for show than out of any real concern for the president's safety.

But to return to the food, Chez Sami has its own group of dedicated fishermen who bring in the best of their daily catch to be displayed in a refrigerator in the cool vaulted entrance for diners to choose a fish, order it by the weight and then instruct the maître d' on how they'd like it cooked. I always order the same thing: tiny red mullet *en friture*, a medium-sized dorade (if there are two or three in our party) or a large wild sea bass (if there are more), to be baked in salt; and when in season, I also order small crabs, to be boiled. The chefs always cook the fish to perfection, keeping it moist and tender. No easy feat given the Lebanese tendency to overcook both meat and fish. The fried fish is served covered with golden triangles of fried pita bread, which I like dipping in the tahini sauce (see page 185), the de rigueur accompaniment for fish, although I prefer my baked fish and boiled crab to be dressed in olive oil and lemon juice.

Unlike other restaurants, Chez Sami's mezze menu is limited to about a dozen dishes, all as excellent as the fish. They are famous for their *fattûsh*, a salad of toasted bread and fresh herbs. In most restaurants, the herbs are chopped but the chefs at Chez Sami keep them whole, adding fresh thyme and rocket to the classic trio of parsley, mint and purslane. I also love their stuffed Swiss chard leaves (see also page 33), a delectable variation on stuffed vine leaves (see page 36), and their *hindbeh* (dandelion leaves or wild chicory cooked in olive oil and served topped with caramelised onions), both as good as any made at home. If you are going to use the herbs whole, as in the recipe below, buy them young and fresh otherwise they will be too tough, and too large. Purslane is now available almost all year round in Middle Eastern shops, and possibly at farmers' markets in spring and summer; the same with fresh thyme. If neither is available, use an equivalent amount of parsley, and a little more mint. I like this salad just as much without the toasted bread, although technically it is no longer *fattûsh*.

Serves 4

2 medium-sized round pita breads (see page 315)
3 tbsp ground sumac (see page 331)
6 tbsp extra-virgin olive oil
200g (7oz) flat-leaf parsley (about 1 bunch), leaves
    picked from the stalks
100g (3½oz) mint (about ½ bunch), leaves picked from
    the stalks
100g (3½oz) purslane (about ½ bunch), leaves picked
    from the stalks
100g (3½oz) spring onions (about 1 bunch), trimmed
    and thinly sliced   *cont.*

181

350g (12oz) small cucumbers (or large if you cannot find
the Middle Eastern variety), cut in half lengthways then
thinly sliced
100g (3½oz) radishes, cut in half and thinly sliced
300g (11oz) cherry tomatoes, halved or quartered
depending on their size
Sea salt
Juice of ½ lemon

Preheat the grill to high or the oven to 200°C (400°F), gas mark 6.

Tear the pita breads open at the seams and toast them under
the grill or in the oven until golden brown. Place on a wire rack
to cool.

Break the toasted bread into bite-sized pieces and put in a mixing
bowl. Sprinkle with sumac, add the olive oil and mix until the
bread is thoroughly coated. (Coating the bread in the oil and sumac
is one way of sealing it and stopping it from going soggy; another
is to mix in the bread at the very last minute after having seasoned
and tossed the salad.)

Put the fresh herbs and other salad ingredients in a salad bowl.
Season with salt and lemon juice to taste and toss all the ingredients
together, then add the toasted bread and toss again. Taste,
adjusting the seasoning if necessary, and serve immediately.

Las Salinas Bread Salad

LAS SALINAS FATTÛSH

A rather nondescript restaurant by the sea in Tyre in the south
of Lebanon, Las Salinas may not be attractive but the food is
definitely worth the detour. They serve incredibly fresh fish, caught
not too far from the restaurant, and their *fattûsh*, the salad of
choice to serve with fish (see page 180), is quite different from any
I have elsewhere. Instead of using lettuce with the herbs, as they

do in some restaurants, they add very finely shredded cabbage, which makes for an even more crisp salad.

Serves 4

1 medium-sized round pita bread (see page 234)
3 tbsp ground sumac (see page 331)
6 tbsp extra-virgin olive oil
1 medium-sized pointed spring cabbage (about 400g/14oz), trimmed and very finely shredded
100g (3½oz) spring onions (about 1 bunch), trimmed and thinly sliced
300g (11oz) small cucumbers (or large if you cannot find the Middle Eastern variety), sliced into medium-thin semicircles
300g (11oz) cherry tomatoes, halved or quartered depending on their size
200g (7oz) flat-leaf parsley (about 1 bunch), most of the stalk discarded, coarsely chopped
100g (3½oz) mint (about ½ bunch), leaves picked from the stalks and coarsely chopped
100g (3½oz) purslane (about ½ bunch), leaves picked from the stalks
Sea salt

Preheat the grill to high or the oven to 200°C (400°F), gas mark 6.

Tear the pita bread open at the seams and toast it under the grill or in the oven until golden brown. Place on a wire rack to cool.

Break the toasted bread into bite-sized pieces and put in a mixing bowl. Sprinkle with the sumac, add the olive oil and mix until the bread is thoroughly coated.

Put the shredded cabbage in a salad bowl and add the rest of the salad ingredients with a little salt. Toss gently together and taste, adjusting the seasoning if necessary, then mix in the toasted bread. Serve immediately.

Wild Chicory in Olive Oil with Caramelised Onions

HINDBEH BIL-ZEYT

Even though this dish is on the menu of most Lebanese restaurants, I only order it at Chez Sami (see page 180) because theirs is almost as good as my mother's. The greens are not cooked to death, for a start. The olive oil they use is excellent and they are generous with the caramelised onions, which really make this dish. It is difficult to get wild chicory in London, except when in season in winter and only in some Middle Eastern shops. If you cannot find it, use frisée. The leaves of the latter are more tender and paler in colour. They require less boiling and the flavour is milder, but they make a good substitute. Spring is the season for foraging for *sliq* or wild greens, a practice known as *tassliq*. People forage for many different varieties, which they prepare in the same way as the recipe below. If you stop at a simple mountain eatery during that time, you may find some on the menu, if you're lucky, because the owners will have been foraging for them.

Serves 4

1kg (2lb 2oz) wild chicory or frisée
Sea salt
100ml (3½fl oz) extra-virgin olive oil
4 medium-sized onions, peeled and thinly sliced
½ lemon, plus extra slices to garnish

Cut the wild chicory (or frisée) into pieces about 6cm (2½in) long. Fill a large saucepan with water and bring to the boil. Add some salt and drop the greens into the water. Boil the chicory for about 5 minutes (2 minutes for frisée) or until just tender. Drain the cooked greens and allow to cool. Squeeze out as much water as you can between the palms of your hands, then separate the pressed leaves. Put in a bowl and cover with a clean tea towel.

Pour the olive oil into a large frying pan and place over a medium heat. When the oil is hot, add the sliced onions and fry, stirring

184

occasionally, until caramelised and a rich brown colour. Be careful not to let it burn – onion can turn from richly caramelised to burned in a matter of seconds. Take the pan off the heat. With a slotted spoon, remove three-quarters of the onions and leave to drain on several layers of kitchen paper. Leave the rest in the pan.

Add the cooked chicory (or frisée) to the pan and place over a medium heat. Sauté for a few minutes, stirring regularly, until the chicory is well blended with the oil and onions in the pan. Taste, adding more salt if necessary, then cover with a clean tea towel and let the mixture cool in the pan.

Transfer to a flat serving platter and squeeze the lemon all over. Scatter the caramelised onions over the top and arrange the lemon slices all around the chicory. Serve at room temperature with pita or any other good bread.

Fish in Tahini Sauce

SAMAK BI-TAHINEH

This dish also goes by the name of *tajen samak* (fish tagine) in restaurants, where it tends to be made differently from at home, with the fish being flaked and mixed in with the sauce. In places such as Chez Sami (see page 180), the flavour may be different too. I suspect they use more spices at Chez Sami, but they are notoriously secretive about their recipes and no one there would tell me how the *tajen samak* is prepared! So here is my version of the dish, using black cod, which is pretty extravagant but it works brilliantly with the sauce and makes for a more elegant presentation. If you find black cod too expensive, however, use Atlantic cod or sea bream fillets instead, or any other white sustainable saltwater fish. My grandmother deep-fried the fish whole, then slipped it into the sauce as it cooked on top of the stove. My mother also fried the fish but she cooked the sauce separately in the oven. I prefer to use fish fillets, which I sear.

185

I then cook the sauce separately and slip the seared fish into it at the last minute so that it doesn't overcook.

Serves 4–6

2 tbsp pine nuts
4 tbsp extra-virgin olive oil
450g (1lb) white fish fillet (such as cod or sea bream –
   see introduction), cut into 6 pieces
3 medium-sized onions, peeled, cut in half and thinly
   sliced
1 tsp ground cumin
Sea salt
Finely ground white pepper

For the tahini sauce
125ml (4½fl oz) tahini
2 garlic cloves, peeled and crushed
Juice of 1½ lemons or to taste

Preheat the oven to 220°C (425°F), gas mark 7.

Spread the pine nuts on a non-stick baking sheet and toast in the oven for 5–7 minutes or until golden brown. Remove from the oven and set aside.

Next make the tahini sauce. Mix the tahini with the garlic in a medium bowl and stir in the lemon juice. The tahini will thicken initially, despite the fact that you are adding a liquid, but don't let this worry you – it will thin out again as you add the water. Slowly add 200ml (7fl oz) of water, stirring all the time, until the tahini sauce is the consistency of single cream.

Put 1 tablespoon of the olive oil in a non-stick frying pan and place over a medium-high heat. When the oil is hot, slide in the fish pieces, skin side down, and cook for about 3 minutes or until the skin is crisp and golden and the fish is almost cooked through. Transfer to a plate and set aside.

Scrape off any bits of fish from the pan then add the remaining oil. Add the onions and cook, stirring occasionally, until soft and very lightly golden. Add the tahini sauce, season with the cumin and a little salt and pepper and mix well. Let the mixture bubble for 3–4 minutes, stirring every now and then, until you see a little oil rising to the surface.

Take the sauce off the heat and slide the fish into it. Gently shake the pan back and forth to coat the fish with the sauce. Return to the heat for a minute or so or until the fish is cooked to your liking. Taste, adjusting the seasoning if necessary. then scatter the toasted pine nuts all over and serve warm or at room temperature.

Spicy Fish

SAMKEH HARRAH

The Silver Shore in Tripoli is another of my favourite fish restaurants, and Tripoli is my favourite city in Lebanon now because it hasn't lost its character like Beirut has. I don't remember my father taking us to any seaside restaurant outside Beirut, and I still can't decide if I love the mountains more than the sea or vice versa, but what is wonderful in Lebanon is that you can go from one to the other in no time at all, regardless of whether you are north, south or east. The recipe below is a hybrid of the *samkeh harrah* my mother makes, with no tahini sauce, and the Silver Shore's version, in which they use more tahini sauce and less fresh coriander. I like both recipes and decided to combine them here.

Serves 6

60g (2oz) pine nuts
Vegetable oil for frying
1kg (2lb 2oz) white fish fillet, about 6 pieces
75ml (3fl oz) extra-virgin olive oil
2 medium-sized onions, peeled and finely chopped
1 green bell pepper, deseeded and finely chopped
100g (3½oz) fresh coriander, most of the stalk
    discarded, finely chopped
100g (3½oz) shelled walnuts, coarsely ground   *cont.*

1 tbsp ground coriander
½ tsp ground cumin
¼ tsp paprika
½ tsp Aleppo pepper (see page 313)
Sea salt

For the tahini sauce
250ml (9fl oz) tahini
8 garlic cloves, peeled and crushed
Juice of 3 lemons

Preheat the oven to 220°C (425°F), gas mark 7.

Spread the pine nuts on a non-stick baking sheet and toast in the oven for 5–7 minutes or until golden brown. Remove from the oven and set aside.

Next make the tahini sauce. Mix the tahini with the garlic in a medium bowl and stir in the lemon juice. The tahini will thicken initially, despite the fact that you are adding a liquid, but don't let this worry you – it will thin out again as you add the water. Slowly add 125ml (4½fl oz) of water, stirring all the time, until the tahini sauce is the consistency of single cream.

Put a little vegetable oil in a frying pan and place over a medium heat. When the oil is hot, slide in the fish fillets, skin down, and cook for about 4 minutes or until the skin is crisp and golden and the fish just cooked. Transfer to a plate and set aside.

Wipe the pan clean and add the olive oil, onions and chopped pepper, then sauté until the onion is golden and the pepper softened. Add the chopped coriander and stir until wilted, then add the ground walnuts and season with the spices and a little salt.

Add the tahini sauce to the onion, herb and nut mixture and let it bubble gently for 3–4 minutes, stirring regularly, until a little oil rises to the surface. Slide the cooked fish into the sauce, gently shaking the pan to coat the fish in the sauce, and leave on the heat for a minute or so. Transfer onto a serving platter, garnish with the toasted pine nuts and serve hot or warm.

Cold Octopus Salad

Throughout the Levant, people prefer to eat fish in restaurants by the sea because it means the fish is freshly caught. There are exceptions, of course, but not in Istanbul where you are spoiled for choice for spots by the water. When I am there I always go to Kıyı in Tarabya, which is very upmarket, and İsmet Baba in Kuzguncuk on the Asian side, which is more simple but on the ground floor of a charming old *yalı* (waterside house) right by a small jetty where you can watch fishermen repair their nets. If you are lucky enough to be seated by the window at İsmet Baba, you can also watch the fish in the water, although more often it will be flotsam floating by. I always go there early for lunch, both to secure a table by the window and to watch their *börek* maker create the largest *börek* roll I have ever seen being made. He works on an elevated platform in full view of the diners and his *börek* is quite unusual, not only because it is a huge fat roll filled with a mixture of cheese and mashed potatoes but also because it is cut into slices and fried. The sheets of *yufka* (as filo is known in Turkey – see page 321) he uses are also larger than any I have seen and the way he handles the pastry, laying one sheet over the other, then spreading the filling and rolling the delicate pastry over the mushy, sticky filling is mesmerising. His *börek* is too difficult to reproduce at home, unlike İsmet Baba's octopus salad, for which the restaurant is also famous. They use regular-sized octopuses for this dish, but I prefer the baby ones which are different from baby calamari – prettier and tastier and with a different texture. If you can't find baby octopuses, however, simply go for a fully grown one, which will be more tender if you buy it frozen. You'll need to defrost it first, then once the meat is boiled, all you have to do is to slice it thinly before serving with the dressing.

Serves 4–6

1 lemon, halved
1kg (2lb 2oz) baby octopuses
Sea salt
Few sprigs of flat-leaf parsley, most of the stalk
    discarded, finely chopped

cont.

For the salad dressing
4 tbsp extra-virgin olive oil
Juice of ½ lemon or to taste
¾ tsp *pul biber* or Aleppo pepper (see page 313)

Bring a large saucepan of water to the boil, then reduce the heat
to low, add the lemon halves and wait until the water is at a bare
simmer. Add the octopuses and some salt and simmer for 15–20
minutes.

Mix the salad dressing in a bowl. When the octopus is done, drain
it thoroughly in a colander before adding to the salad dressing with
the parsley. Mix together well. Taste, adjusting the seasoning if
necessary, and serve warm, at room temperature or slightly chilled.

Lebanese Steak Tartare

KIBBEH NAYEH

Qal'at el-Rummiyeh in Qley'at is about 10 minutes' drive from my
mother's home. The restaurant itself is not beautiful but it is high
up in the Lebanese mountains, overlooking a dramatic valley
leading to the sea in the distance; and the owners raise their own
lambs, butchering them in situ. As a result, their raw meat dishes
are incredibly fresh. I often go there with my mother, and despite
us often being on our own, I insist on ordering almost as many
dishes as my father used to order for the whole family. And like
he did, I engage in conversation with the maître d', asking what is
best or in season; and seeing all the mezze dishes being brought to
our table and covering it in a vibrant display never fails to bring
back memories of those delightful meals I so enjoyed as a child.
I always order the same dishes except for seasonal specialities; and
I often ask for a second order of *habrah nayeh* (very finely minced
raw meat with hardly any seasoning), which they serve with a very
fluffy, almost ethereal garlic dip (*tûm*). I also adore their raw
kibbeh and *kafta* (also made with minced meat). And if the raw
liver is from a freshly slaughtered lamb, I order it as well and I ask

my mother to make me liver bites, just as my grandmother used to do (see page 116) except that she adds fresh mint leaves.

For *kibbeh nayeh* (like *habrah nayeh* but with burghul added to the mixture), you need to have a good relationship with your butcher so that he doesn't mind boning a leg of lamb, trimming the meat of all the fat and sinuous nerves and passing it through the fine mincer twice. I do not advise making *kibbeh nayeh* with ready-minced meat from the supermarket, however lean. You need to know that the meat is very fresh and that it comes from a superior cut. If your butcher is not prepared to do the work, then have him bone and skin the leg and you do the rest, using meat from only the top part of the leg for the *kibbeh nayeh* and reserving meat from the bottom part for regular mince or a stew.

Serves 4–6

500g (1lb 1oz) lamb from the top part of the leg, skinned
Sea salt
1 small onion, peeled and finely grated
2 tsp ground cinnamon
1 tsp Lebanese seven-spice mixture (see page 331)
1 tsp ground allspice
½ tsp finely ground black pepper
Sea salt
120g (4oz) fine burghul, rinsed under cold water and
    drained

For the garnish
Spring onions, trimmed
Fresh mint leaves

Trim the meat of any fat and as many white ligaments as you can. Then put the meat through a fine mincer twice. You can mince the meat in a blender, if you prefer, but you need to be careful not to process it too much or it will become too smooth and lose texture. Alternatively, ask if your butcher will prepare the meat and mince it for you.

Prepare a bowl of lightly salted water and have it at hand.

Put the grated onion in a mixing bowl. Add the minced meat with the spices and some salt and with mix well using your hand. Add the burghul and mix it in, dipping your hand every now and then into the salted water to moisten both your hand and the *kibbeh* mixture. Knead for about 3 minutes or until you have a smooth meat paste. Taste and adjust the seasoning if necessary. Serve immediately drizzled with olive oil and accompanied by spring onions, fresh mint leaves and some pita bread.

Chickpea Fatteh

FATTET HOMMUS

My father took us only to elegant restaurants. Eating out for him was a treat and not a necessity – my mother was and still is a wonderful cook – and as far as he was concerned, modest eateries were for workers and travellers and not places where well-to-do families went. As I grew older and became independent, I was able to escape my parents' control and to eat wherever I wanted – particularly on the street or in simple cafés/restaurants specialising in one particular dish or in a specific meal such as breakfast. I love eating at these places as much as, and sometimes more than, at elegant restaurants. One of my favourites is El-Soussi, a simple breakfast café in west Beirut named after its owner who specialises in *fatteh* (from the Arabic verb *fatta*, meaning to break or crumble). *Fatteh* is a composite dish made up of different layers (see page 192), starting with toasted or fried pieces of pita bread and finishing with yoghurt mixed with crushed garlic and garnished with toasted pine nuts. In between you can have chickpeas, alone like at el-Soussi, or chickpeas and meat, or aubergines. The dish brings together a wonderful mixture of different tastes, textures and temperatures, with crunchy contrasting with velvety, hot with cold, and subtle with intense.

The café is a very basic place with plastic tables and chairs arranged haphazardly in a bare room. Next door, the Zen-like El-Soussi presides over the tiniest kitchen where he tends a large pot of chickpeas on one big burner in the window and a frying pan on a small burner on the counter in which he fries eggs with *qawarma* (lamb 'confit' – see page 115) and lamb's testicles. It is

almost as if he had a toy kitchen right next to a 'proper' one. He
serves a few other dishes, including *fûl medammes*, another typical
Arab breakfast dish, made with boiled fava beans and originally
from Egypt. Sometimes *fûl* is served without a garnish, but
El-Soussi tops his with chopped tomatoes. His *fûl* is very good but
I never order it there. Not because I don't like it, nor because he
serves his Lebanese-style, adding chickpeas to the broad beans, but
because I always wait until I get to Aleppo to have my *fûl* at Hajj
Abdo, a wonderful old man whose *fûl medammes* is the best
(see page 216).

Serves 6

200g (7oz) dried chickpeas, soaked overnight in cold
    water (enough to cover the chickpeas by 2–3 fingers)
    and ½ tsp bicarbonate of soda
1 cinnamon stick
1 large round pita bread (see page 234)
40g (1½oz) unsalted butter
60g (2oz) pine nuts
2 large garlic cloves, peeled and crushed
900g (2lb) plain yoghurt
Sea salt

Rinse the chickpeas under cold water, then place in a saucepan
and cover well with fresh water. Add the cinnamon stick and place
over a medium heat. Bring to the boil, then lower the heat to
medium-low, cover the pan with a lid and cook for 1 hour or until
they are tender. Then add salt to taste (adding salt before the end
of cooking will harden the skins) and keep warm.

Meanwhile, preheat the grill to high or the oven to 200°C (400°F),
gas mark 6.

Tear the pita bread open at the seams and toast it under the grill
or in the oven until golden brown. Place on a wire rack to cool.

Melt the butter in a frying pan and sauté the pine nuts, stirring
constantly, until golden brown. Remove with a slotted spoon onto
a double layer of kitchen paper and leave to drain.

Mix the crushed garlic into the yoghurt, adding salt to taste.

Break the toasted bread into bite-sized pieces and spread over the bottom of a deep serving dish. Remove the chickpeas with a slotted spoon and spread over the bread. Cover with the seasoned yoghurt and garnish with the sautéed pine nuts before serving immediately.

Khawali Hommus

HOMMUS KHAWALI

Even though Damascus has many restaurants, including the largest in the world (the Damascus Gate, with over 6,000 seats, as confirmed by Guinness World Records), few are good. Khawali, just off Straight Street and occupying a whole building originally constructed in the fourteenth century, was until recently the only excellent restaurant in town. The main dining area is an enchanting courtyard with a fountain in the centre that sometimes is filled with flowers floating in the water, usually left over from private parties. The clientele at Khawali is made up of the political elite, members of Damascene high society, and some tourists, all enjoying the restaurant's specialities, such as *hommus Khawali*, where the classic mixture of chickpeas, tahini and lemon juice is jazzed up with pepper paste (*muhammara* is both the name of the paste and the name of a dip made with the paste – see page 205) and pomegranate syrup to give the dip a touch of heat and a hint of sweetness that make it totally irresistible, among the best hommus I have ever had. Also, Khawali was among the first to serve the now ubiquitous mint lemonade where fresh mint leaves are whizzed with freshly made lemonade to produce a supremely refreshing drink.

Serves 4–6

1 × 660g jar of chickpeas, drained and rinsed
   (425g/15oz drained weight)
100ml (3½fl oz) tahini
Juice of 1 lemon or to taste
1 garlic clove, peeled and crushed

1 tbsp Aleppo pepper paste (see page 313)
½ tbsp pomegranate syrup (see page 327)
¼ tsp ground cumin
Fine sea salt
Aleppo pepper for sprinkling
Extra-virgin olive oil for drizzling

Place the chickpeas in the food processor. Add the tahini, lemon juice, garlic, pepper paste and pomegranate syrup and process until very smooth.

Transfer to a mixing bowl. Add the cumin and salt to taste and mix well. If the hommus is too thick, thin it by adding a little water or a little more lemon juice, unless it is tart enough already. Taste and adjust the seasoning if necessary.

Spoon the hommus into a shallow serving bowl and, using the back of a spoon, spread it across the dish, raising it slightly at the edges and in the centre, so that you have a shallow groove in between. Sprinkle a little Aleppo pepper over the raised edges and in the middle and drizzle a little olive oil in the groove. Serve with pita bread.

Minty Labneh Dip

KISHKEH

The first time I had this dip was more than 20 years ago in a wonderful restaurant in Aleppo that is now an equally wonderful hotel. The hotel, which went by the name of Dar Yasmine as a restaurant, is now known as Yasmeen d'Alep – information that is sadly of no practical use until the situation improves in Syria. I was familiar with *labneh*, or strained yoghurt, as I'd grown up on it. But I had never had it mixed with burghul and mint before and I was intrigued by the name *kishkeh* on the menu because it sounded like *kishk* (see page 120), although I didn't know they were related. When the waiter explained what it was, the name

195

made sense as it was more or less the fresh version of *kishk*, where burghul and yoghurt are mixed and left to ferment before being dried. You can use fresh or dried mint for this dish. At Dar Yasmine and elsewhere in Syria they use dried mint, whereas I alternate between the two. I also use fine burghul but you can use medium grade, if you prefer. I suggest you prepare the dip a little ahead of time. The burghul soaks up a lot of the moisture from the *labneh* and you may need to adjust the consistency by adding a little water and adjusting the seasoning if needed.

Serves 4–6

250g (9oz) *labneh* (to make it yourself, see page 104)
2–3 tbsp fine burghul, rinsed under cold water and
  drained
1 tbsp dried mint
Sea salt
Extra-virgin olive oil, for drizzling

Mix the *labneh*, burghul and dried mint in a mixing bowl. Add salt to taste, then cover with a clean tea towel and let the mixture sit for about 30 minutes. Mix again, adding a little water if you think the dip is too thick and more salt if necessary.

Spoon the dip into a shallow serving bowl and, using the back of a spoon, spread it across the dish, raising it slightly at the edges and in the centre, so that you have a shallow groove in between. Drizzle a little olive oil in the groove and serve with good bread or crisp crudités.

Grilled Aubergine Salad with Tahini Sauce

BATINJAN KHAWALI

This salad is another speciality of Khawali, one of my favourite restaurants in Damascus, who give their own name to this dish, as they do to their superlative hommus (see page 194).

Serves 4

2 large aubergines (about 600g/1lb 5oz total weight)
100g (3½oz) spring onions (about 1 bunch), trimmed and thinly sliced
1 ripe firm medium-sized tomato, deseeded and diced into small cubes
Few sprigs of flat-leaf parsley, most of the stalk discarded, finely chopped
2 tbsp pomegranate syrup (see page 327)
2 tbsp extra-virgin olive oil
Handful of walnut halves, coarsely chopped, to garnish

For the tahini sauce
125g (4½oz) tahini
Juice of 1 lemon or to taste
2 garlic cloves, peeled and crushed
Sea salt

First make the tahini sauce. Put the tahini in a mixing bowl and gradually whisk in the lemon juice, alternating it with 75ml (2½fl oz) of water. Taste from time to time to make sure that you get the right balance of tartness while keeping the consistency like that of creamy yoghurt. The tahini will first thicken to a purée-like consistency before starting to dilute again. Add the crushed garlic and a little salt. Taste and adjust the seasoning if necessary.

Preheat the grill to high or start a charcoal fire on a barbecue.

Prick the aubergines in a few places and grill or barbecue them until the skin is charred and the flesh is very soft. Cut the aubergines in half lengthways and scoop out the flesh. Let the flesh drain in a colander for about 30 minutes to get rid of the excess liquid, then dice into bite-sized chunks. Put in a bowl with the spring onions, tomato and parsley and carefully mix, making sure you do not mash up the aubergines too much.

Mix the pomegranate syrup with the olive oil and pour over the aubergines. Add salt to taste and toss together. Spoon the salad into a serving dish and drizzle as much tahini sauce as you would like over it. (At Khawali, they mould the salad in a timbale and invert it on a plate before drizzling with the sauce.) Garnish with the chopped walnuts and serve with good bread.

Turkish Kebabs

ŞIŞ KEBABI

Turkey has distinct regional cuisines but you don't need to travel all over the country to taste these. All you need to do is to go to Çiya in Kadıköy in Istanbul to eat chef Musa Dağdeviren's food. Dağdeviren travels throughout Turkey researching regional specialities which he then reproduces in his three Çiya restaurants, all gathered in a cluster on a pedestrian street on the Asian side of the city. The main Çiya is a glorified *esnaf lokantası* (see page 224) with all the dishes on display, each kept in the large pot it has been cooked in. The food is served in very pretty metal bowls, rather than regular china, the way it was served in the past and still is in some parts of south-eastern Turkey, which is where Musa comes from. The last time I ate there, Musa made me taste lamb kebabs wrapped in apricot leather (see page 322) which he grilled over charcoal and served with a chunky tomato sauce. The apricot leather was slightly burned in places and melting in others, making for a wonderful contrast between bites. Musa also serves stuffed vegetables made with dried aubergines and peppers, which are quite exquisite, the dried vegetables giving the dish a more pronounced flavour than if it had been prepared with fresh ones. His *kissir* (see page 29) is better than any I have eaten at a restaurant, while the big puffy bread they bring to the table straight out of the oven (a little like a giant pita but thinner and dusted with sesame and nigella seeds) is perfect for scooping up dips and salads or wrapping around kebabs. The recipe below is for regular kebabs, but if you want to give it the Çiya apricot-leather twist, you could wrap the kebabs in apricot leather before grilling.

At Borsa, another restaurant in Istanbul with several branches dotted all over the city, they serve their equally delicious kebabs with thick-skinned yoghurt, which reminds me of the yoghurt my Syrian aunt used to make with the milk from her own cow. She would milk her cow, which she kept in a barn on one side of the courtyard, early in the morning and I often went with her, carrying the tin pail for the milk. My aunt kept a stool by the door which she moved near to the cow as we entered. I stood behind her, both a little scared of the cow and fascinated by how the milk spurted out of her udders as my aunt squeezed on them. Every now and then I mustered enough courage to try milking, but I didn't know how to get the milk out of the poor animal, despite squeezing hard on her udders. The same happened when I tried to milk a camel in Dubai not so long ago; I felt so sorry for the poor beast having to put up with my clumsy handling! I guess I am not made for that kind of life.

But to go back to kebabs, the two other places in Istanbul where I love eating them are Ulus 29 and Hamdi, the whole dining experience enhanced by the spectacular views from both restaurants. Situated on top of a hill in Bebek, a chic neighbourhood on the Bosphorus, Ulus 29 offers a sweeping view of both the sea and the Asian side of the city, while Hamdi is right on Eminönü Pier, overlooking the Galata Bridge and all the activity there on both land and water.

Serves 4

800g (1¾lb) lamb from the leg, skinned, trimmed of most
   of the fat and cut into 3cm (1¼in) chunks
20–24 cherry tomatoes   *cont.*

For the marinade
3 garlic cloves, peeled and crushed
3 tbsp extra-virgin olive oil
1 tbsp tomato purée
½ tsp paprika
¼ tsp cayenne pepper
¼ tsp ground allspice
¼ tsp ground cinnamon
¼ tsp ground cumin
1–2 tbsp fresh thyme leaves
Sea salt
Finely ground black pepper

8 long metal skewers

Put all the marinade ingredients in a large bowl, season with salt and pepper and mix well. Add the lamb and toss in the marinade so that the meat is well coated and leave to marinate for at least 2 hours.

Preheat the grill to high or start a charcoal fire on a barbecue.

Thread the meat onto seven of the skewers and the tomatoes onto the eighth one. Grill over a high heat for 3–4 minutes on each side or until the meat and tomatoes are done to your liking. Serve immediately with good bread.

Stuffed Aubergines Fatteh
FATTET AL-MAKDUSS

For a long time Khawali (see page 194) was the only restaurant to eat in and be seen at in Damascus, but its place has now been usurped by Naranj, a relative newcomer on Straight Street further down towards Bab Sharqi (Eastern Gate). It is now the restaurant of choice for the top echelon of Damascene society. When the president wanted to entertain Brad Pitt and Angelina Jolie (who were attending the city's film festival a couple of years before the Syrian uprising), he chose the courtyard of the nearby Talisman hotel as the setting, and had the food brought over from Naranj, asking their waiters to serve it. All the hotel staff and those staying there, including me, had to make themselves scarce while the president, his wife and their glamorous guests enjoyed their meal. Luckily, I was out for the day visiting the ruins of Bosra in the south, otherwise I might have protested! Even after the revolution started, Naranj kept its place as the government's restaurant of choice (apparently because the owner is an ex-Mukhabarat or secret service man), and when Kofi Annan went to Damascus to try to broker a peace deal between the opposition and the government, they took him to Naranj, along with their TV cameras to advertise the whole event.

Naranj, like Khawali, is also converted from an old house, albeit a less ancient one. It is larger and glitzier, with a delightful roof terrace. The waiters are elegantly dressed in a modern take on the traditional 'abaya (long robe-like garment) and the restaurant has the decided advantage of serving alcohol, which they don't at Khawali. The menu features such regional specialities as haraq osba'u (see page 203) and fattat al-makduss (a variation on El-Soussi's fatteh on page 192), where the hot element of the dish (as in heat rather than spiciness) is baby aubergines stuffed with meat. In the Syrian version, the yoghurt is mixed with tahini and the bread is fried, although I prefer to toast mine in the oven instead.

Serves 4

For the lamb broth
500g (1lb 1oz) lamb from the shanks, cut into medium-sized chunks
1 cinnamon stick
1 large onion, peeled and quartered
Sea salt
3 large ripe tomatoes, peeled, deseeded and finely chopped

For the stuffed aubergines
100g (3½oz) unsalted butter
60g (2oz) pine nuts

cont.

300g (11oz) freshly minced lean lamb, from the
    shoulder or neck (either ask your butcher to mince
    the lamb or do it yourself using the fine attachment
    on a meat grinder)
½ tsp ground allspice
½ tsp ground cinnamon
Finely ground black pepper
1kg (2lb 2oz) small aubergines, trimmed and cored
    (see page 30)
3 medium-sized round pita breads (see page 234)
2kg (4lb 4oz) plain Greek yoghurt (sheep's or goat's)
2 tbsp tahini
2 garlic cloves, peeled and crushed
Few sprigs of mint, leaves picked off the stalks,
    finely chopped

First make the lamb broth. Put the meat from the shanks in a large saucepan and cover with water. Place over a medium-high heat and bring to the boil, skimming away any scum that rises to the surface. Add the cinnamon stick, onion and some salt, then reduce the heat and simmer, covered with a lid, for about 30 minutes or until the meat is half cooked. Add the chopped tomatoes and continue simmering until the meat is done. Keep hot in the pan.

Meanwhile, prepare the stuffed aubergines. Put half the butter in a frying pan and place over a medium heat. Add the pine nuts and sauté, stirring constantly, until golden brown. Transfer with a slotted spoon onto a plate and add the minced lamb. Cook, stirring the meat and mashing it with the back of a wooden spoon so as to break up any lumps, until there are no traces of pink, then add the allspice, cinnamon and some salt and pepper. Return half the toasted pine nuts to the pan, reserving the rest for garnishing, and mix well. Allow to cool before you stuff the aubergines.

Take hold of a cored aubergine and hold it upright, cupping your hand around it. Scoop up a little of the stuffing with your other hand and gently push it inside the aubergine, using your finger to force it down. Every now and then, shake the vegetable in a downward motion to make sure the filling is well inside it (or push the filling in further with your little finger). Stuff the remaining aubergines in the same way.

Melt the remaining butter in a saucepan over a medium heat. Add the stuffed aubergines and gently sauté until they become pale in colour. Pour in 375ml (13fl oz) of the meat broth and simmer for about 1 hour or until done. Keep hot while you prepare and assemble the rest of the dish.

Preheat the grill to high or the oven to 200°C (400°F), gas mark 6.

Tear the pita breads open at the seams and toast them under the grill or in the oven until golden brown. Place on a wire rack to cool.

Mix the yoghurt with the tahini, crushed garlic and chopped mint. Spread the toasted bread over the bottom of a deep serving dish. Remove the meat from the hot broth and spread over the bread. Then arrange the stuffed aubergines over the bread and meat and cover with the yoghurt. Garnish with the reserved toasted pine nuts and serve immediately.

Lemony Lentils with Pasta and Croutons

HARAQ OSBA'U

I used to love going to Naranj (see page 200) until I realised it belonged to an ex-secret service man and was the place of choice of the Syrian regime who wined and dined their guests there while their army and *shabbiha* were killing the people. Regardless, the food at Naranj was, and I suppose still is, exquisite. They specialise in serving typical regional dishes from all over Syria, including this particular one from Damascus with its amusing name, which means 'he burned his finger'. According to Sonia Khandji, who gave me the recipe below, it came to be known as this because cooks tend to burn their fingers when arranging the hot fried bread over the lentils. If you don't feel like making the dough, you can buy fresh pasta and use it instead. It will not be quite the same, but it is a respectable substitute.

203

Serves 4–6

For the pasta
150g (5oz) plain flour, plus extra for dusting
Fine sea salt

500g (1lb 1oz) brown lentils, soaked for 30 minutes in cold
   water (enough to cover the lentils by 2–3 fingers)
100ml (3½fl oz) extra-virgin olive oil
3 medium-sized onions, peeled and thinly sliced
Juice of 1 lemon
Sea salt
200g (7oz) fresh coriander (about 1 bunch), most of the
   stalk discarded, finely chopped
2 cloves garlic, peeled and crushed
Vegetable oil for frying

First make the pasta dough. Mix the flour and ½ teaspoon of salt in
a large mixing bowl and make a well in the centre. Gradually add
90ml (3fl oz) of water and mix with the flour until you have
a rough ball of dough. Transfer the dough onto a lightly floured
work surface and knead for 2–3 minutes. Invert the bowl over
the dough and leave to rest for 15 minutes.

Knead the dough for a few more minutes, lightly flouring your
hands every now and then, until the dough is smooth and elastic.
Shape into a ball, then sprinkle a clean bowl with a little flour and
place the ball of dough in it. Cover with cling film and let it rest
while you prepare the rest of the dish.

Drain the lentils and put in a large saucepan, add 1 litre (1¾ pints)
of water and place over a medium heat. Bring to the boil, then
lower the heat and simmer for 15–45 minutes, depending on the
type of lentils you are using – some will take longer to cook than
others.

While the lentils are cooking, roll out the dough and cut into long
strips and the strips into small squares with sides about 2cm (just
under 1in). Spread the pasta squares over a clean tea towel to let
them dry a little. You will be adding half to the lentils and frying
the other half to use as a crouton garnish. (This is what they do at
Naranj, whereas Sonia fries all the pasta to add at the end.)

LEVANT

Next add 75ml (2½fl oz) of the olive oil and the onions to a large frying pan and place over a medium heat. Fry until golden brown, then transfer half the onions onto several layers of kitchen paper to drain the excess fat – you will use these for garnishing. Reserve one-third of the chopped coriander for scattering over the finished dish and, in a separate pan, sauté the rest with the crushed garlic in the remaining olive oil until they become aromatic.

Five minutes before the lentils are ready, add half the pasta, the fried onions and their oil, the lemon juice and the coriander and garlic mixture. Add salt to taste and simmer for another 5 minutes. Take off the heat and allow to cool while you fry the remaining squares of pasta until golden brown in a little vegetable oil. Serve the lentils garnished with the pasta croutons and reserved fried onions and chopped coriander.

Aleppine Muhammara

Here is the classic Aleppine version of *muhammara*, which comes from Maria Gaspard Samra, once the chef at the Mansouriya, Aleppo's finest boutique hotel and now a private chef who did demonstrations for my culinary groups in Syria before the revolution. Hers is very similar to the *muhammara* served at the Club d'Alep, a private and very exclusive dining club in Aleppo that you can go to only if you are invited by a member. I normally use a thick pepper paste (see page 313) that I buy in Aleppo or Gaziantep, but you can use a commercial Turkish brand instead, sold in Middle Eastern shops either in a tin or jar and either mild or hot. It may be a little too watery compared to those sold in the souks, but it will have to do if you can't get a more artisanal one. You can, if you want, add Aleppo pepper (see page 313) to enhance the flavour.

125g (4½oz) fine golden breadcrumbs
300g (11oz) Aleppo pepper paste, plus ½ tbsp Aleppo
   pepper (see page 313) (optional)
1½ tbsp ground cumin
Juice of ½ lemon or to taste
1 tbsp golden granulated sugar
1½ tbsp pomegranate syrup (see page 327)
2 tbsp extra-virgin olive oil
½ tbsp tahini
125g (4½oz) shelled walnuts, coarsely ground
Sea salt

Put the breadcrumbs, pepper paste and 125ml (4½fl oz) of water in a mixing bowl and mix well. Add the remaining ingredients (plus the Aleppo pepper if your pepper paste is not up to scratch), season with salt to taste and mix well. If the *muhammara* is too thick, add a little more water or lemon juice if you want it to be more tart (although it is not supposed to be).

Taste and adjust the seasoning if needed, then serve with pita or another good type of bread or cover and refrigerate to serve later. Like Mohamed's *muhammara* (see page 206), this will also last for a couple of days – even longer, in fact, given that it contains no onion and fresh peppers.

Mohamed's Muhammara

There are different ways of preparing *muhammara*, with raw peppers, or grilled peppers or simply pepper paste, the latter being the classic Aleppine way (see page 205). I had been searching for a recipe for *muhammara* for quite a while when I tasted Mohamed's version, which I like as much as the classic version. He makes it quite differently, using a mixture of nuts rather than just walnuts, and he not only very kindly gave me his recipe, but also showed me how to make it in the kitchens of his restaurant, Al Waha, which is my favourite Lebanese eating place in London. Mohamed sautés the different nuts separately and chops them by hand, but I am too impatient for this and roast the nuts in a hot oven before chopping them in a food processor. *Muhammara* is more of a spread than a dip. If you would like the mixture to be softer, however, simply omit the step in which the peppers and onion are squeezed dry.

Serves 6

60g (2oz) shelled walnuts
30g (1oz) raw shelled pistachios, plus extra to garnish
30g (1oz) raw cashews
30g (1oz) pine nuts
30g (1oz) flaked almonds
45g (1½oz) fine golden breadcrumbs
½ tsp sea salt
¾ tsp cayenne pepper or to taste
2½ red bell peppers, trimmed and deseeded
1 small Spanish onion, peeled and quartered
170ml (6fl oz) extra-virgin olive oil

Preheat the oven to 220°C (425°F), gas mark 7.

Spread the walnuts, pistachios and cashews on one non-stick baking sheet and the pine nuts and flaked almonds on another and toast in the oven until golden: 6–7 minutes for the walnut mixture and 5 minutes for the pine nuts and almonds. Remove from the oven and allow to cool.

Place the walnuts, pistachios and cashews in a food processor and pulse until medium-fine. Transfer to a large mixing bowl, then add the pine nuts, almonds, breadcrumbs and seasonings and mix well.

Place the peppers and onion in the food processor and process until fine. Transfer to a bowl and, using your hands, squeeze out all the excess liquid, reserving the juices. Add to the nuts, together with the olive oil, and mix well. If the mixture is too dry, use some of the reserved juices to thin it. Taste, adjusting the seasoning if necessary, and serve immediately with pita bread, or place in a sealed container and refrigerate to serve later. *Muhammara* will keep for a couple of days in the fridge.

Pistachio Kebabs

FISTIKLI KEBAB

I am ambivalent about the way mezze are served in some restaurants in Turkey, with the waiter bearing a large tray with every dish on it. You choose which ones you want and he just lifts them off the tray and puts them on your table. It is quick and practical, but I can't help wondering how long the food has been sitting uncovered and possibly unrefrigerated. At Hamdi (see page 199), they serve mezze in the same way and I have to admit that I'm not that keen on them, but I do like their kebabs, in particular the *fıstıklı* ones (in which the meat is mixed with pistachios). For really exceptional kebabs, I travel all the way to the south-east to eat at İmam Çağdaş in Gaziantep. The town is Turkey's kebab and baklava capital and İmam Çağdaş is the undisputed king of both. I love everything about the place: the owners, Burhan Bey and his adorable father, who takes me to the back to watch the kebab makers wield the *zirh* (a large sabre-like knife with a wide curved blade) with great dexterity, or upstairs to the baklava kitchens, where everything is still made by hand and where they bake the baklava in a wood-fired oven. All the meat is minced by hand, and if you are lucky enough to be allowed into the kebab kitchen, a few steps down from where the barbecue chefs are wrapping the minced meat around the skewers and grilling it, you can watch several men, each rocking his amazing *zirh*, back and forth, over a mound of meat, parsley or tomatoes. They all work to the same rhythm, as if they were dancers, and they stay totally absorbed by what they are doing regardless of what is going on around them, which is no bad thing. The knives they use could easily cut off one of their fingers in one fell swoop in one distracted moment. As for the grill chefs, they consistently cook the meat to perfection, never overdoing it.

As I watch them, I remember barbecue lunches at home, with my uncles and grandmother grilling the meat out on the balcony, fanning the embers of the charcoal fire to keep them glowing. But the taste of our grilled meat was very different; my grandmother used a lot of garlic in her marinade, whereas the marinade is plainer at İmam Çağdaş. Their menu includes several types of kebabs, all of them consisting of minced meat except for an outstanding one in which the meat (lamb fillet) is cut into chunks and grilled pink – rather unusual in that part of the world. Apart from the different kebabs, you can have one of two salads, both chopped very small: one spicy and the other dressed with pomegranate syrup (see page 327) and more like a salsa than a salad. They also serve the best *lahmacun* (very thin meat 'pizza') in town, which I eat Turkish-style – wrapped around mashed-up grilled aubergines and fresh parsley. Even their *ayran*, a frothy, slightly sour yoghurt drink, is sensational. They serve it in gorgeous tin bowls that you sup from with a tin spoon, its handle embossed with their elegant 1950s-style Çağdaş logo. I've never found out if the logo was designed then and never changed or if it is a retro design. And of course, you can finish with some of their own baklava, considered to be the best in Turkey.

Serves 4

Sea salt
500g (1lb 1oz) freshly minced lean lamb, from the shoulder or neck (either ask your butcher to mince the lamb or do it yourself using the fine attachment on a meat grinder)
1 medium-sized onion, peeled and very finely chopped
Few sprigs of flat-leaf parsley, most of the stalk discarded, very finely chopped
100g (3½oz) raw shelled pistachios, ground medium-fine
2 garlic cloves, peeled and crushed
1 tsp finely ground black pepper
½ tsp *pul biber* or Aleppo pepper (see page 313)

6 flat metal skewers

Prepare a small bowl of lightly salted water and keep this to hand. Put the minced meat in a mixing bowl, then add the remaining ingredients and some salt. Mix together with your hand, wetting it in the salted water every now and then, until the mixture is well blended. Pinch off a little of the mixture and sear in a hot pan to taste, adjusting the seasoning if necessary.

At this stage you have the choice of wrapping the mixture around skewers, as on page 139, or simply shaping it into medum-sized balls or patties. I normally bake my meatballs in a hot oven (preheated to 220°C/425°C/gas mark 7) for a few minutes to keep the inside moist, or I sear the patties in a frying pan, for 1½–2 minutes on each side, as you would with hamburgers. Still, the traditional way to serve these kebabs is on skewers and grilled over charcoal, which you could do on a barbecue, cooking the skewers for 2–3 minutes on each side.

Chelow Kebab

Iran does not have a restaurant culture. To sample the best of Iranian cooking, you need to go into people's homes. If you eat out, then apart from a few exceptions, you'll be served kebabs and rice, along with side dishes such as pickles, yoghurt and cucumber, or yoghurt and elephant garlic salad, and quartered cucumbers or other crudités. The kebabs generally consist of chunks of meat (*tikkeh kabâb*), minced meat (*kabâb kubideh*) or chicken (*jujeh kabâb*). Below are recipes for the plain rice and these three different types of kebab, together with the cucumber and yoghurt dip – the most common items on the menu of an Iranian restaurant. As for the pickles, you can buy them ready-made from Iranian shops or make your own following the recipes on page 98.

Plain Rice
POLOW

The Iranian way of cooking rice is one of the best there is and, like my Iranian friends, I prefer to use rice grown in Iran, but good Pakistani or Indian basmati is also fine. They have three basic ways of preparing rice but *polow*, where the rice is parboiled then drained and steamed, is the one you'll have in almost every restaurant you go to. What is interesting about eating out in Iran is that, while the rest of the food may be very variable in quality, you will be served excellent rice wherever you go, even in the most modest cafés or restaurants. No self-respecting Iranian would eat rice that is not properly cooked. One thing is for sure, though; it is unlikely that you will get any *tahdig* – the delicious crust of rice that forms in the bottom of the pan – in most restaurants. If they make it, they keep it for themselves, although I suspect it is much easier for them to make large quantities of rice without bothering with the *tahdig*.

Serves 4–6 to accompany stews and kebabs

500g (1lb 1oz) basmati rice
Sea salt
75ml (3fl oz) vegetable oil
Good pinch of saffron threads, soaked in 6 tbsp water
60g (2oz) unsalted butter, melted

Put the rice in a sieve and rinse under cold water. Place in a large bowl and add enough cold water to cover it by two fingers. Stir in 2 tablespoons of salt and leave to soak for 2 hours.

Bring 2 litres (3½ pints) of water to the boil in a large saucepan. Drain the rice and add to the boiling water with 3 tablespoons of salt. Bring back up to the boil and boil for 3 minutes, then drain the rice.

Wipe the pan clean and place over a medium heat. Add the oil and half the saffron water. As soon as it starts sizzling, sprinkle a layer of rice over the bottom of the pan. Sprinkle another layer of rice and another, keeping the rice away from the sides of the pan so that it does not stick, until you have built up a pyramid.

With the handle of a wooden spoon, make a hole in the middle and pour in the melted butter and remaining saffron water. Wrap the lid of the saucepan in a clean tea towel and place over the pan so that it is tightly covered. Leave on a medium heat for 3 minutes, then reduce the heat to low and let the rice steam for 1 hour or a little longer. The finished rice should be light and fluffy.

Take the pan off the heat and dip the bottom in iced water to loosen the crust, or *tahdig*, as it is known in Persian. Spoon the saffron-coloured rice into a small bowl and the rest of the rice into a serving dish. Scatter the saffron rice all over the rice in the serving dish. Remove the *tahdig* from the pan, break it into chunks and arrange around the rice. Serve immediately with the kebabs of your choice.

Iranian Minced Meat Kebabs

KABÂB KUBIDEH

Minced meat kebabs are one of three basic types of kebab that you can order in an Iranian restaurant. The meat is wrapped around beautiful flat metal skewers that are kept in their own case like a prized set of silver cutlery. The skewers are twice as wide as those used by Lebanese, Syrians and Turks, and usually longer, and as a result the kebabs are longer and larger too.

Serves 4

Sea salt
500g (1lb 1oz) freshly minced lean lamb, from the
    shoulder (either ask your butcher to mince the lamb or
    do it yourself using the fine attachment on a meat
    grinder)
1 tsp fine breadcrumbs
1 medium-sized onion, peeled and finely grated
¼ tsp ground turmeric
Unsalted butter, to serve
Ground sumac (see page 331) for sprinkling
Finely ground black pepper

4 long flat metal skewers

Prepare a small bowl of lightly salted water and keep this to hand. Put the meat in a mixing bowl with the rest of the ingredients and season with salt and pepper. Mix together with your hand, wetting it in the salted water every now and then, until the mixture is well blended. Pinch off a little meat and sear in a hot pan to taste, then adjust the seasoning if necessary. Wrap equal quantities of meat around the skewers following the instructions on page 139.

Preheat the grill to high or start a charcoal fire on a barbecue.

Grill or barbecue the skewers for for 2–3 minutes on each side or until the meat is done to your liking. Serve with the *polow* (see page 210), with more butter added to the hot rice, and sprinkled with sumac for extra seasoning.

Chicken Kebabs

Jujeh Kabâb

Chicken is another popular type of kebab. Depending on the restaurant, you will be served boneless pieces, both dark and white meat, or you will get joints of poussin, which I prefer – *jujeh* means 'young chicken', in fact – and have included in the recipe below.

Serves 4

2 poussins, jointed into 8 pieces (reserving the
   carcass for stock or soup)
Unsalted butter, to serve
Ground sumac (see page 331) for sprinkling

For the marinade
Pinch of saffron threads soaked in 1 tsp water for
   15 minutes
1 small onion, peeled and finely grated
Juice of ½ lemon
Sea salt
Finely ground black pepper

Put the saffron water, grated onion and lemon juice in a large mixing bowl and season with salt and pepper. Add the poussin pieces and mix together so that the meat is well coated in the marinade, then let it marinate for 2 hours or preferably longer.

Preheat the grill to high or the oven to 220°C (425°F), gas mark 7, or start a charcoal fire on a barbecue.

Grill or barbecue the marinated chicken pieces for 10 minutes on each side. Or spread the pieces on a non-stick baking sheet and roast them in the oven for 30 minutes. Serve with the *polow* (see page 210), with more butter added to the hot rice, and sprinkled with sumac for extra seasoning.

Shish Kebabs

TIKKEH KABÂB

Chunks of marinated meat threaded onto skewers and grilled or barbecued are the third main type of Iranian kebab. This is the most risky variety to order in a restaurant, however, because if the meat is not good quality, it will be tough and chewy. Indeed, unless I know the restaurant, I always order *kubideh* or *jujeh* (see pages 212 and 213) instead. Home-cooked *tikkeh* are another matter entirely, of course, especially if you use meat from a leg of lamb or if you use the fillet.

Serves 4

500g (1lb 1oz) lamb from the top part of the leg,
     cut into 3–4cm (1¼–1½in) cubes

For the marinade
Pinch of saffron threads, soaked in 1 tsp water for
     15 minutes
2 medium-sized onions, peeled and finely grated
Juice of 2 lemons
Sea salt
Finely ground black pepper

4 long flat metal skewers

Put the saffron-infused water in a large mixing bowl. Add the grated onion and lemon juice and mix well, season with salt and pepper. Add the lamb, mixing together so that the meat is well coated in the marinade, and let it marinate for at least 2 hours or preferably longer.

Preheat the grill to high or start a charcoal fire on a barbecue.

Thread the marinated pieces of meat onto the skewers and grill or barbecue for 3–4 minutes on each side or until the lamb is done to your liking. Serve with the *polow* (see page 210), with more butter added to the hot rice, and sprinkled with sumac for extra seasoning.

Yoghurt and Cucumber Dip
MAST-O KHIYAR

In most of the kebab restaurants I've visited in Iran, there is a buffet table on which they have a bowl of this dip, alongside bowls of pickles (*torshi*) and platters of crudités that include cut-up carrots and cucumbers. You help yourself to as much as you want to eat with your order of *chelow kabâb*. The recipe below can be varied by using 100g (3½oz) of elephant garlic (*musir*), milder than regular garlic and available sliced and dried in Iranian shops, instead of the clove of garlic. You will need to rehydrate the *musir* first by putting it in a saucepan over a high heat and bringing it to the boil. Lower the heat and simmer for 20 minutes, then drain and rinse the garlic under cold water and place on a clean tea towel to dry before finely chopping and mixing with the other ingredients.

Serves 4 as an accompaniment

500g (1lb 1oz) plain yoghurt (preferably goat's)
1 garlic clove, peeled and crushed
2–3 tbsp dried mint, plus extra to garnish
3 mini cucumbers, grated and strained of any
    excess liquid
Sea salt

Mix the yoghurt with the garlic and dried mint. Add the grated cucumber and season with salt to taste. Taste, adjust the seasoning if needed, and transfer to a serving bowl. Garnish with a little dried mint and serve.

Fûl Medammes

Hajj Abdo's café in Aleppo is as modest as El-Soussi's (see page 192) and his choice even more limited. Just *fûl medammes*, which you can have with tahini or with lemon juice. The *fûl* is served with raw onion, sliced tomatoes and pita bread. Everyone scoops up the beans with pieces of bread, never touching a piece of cutlery, eating it with the onion and tomatoes. I always make a mess when I try eating *fûl* like this, with the pita flopping around and the sauce dribbling everywhere, and I end up asking for a spoon. Perhaps one day I will get the hang of it, the way I eventually learned to eat rice gracefully with my hand. Hajj Abdo's café is in Jdaydeh, a Christian Armenian neighbourhood with narrow cobbled streets lined with lovely old buildings, and a large open area called Sahet el-Hatab (Square of the Logs) where people gather in the evening. Children play ball, young couples whisper sweet nothings to each other without getting too close – they are, after all, in a strict Muslim country – and old men sit on benches, fiddling with their worry beads and chatting. Hajj Abdo is on one side of the square and Zmorod, an elegant restaurant in a converted old Ottoman house, is down a narrow lane on the other side. Within the few minutes it takes to go from the one to the other, you leave a world of simplicity to one of opulence. I enjoy both equally, I have to say, and fortunately I don't have to make a choice between the two. Hajj Abdo is open from early morning till early evening and Zmorrod is open from early evening till late, although such information isn't really relevant until the situation in Syria improves and visitors can go there again. Sadly, Hajj Abdo's café was completely burned in the fighting between regime forces and rebels and he has moved to Egypt. I am still not sure if Zmorrod has escaped the destruction wreaked on that part of Aleppo.

Serves 4

350g (12oz) dried fava beans, soaked overnight in cold water (enough to cover the beans by about 5cm/2in) and 1 tsp bicarbonate of soda
Sea salt

2 tbsp Aleppo pepper paste (see page 313), diluted
     with 3 tbsp water (optional)
Extra-virgin olive oil, for drizzling

For the tahini sauce
125ml (4½fl oz) tahini
1 garlic clove, peeled and crushed
Juice of 1 lemon or to taste

Drain the soaked fava beans and rinse under cold water. Put in a
large saucepan and add about 1 litre (1¾ pints) of water. Place
over a medium heat and bring to the boil, then reduce the heat to
low and simmer for 2½–3 hours or until the beans are very tender
and the cooking liquid has thickened. Add salt to taste – it's best
not to add salt until the very end or the skins will harden.

Make the tahini sauce by mixing the tahini with the crushed garlic
and lemon juice, then gradually add 190ml (6½fl oz) of water until
the mixture is a little thinner in consistency than double cream.

To serve the *fûl*, first divide the tahini sauce between four serving
bowls. Add a serving of hot beans together with a little of their
cooking liquid. Spoon a little diluted pepper paste over the top,
drizzle with olive oil and serve immediately with pita bread.

Meat Kebabs in Cherry Sauce

KABAB KARAZ

Zmorod is possibly the best restaurant in Aleppo; the Club d'Alep,
a private establishment, is as good if not better, but it is out of
bounds to visitors unless you are friends with a member. You enter
Zmorod through a narrow door leading into a tiny entrance hall
which doesn't prepare you for the fabulous courtyard beyond with
carved alcoves on every side. Even though I have been there many
times, I am always amazed by the splendour hidden behind the
modest entrance. It was once a private home, and judging by the

elaborate wall decorations and woodwork, it must have been a rather grand one. Until Zmorod opened, the best of Aleppine cuisine could only be enjoyed at friend's homes or at the Club d'Alep. But Dalal Touma, the splendid owner of Zmorod, changed all that and made it possible for foreign visitors, and Syrians alike, to enjoy the best of local cooking in a delightful restaurant setting. And her cherry kebabs are almost as good as those of my friend Lena Antaki, who has one of the best tables in Aleppo.

Serves 4

500g (1lb 1oz) freshly minced lean lamb, from the shoulder or shanks (either ask your butcher to mince the lamb or do it yourself using the fine attachment on a meat grinder)

½ tsp Lebanese or Syrian seven-spice mixture (see page 331) or ground allspice

Sea salt

Handful of pine nuts, plus extra toasted (see page 41) to garnish

1 tbsp unsalted butter

1 tsp unbleached plain flour

1kg (2lb 2oz) fresh sour cherries, pitted, or 500g (1lb 1oz) dried sour cherries soaked overnight in 500ml (18fl oz) water and then drained

2–3 medium-sized round pita breads (see page 234), opened at the seams and cut into medium triangles

2 tbsp finely chopped flat-leaf parsley, to garnish

Mix the meat with the spices and season with salt. Roll the mixture into small meatballs, each smaller than a walnut, and press a pine nut inside each. Melt the butter in a frying pan over a medium-high heat, then sauté the meatballs until they are browned all over and transfer to a sieve to drain off the excess fat.

Add the flour to the remaining butter in the pan and stir for a minute or so. Add the pitted cherries (or soaked dried cherries). Season with a little salt and stir for a few minutes. Let the cherries simmer on a low heat for about 20 minutes or until mashed up and completely softened.

When it is time to serve the kebabs, add the meatballs to the cherry sauce to heat them through. Serve over torn pieces of pita bread, garnished with toasted pine nuts and chopped parsley.

Kibbeh in Sumac Sauce
KIBBEH SUMMAQIYEH

Aside from Zmorod (see page 217), the other restaurant in Aleppo where you can enjoy excellent local dishes is Bazar el-Sharq, set in the armoury of the old Aleppo Governorate building. There you can order classic dishes such as *kibbeh summaqiyeh* (*kibbeh* balls cooked in a sumac sauce with aubergines and diced lamb) and *ma'jouqa* (an amazing meat pie filled with vegetables), all cooked to perfection by chef 'Emad, who has been presiding over the kitchen for years. Despite the magnificent vaulted rooms, the restaurant is not particularly elegant but the excellent food more than makes up for the drab surroundings. Sadly this restaurant has also disappeared because of the fighting.

Serves 4–6

½ quantity of uncooked *kibbeh* (see page 42)
½ quantity of cooked *kibbeh* stuffing (see page 42), with 1 tbsp finely chopped walnuts mixed in

For the sauce
50g (2oz) whole sumac berries (see page 331)
1kg (2lb 2oz) lamb from the shanks, cut into medium-sized chunks
3 medium-sized onions, peeled, one kept whole and the others thinly sliced
Coarse sea salt
4 tbsp extra-virgin olive oil
750ml (1⅓ pint) tomato passata

cont.

350g (12oz) small aubergines (or 1 largish aubergine),
   peeled to create a striped effect, cut in half lengthways
   and then cut across into medium-thick chunks
30g (1oz) unsalted butter
2 tsp dried mint
5 garlic cloves, peeled and crushed
Juice of 1 lemon or to taste
½ tsp finely ground black pepper

Divide the *kibbeh* into 20 equal-sized pieces and roll them into balls, each the size of a large plum. (Keep them round, following the Syrian style, rather than moulding them into oval patties as on page 53.) Lightly moisten your hands in salted water (dipping them in the bowl of water used during the preparation of the *kibbeh*) and place a *kibbeh* ball in the palm of one hand. With the index finger of your other hand burrow a hole into the ball while rotating it – this makes the hollowing out easier and more even. You should produce a thin meat shell resembling a topless egg. Be careful not to pierce the bottom or sides of the *kibbeh* shell.

Put 1½–2 teaspoons of stuffing inside the *kibbeh* shell, gently pushing the stuffing in with a finger, then pinch the open edges together and mould back into a fully rounded shape in your hands. Put the finished ball on a non-stick baking sheet. Continue making the balls until you have used up both *kibbeh* mixture and stuffing. Place the *kibbeh* balls in the fridge or freezer to firm them up.

Meanwhile, prepare the sauce. Put the sumac berries in a small saucepan. Add 375ml (13fl oz) of water and bring to the boil. Remove from the heat and leave to infuse while you prepare the rest of the ingredients for the sauce.

Put the meat and the whole peeled onion in a large saucepan and add 1 litre (1¾ pints) of water. Place on a medium heat and bring to the boil, skimming away any scum that rises to the surface. Add 1 tablespoon of salt, then reduce the heat and simmer, covered with a lid, for 1 hour or until the meat is very tender. Discard the onion.

Put the olive oil and sliced onions in a wide saucepan and fry over a medium heat until lightly golden. Strain the lamb stock, reserving the meat, and add to the onions, followed by the passata. Strain the sumac liquid and add it to the pan before bringing back up to the boil and adding the butter. Reduce the heat and let the pot bubble gently for 15 minutes.

Add the aubergines and the stewed lamb and cook for about 15 minutes or until the aubergines are nearly done. Then add the mint, garlic and lemon juice and drop the *kibbeh* balls into the sauce. Season with more salt if necessary and the black pepper and simmer for another 5 minutes or until the *kibbeh* balls are cooked through. Taste, adjusting the seasoning if needed, and serve very hot in soup bowls accompanied by good bread.

Siddiq's Kibbeh

KIBBET SIDDIQ

Shawarma (see pages 147 and 150) is a very common street food, formerly just in the Levant but now all over the world. Most places cook their *shawarma* at a gas-fired vertical grill, but at Siddiq, an unpretentious restaurant in a delightful, little-known (at least for those visiting from abroad) part of Damascus called Qanawat, they grill the meat over charcoal. The restaurant is tucked away in a quiet narrow lane off a charming pedestrian street shaded by trellised vines and lined with shops – grocers selling every kind of spice cheek by jowl with vendors of outlandish ladies' fashions. The restaurant, once someone's family home, has a pleasant courtyard and two airy rooms on either side. One is the kitchen with the charcoal-fired vertical spit where the *shawarma* is cooked in full view of customers, while the other room takes the overspill of diners when the courtyard is full. Seated at a table to one side of a large flat-screen television, and totally oblivious to the loud noises coming from it, the owner benevolently watches over his clientele, making sure they are well looked after.

The great thing about Siddiq is that you never have to worry about what to order. Their set menu consists of a few mezze dishes, followed by *shawarma* then fruit or *qatayef* (see page 164). All you can do is ask for fewer mezze dishes if you are not very hungry, or more dishes if you are. The service is fast: within minutes of being

221

seated, you are brought plates of hommus, *baba ghannuge*, salad, chips, cheese *börek* (in the form of puffed-up squares, unlike the Turkish and Lebanese versions, which are finger-shaped) and two types of *kibbeh* balls, one stuffed with spiced tail fat (see page 137) and the other with minced meat seasoned with pomegranate syrup (see page 48).

Every time I eat grilled *kibbeh* there, I remember my aunt Jamileh in Mashta el-Helou, who was married to my father's only brother. Unlike my gorgeous mother, who had a model's figure, 'Ammto Jamileh was very fat. We didn't like her much. Not only was she unattractive, but she was also not very kind. Still, this didn't stop us from enjoying her *kibbeh* balls, which were very different from my mother's or grandmother's. Instead of making torpedo-shaped balls, she made hers by flattening each piece of the meat mixture into a disc on which she piled seasoned tail fat before laying another thin disc of *kibbeh* on top to form a domed shape. She then grilled the *kibbeh* over charcoal in a *manqal* (see page 14) that she set up in the courtyard by a low stool. As she sat down on the stool, her flesh draped over the sides and we would start giggling. Then she started sweating as she fanned the fire, which made us giggle all the more, impatient for the first batch to come off the fire, so that we could nab our portion and run off. I guess we were not very nice either. Siddiq's *kibbeh* is shaped differently from my aunt Jamileh's and stuffed with meat rather than tail fat, but it is just as good.

Serves 4–6

1 quantity of uncooked *kibbeh* (see page 41)
1 quantity of uncooked *kibbeh* stuffing (see page 42), with no pine nuts and with 1 tbsp pomegranate syrup added at the end
50g (2oz) unsalted butter, melted, for brushing

Preheat the oven to 220°C (425°F), gas mark 7.

Divide your *kibbeh* into 24 pieces, with 12 a little larger than the other 12, and roll into balls. Then take one of the smaller balls and flatten into a disc measuring about 10cm (4in) in diameter. Place on a sheet of cling film and pile 2 tablespoons of stuffing into the centre. Take one of the larger balls and flatten into a disc a little larger in diameter and carefully lay over the filling, aligning the edges with those of the bottom disc. Press on the edges to seal and then shape the top into a rounded dome.

Lift the cling film with the *kibbeh* ball to remove it from your work surface. Carefully take the *kibbeh* off the plastic and lay on a non-stick baking sheet (or one lined with baking parchment). Brush with the melted butter before filling and shaping the remaining *kibbeh* balls in the same way. Brush them all again with melted butter and bake in the oven for about 15 minutes or until just done. Serve hot as part of a mezze, or with a yoghurt and cucumber dip (see page 215) as a main course.

Eskenderun's Shanklish Salad

I discovered Eskenderun thanks to my friend Lina Sinjab, the BBC's correspondent in Damascus who knows all the best spots to eat in the city. When I first walked into the tiny restaurant, I wondered if I had come to the right place. It had only two tables, and a few straggly chairs covered in red plastic. The food was displayed in a refrigerator at the back with a charcoal grill behind it, making it look more like a take-away than a restaurant. I was about to walk out, when Ahmed, the owner, whom I had called earlier to book a table, came to greet me and the two friends I had with me. We sat down, wondering what kind of lunch we were going to be served, but all it took was one bite of their *baba ghannuge* (which in Syria confusingly means a grilled aubergine salad and not the Lebanese dip) for us to realise that the meal was going to be exceptional. The aubergines had an intense smoky flavour from being grilled over charcoal, and the well-judged pomegranate dressing gave the salad a subtle sweet and sour flavour. Everything we had was very fresh, and beautifully seasoned. And it had been a long time since I had eaten a proper *shanklish* (a fermented curd cheese, the Levantine answer to Roquefort – see page 330) and theirs was pungent and spicy, as it should be – it can be fairly bland – and more soft than crumbly, just like the one my aunt Zahiyeh used to make in Mashta el-Helou (see page 121).

223

Serves 4

200g (7oz) *shanklish* (see page 121), crumbled
2 medium-sized firm ripe tomatoes, diced into small
   cubes
1 small Spanish onion, peeled and very finely chopped
4 tbsp extra-virgin olive oil

Put all the ingredients in a mixing bowl and mix well. Serve with
good bread.

LEVANT

Stewed Lamb on a Purée of Smoky Aubergines

HÜNKAR BEĞENDI

An *esnaf lokantası*, or 'restaurant of the working people', is a
Turkish eatery where the food is displayed in large metal trays and
kept in hot cabinets for customers to see what's being served that
day – a great system for visitors who don't speak the language.
Some are very unappealing, with greasy trays and wizened pieces
of meat and vegetables that have been sitting in the heat for far too
long, while others have wonderful displays that make you want
to try everything. And at Özkonak in Cihangir, a charming and
tranquil neighbourhood where you'll find one of the best pickles
shops in Istanbul, I'm tempted to eat everything. The food, limited
to half a dozen dishes, is displayed at the back. It is always
seasonal, and in the spring they have the most sensational artichoke
hearts cooked in olive oil with diced potatoes, carrots, fava beans
and fresh dill. They also have classics, like this dish here – *hünkar
beğendi* or succulent lamb shanks served on a velvety aubergine
purée. As for the atmosphere, it is as relaxed as the neighbourhood,
and very friendly. The old owner, who is permanently stationed by
the door, either sitting at a small table or standing by it, greets
everyone with a big smile. His clientele is made up of locals, some
enjoying a leisurely meal, others a quick bite or a pudding.

Özkonak is known for its *kazandibi* (see page 226), which is displayed with other desserts in the windows either side of the entrance door.

Serves 4

25g (1oz) unsalted butter
3 medium-sized onions (about 300g/11oz total weight), peeled
4 lamb shanks
2 tbsp tomato purée
1 tbsp red wine vinegar
1 bay leaf
2 sprigs of thyme, leaves picked from the stalks
1 tsp Aleppo pepper (see page 313)
¼ tsp ground cinnamon
¼ tsp finely ground black pepper
Sea salt

For the aubergine purée
4 medium-sized aubergines (about 1kg/2lb 2oz total weight)
Juice of 1 lemon
100g (3½oz) unsalted butter
50g (2oz) plain flour
500ml (18fl oz) full-cream organic milk, boiled and cooled
50g (2oz) *kaçar* (see page 1) or pecorino cheese, grated

Melt the butter in a saucepan and add the onions. Sauté until lightly golden, then add the lamb shanks and lightly brown them all over. Add the remaining ingredients and season with salt. Pour in 1 litre (1¾ pints) of water and bring to the boil, then reduce the heat to medium-low, cover the pan with a lid and let it bubble gently for 1½ hours.

While the meat is cooking, start preparing the aubergine purée. First preheat the grill to high.

Prick the aubergines in several places and place under the grill to cook until the skin is charred and the flesh is very soft. Cut the aubergines in half lengthways and scoop out the flesh. Let the flesh drain in a colander for about 15 minutes, then marinate in 1 litre (1¾ pints) of water mixed with the lemon juice. Drain the aubergines well and mash with a fork or a potato masher.

Melt the butter in a medium-sized pan over a medium heat, add the flour and stir for a couple of minutes to form a roux. Take the pan off the heat, then add the mashed aubergines and stir energetically to mix in with the roux. Return the pan to the heat and stir in the milk. Cook for 2–3 minutes, stirring constantly, until you have a creamy purée. Then add the cheese and stir for another minute or so.

Using a slotted spoon, remove the lamb shanks from the broth and arrange in the middle of a serving dish. Arrange the aubergine purée around the meat and serve very hot with good bread.

Caramelised Milk Pudding

KAZANDIBI

Kazandibi, a milk pudding made with shredded chicken breast, is an acquired taste for some, but I love experiencing the texture of the meat without any of the taste. The extraordinary use of meat in a dessert may appear outlandish, but *kazandibi* is one of the great Turkish desserts, and thanks to my friend Hande, who owns the Istanbul Culinary Institute, I now know where to go for the best *kazandibi* in town, at Özkonak (see page 224). Last time I was there, I was greedily enjoying my second serving of the pudding when I noticed a young girl sitting across from me, tucking into a plate of stuffed vegetables. There was something rather strange about her. She looked fearful and was eating far too quickly, even by my standards – I eat very quickly. I wondered what it was that was making her so anxious. Admittedly she was a bit young to be there on her own, but everyone was very friendly. I left still wondering about her until I saw her later in the day, begging for money in the Pera district. I guess the old man had kindly fed her for free, which did not surprise me. Turks are amongst the most generous people in the Middle East, even more hospitable, if anything, than my fellow countrymen and women, who are famous for their gracious welcome of strangers.

Serves 4

100g (3½oz) pudding rice, soaked overnight in 100ml
    (3½fl oz) cold water
1 small breast of chicken, without the skin
1 litre (1¾ pints) full-cream organic milk
200g (7oz) golden caster sugar
Ground cinnamon for sprinkling

Put the soaked rice and its water in a food processor and process until completely pulverised. Drain in a fine sieve to collect the starchy water, or *sübye* – the basis of many milk puddings. You can use rice flour instead but the pudding will not be as smooth or set as well.

Put the chicken breast in a small saucepan and cover with water. Place over a medium heat and bring to the boil, skimming away any scum that rises to the surface. Reduce the heat, then cover the pan with a lid and simmer for 30 minutes or until the chicken is completely cooked through.

Drain the meat and put in a bowl full of cold water. Leave to cool for a short while then separate into very fine shreds – the meat should almost disappear in the dessert. Soak the shredded chicken in cold water.

Heat the milk and as it comes to the boil, reduce the heat to low. Add the *sübye*, stirring constantly, and continue stirring for about 15 minutes or until the milk starts thickening. Add the sugar and continue stirring for another 10 minutes. Drain the shredded chicken well and add to the milk, then cook for another 10 minutes, stirring regularly.

Put a medium-sized non-stick saucepan on a medium-high heat and when the pan is hot, pour the milk dessert into it. Cook for about 10 minutes or until the bottom is browned but not burned. Lift a corner with a spatula to check on how the colour is developing.

When the bottom has coloured properly, take the pan off the heat. Cover with a clean tea towel and allow to cool. Cut into quarters, which you can roll up if you like or are able to – like a fat Swiss roll – and serve sprinkled with cinnamon.

At the Bakery

When I look back at photographs of myself as a child and see how chubby I was, I fall into a kind of nostalgic rêverie, thinking of all the dishes I loved to eat, all of them prepared by my mother, grandmother or aunt, except for one of my favourite breakfasts, *manqûsheh*, a flat bread topped with olive oil and *za'tar* (see page 333). Lebanese home-cooks, at least those living in the city, did not bake their own bread. Each neighbourhood had several bakeries that catered to the community's bread needs. But if home-cooks did not bake their bread, they baked their own savoury pastries, at least in part. They would prepare the filling or topping at home to take to the baker for him to use with his own dough and bake in his ovens. My mother was no different. She would send a maid with the topping for *manaqish* (plural for *manqûsheh*) to the bakery and I, being the family's dedicated kitchen pest, often tagged along, not just to watch the action at the bakery but also to have one of the breads straight out of the oven. We never told my mother I ate there. I didn't want her to say one *manqûsheh* was enough, nor to tell me off for eating outside. She was rather strict.

I never had any problems convincing the maid of the moment to keep my secret. They were all very kind, although I have vivid memories of only two. One, a pretty young girl from the mountains who had the most gorgeous long chestnut-coloured hair, until that is my mother and grandmother cruelly sheared it off one day when they realised it was her who had given us nits, and not someone at school. They then sent her back to her family, and replaced her with Omm Yussef, whom I adored. She was a middle-aged, portly Druze woman from the Huran mountains in Syria who arrived every morning wearing all her finery, layer upon layer of black embroidered clothes, typical of her region, which she then proceeded to remove one by one until she got down to her black satin underwear. Nothing sexy mind you. They were more like pyjamas than skimpy lingerie! And all the while, she jingled the many gold bracelets she wore around her wrists – they were her pension and all her savings went into adding to them. Every day, I would sit and watch her peel off her clothes while making her own music, never tiring of the scene.

231

Omm Yussef knew not to undress on *manaqish* day until after we came back from the bakery. By the time she got to us, my mother had the *za'tar* and olive oil already mixed in a bowl, which she placed in the middle of a large round metal tray – you couldn't expect the baker's *za'tar* and olive oil to be as good as the one you had at home. Omm Yussef picked the tray up and placed it on her head. She then grabbed my hand and we walked up the street to the baker. Sometimes we had to wait alongside our neighbours or their maids who had also brought their own topping or fillings to be used with the baker's dough. Other times, the bakery would be empty and we were served immediately. It really depended on what was happening in the neighbourhood – big family gatherings or celebrations meant the baker had to make dozens and dozens of *manaqish* or other savoury pastries such as *lahm bil-ajine* (meat pizzas) or *fatayer* (pastry triangles filled with greens, *labneh* or cheese).

When it came to our turn, Omm Yussef made sure to remind the baker, on my mother's instructions, to be generous with our *za'tar* topping. He already knew that from our previous visits, but my mother never failed to insist she should remind him. As soon as the first lot of *manaqish* came out of the oven, the baker folded one in half, wrapped it in paper and handed it to me, patting me on the head. He liked to see me eat. He then lined our tray with paper and spread the rest of the *manaqish* on it. When we had them all, Omm Yussef lifted the tray back onto her head and we walked home where my mother had already laid the table for breakfast with tomatoes, cucumbers, olives, *labneh* and fresh mint, all of which she put inside the *manqûsheh* to make one of the best wraps ever. I sat down with my siblings to my second *manqûsheh* with all the different garnishes, smiling naughtily at Omm Yussef while she peeled off her clothes.

Such small bakeries, providing both bread and an oven to the neighbourhood were the only ones I knew as a child. There are still some today, although many have now been edged out by large industrial bakeries with branches everywhere that produce industrial quantities of breads, as well as savoury pastries and *ka'k* (different shaped rusks leavened with fermented chickpea flour that are normally consumed for breakfast with hot milk). Naturally none of these bakeries produce breads or pastries that are as good as those made by the smaller bakers but most people in Lebanon, like everywhere else in the world, prefer to go for convenience and are happy to buy their breads and other baked goods from the chain bakeries. In fact, there is a noticeable difference between Levantine bakers and their Western counterparts. Whereas Western bakers do both savoury and sweet baking, those in the Levant only do savoury, leaving all the sweet stuff to specialist sweet-makers and if you are looking for recipes for sweets, you will need to go to the chapter devoted to sweet-makers.

Fortunately, there are still enough individual bakers in most neighbourhoods including a kind that didn't exist when I lived in Beirut: tiny, hole-in-the-wall bakeries that are mostly manned by women and where the bread (known as *marqûq*, see page 5) is baked over a *saj* (a kind of inverted wok). The *saj* was once heated by wood fire but most are now fired by gas. The same can be said of the regular bakery ovens that are now also mostly gas-fired.

Pita Bread

KHOBZ 'ARABI

It is rare nowadays to find a pita bread bakery where the process is not completely automated, from when the dough is put into the cutting machine to when the loaves are baked and either dropped piping hot at the sales window to be sold straight away or spread out to cool before being packed into plastic bags to be delivered to shops and restaurants. One of my favourite pita bread bakeries is in Aleppo, next to the hotel where I used to stay. The large dark room is almost completely taken up by a snaking conveyor belt that starts at the dough-cutting machine then climbs up to the rollers, two sets, one on top of the other. The first rolls out the dough into ovals that are swivelled and transferred to the second set below to be rolled out into perfect circles. The discs of flattened dough are then slowly conveyed into the blazing oven where they puff up and bake in seconds before being ejected onto the cooling conveyor belt, made up of slats with gaps between to allow air to circulate. The cooling belt also climbs but this time to carry the loaves to the sales window. There they are taken off the belt and sold piping hot to customers waiting outside who spread them out on mats on the pavement to cool them before carrying them home. (If the pita is not cooled before being packed, the two layers of the loaf will stick together.) Loaves are also handed to packers inside the bakery who spread them out on the floor and let them cool before bundling them into packs of 12 and stuffing them into plastic bags. The system is ingenious and I wonder if it existed when I was a child. I don't remember ever seeing it then. In the bigger industrial bakeries, the cooling conveyor belt ferries the loaves to a large packing room behind the bakery where muscly men spend the whole morning stuffing stacks of pita breads into branded bags that are sold in the shop section of the bakery or sent out in trucks to supermarkets.

Using the same pita dough, you can make both bread, as in the recipe below, or 'pizza' with different toppings (see page 240). You can also vary the basic recipe to make different regional styles of bread, such as *mishtah* (see page 236), which you can use as a base with the same range of toppings.

Makes 10 individual breads

500g (1lb 1oz) unbleached plain flour, plus extra for
  dusting
1 heaped tsp (½ × 7g sachet) fast-action yeast
2 tsp fine sea salt
60ml (2fl oz) extra-virgin olive oil, plus extra for greasing

Mix the flour, yeast and salt in a large mixing bowl. Make a well
in the centre and pour the oil into it. Using the tips of your fingers,
rub the oil into the flour until well incorporated.

Gradually add 310ml (10½fl oz) of warm water, bringing in the
flour as you go, then knead until you have a rough, rather sticky
ball of dough.

Sprinkle your work surface with flour. Transfer the dough to it
and dust with a little flour. Knead for 2–3 minutes, sprinkling with
more flour if the dough sticks. Invert the bowl over the dough and
leave to rest for 15 minutes. Remove the bowl and knead for a few
more minutes or until the dough is smooth and elastic and rather
soft. Shape the dough into a ball and place in an oiled bowl,
turning the dough to coat all over with oil. Cover with cling film
and let it rise in a warm, draught-free place for 2 hours.

Fold after the first hour to strengthen the dough and make it rise
better. The best way to do this is to first dust your hands and work
surface with flour, then invert the bowl over one hand to let the
dough drop onto your palm. Gently slide it onto the work surface
and pat it into a thick flat circle. Fold one-third of the dough over
from your right. Fold the left third over, then fold the top third
over and the bottom one over it. Return to the bowl, with the
folded sides down, and leave to finish rising. By the end, the dough
should have doubled in size.

Transfer the dough to your work surface. Divide into ten equal-
sized pieces, each weighing just under 90g (3oz). Roll each piece
of dough into a ball, cover with a tea towel that is wet but not
dripping and leave to rise for 45 minutes.

Roll out each ball of dough to a disc about 15cm (6in), dusting
your work surface and the dough with flour every now and then

235

and making sure you form even circles. A good way to achieve this is to give the disc a quarter turn between each rolling out. You can also use a pasta machine to roll out each piece of dough. Transfer to non-stick baking sheets (or ones lined with baking paper or a silicone mat). Cover the discs of dough with a floured baker's couche or tea towel and leave to rest for 15–20 minutes.

Preheat the oven to its highest setting.

Bake in the oven for 6–8 minutes or until well puffed and very lightly golden. The baking time will vary depending on how hot your oven is. I suggest you start checking the pita breads after 5 minutes. You may have to bake them in separate batches if your oven is not large enough. These are best served immediately or at least still warm. Alternatively, you can let them cool on a wire rack and freeze them for later use. When you are ready to serve them, simply defrost them in the bag before removing from the bag and reheating in a warm oven.

Spicy Pita
MISHTAH

Mishtah is an interesting flatbread that is little known outside southern Lebanon. I had never eaten it until a few years ago when I met my friend Nayla Audi, whose family comes from that part of the country – her father and his father before him represented their constituency in parliament. I was researching my baking book then and Nayla gave me some *mishtah* she had in her freezer in Beirut. Unlike pita, it is not a pocket bread, just a thin flatbread. But it has texture because of the *jrish* (cracked wheat – see page 320) mixed in with the flour and a wonderful, rather unusual flavour due to the spices in the dough. I was curious to see how it was made and Nayla very kindly took me to her local baker before giving me a spectacular lunch at her father's nineteenth-century house where the family graveyard is just off the courtyard. The old baker, Jawwad Yussef Daher, let us into the primitive bakery to watch the ladies make not only *mishtah* but also *marqûq* bread (see page 315). And he gave me the following recipe that can be used to make *manaqish* on page 240. Since then, I have visited other bakeries, including one where the baker made a very long *mishtah* which he sold by the piece, a little like the long focaccias of Rome or Puglia. Each baker has his own formula: some make a softer and spongier version of the bread, while others might use less cracked wheat or fewer spices. So you can vary the recipe slightly (at least as far as the cracked wheat, seeds and spices are concerned) to make a *mishtah* to your taste. If you want it softer and spongier, for instance, either leave it to rise for longer or use more yeast, and when you flatten it, make sure it is a little thicker than what I suggest here.

Makes 6 individual breads

500g (1lb 1oz) wholewheat flour, plus plain flour
for dusting
2¼ tsp (1 × 7g sachet) fast-action yeast
1 tsp fine sea salt
3 tbsp anise seeds
3 tbsp sesame seeds
½ tsp ground *mahlab* (see page 322)
½ tsp ground aniseed
½ tsp *daqqaat ka'k* (a special spice mixture from the
south) (optional)
100g (3½oz) organic *jrish* (cracked wheat – see page 320),
soaked in cold water for 1 hour and drained
Extra-virgin olive oil for greasing

Mix the flour, yeast, salt and spices in a large mixing bowl. Be sure to distribute the spices evenly at this stage as it may be more difficult to do that when kneading the dough.

Stir in the cracked wheat and make a well in the centre. Gradually add 250ml (9fl oz) and 1 tablespoon of warm water, bringing in the flour as you go, then knead until you have a rough ball of dough.

Transfer the dough to a work surface lightly dusted in flour. Knead for 3 minutes, sprinkling with a little flour if the dough sticks. Invert the mixing bowl over the dough and leave to rest for

237

15 minutes. Knead for 3 more minutes or until the dough is smooth and elastic. Grease a large bowl with a little olive oil. Shape the dough into a ball and place in the bowl, turning it to coat all over with oil. Cover with cling film and leave to rise in a warm, draught-free place for 2 hours. Fold after the first hour (see page 235). By the end, the dough should have doubled in size.

Transfer the dough to your work surface. Divide into six equal-sized pieces and roll each into a ball. Cover with a tea towel that is wet but not wringing and leave to rise for 45 minutes.

Flatten each ball in your hands into a disc about 20cm (8in) in diameter. Transfer to non-stick baking sheets (or ones lined with baking paper or a silicone mat). Cover with a floured baker's couche or tea towel and leave to rest for 10–15 minutes. If you are going to make *manaqish* (see page 240), spread the *za'tar* and oil mixture over each disc as soon as you flatten it, making sure you oil the edges, and then leave uncovered.

Meanwhile, preheat the oven to its highest setting.

Bake in the oven for 10–12 minutes or until lightly golden. Serve warm or cool on a wire rack to serve at room temperature.

Lebanese Morning Bread

KHOBZ AL-SABAH

The following recipe, a variation on pita (see page 234), is from the same baker who gave me the recipe for *mishtah* (see page 236). I've never asked him why he calls it morning bread, but I guess it is because it is eaten mostly for breakfast. He uses three different types of flour in the dough to give the bread more texture.

Makes 12 individual breads

500g (1lb 1oz) unbleached plain flour, plus extra
   for dusting
100g (3½oz) wholewheat flour
100g (3½oz) fine cornmeal
2¼ tsp (1 × 7g sachet) fast-action yeast
4 tsp fine sea salt

Mix the flours, cornmeal, yeast and salt in a large mixing bowl.
Make a well in the centre and gradually add 375ml (13fl oz) and
1 tablespoon of warm water, bringing in the flour as you go.
Knead until you have a rough ball of dough.

Dust your work surface with a little flour and transfer the dough
onto it. Knead for 3 minutes, sprinkling with a little flour if the
dough sticks. Invert the bowl over the dough and leave to rest for
15 minutes. Knead for another 3 minutes, or until the dough is
smooth and elastic. Roll into a ball and place in a clean, lightly
floured bowl. Cover with cling film and leave to rise in a warm,
draught-free place for 2 hours. Fold after the first hour (see page
235). By the end, the dough should have doubled in size.

Transfer the dough to your work surface and divide into 12 equal-
sized pieces. Roll each into a ball and place on a lightly floured
tray. Cover with a tea towel that is wet but not dripping and leave
to rise for 45 minutes.

Roll out each ball of dough into a disc about 15cm (6in) in
diameter. Transfer onto a large non-stick baking sheet (or one lined
with baking parchment or a silicone mat). Cover with a floured
baker's couche or tea towel and leave to rest for about 15 minutes.

Meanwhile, preheat the oven to its highest setting.

Bake in the oven, in batches if necessary, for 6–8 minutes or until
puffed up and very lightly golden. The baking time may vary,
depending on how hot your oven is. As with pita bread (see page
234), I suggest you check the breads after 5 minutes. Again, these
are best served immediately or still warm. Alternatively, you can
let them cool on a wire rack and freeze them for later use.

Lebanese 'Pizza'

MANAQISH BIL ZA'TAR

Manaqish topped with *za'tar* or *kishk* make the quintessential Lebanese breakfast. Throughout most of the country, they are made with the same dough as pita (see page 234) or *marqûq* (see 'bread' on page 315), while in the south they are often made with *mishtah* dough (see page 236), which gives them a more interesting flavour as well as texture. All versions are incredibly moreish and perfect for any time of day, whether breakfast, lunch or a mid-morning snack.

Makes 8 individual breads

1 quantity of pita or *mishtah* dough (see pages 234 and 236)

For the za'tar topping
6 tbsp *za'tar* (thyme mixture – see page 333)
125ml (4½fl oz) extra-virgin olive oil, plus extra for brushing

For the kishk topping
150g (5oz) *kishk* (dried yoghurt – see page 210)
4 tbsp toasted sesame seeds (to toast them yourself, see page 329)
1 small onion, peeled and very finely chopped
190–250ml (6½–9fl oz) extra-virgin olive oil
1 medium-sized ripe tomato, deseeded and diced into small cubes
Pinch of fine sea salt
Pinch of cayenne pepper

Following the instructions in the recipes on pages 234 and 236, shape the pita or *mishtah* dough into discs about 17.5cm (7in) in diameter and leave to rise/rest.

Meanwhile, mix the *za'tar* and olive oil in a bowl or mix together the ingredients for the *kishk* topping.

Raise the edges of the discs of dough to form an outer lip by pinching them upwards and prodding with your finger to make dimples all around the edge of the dough. Divide the topping of your choice between the breads, spreading it over each circle of dough. Brush the edges with oil and leave to rest for 15–20 minutes.

In the meantime, preheat the oven to its highest setting.

Bake in the oven for 7–10 minutes or until golden. *Manaqish* are best served immediately or warm; if made with the *za'tar* topping, they can be accompanied with *labneh* (see page 104), olives and fresh mint, although they are just as delicious served on their own.

Sweet Holy Bread

Qorban

You find this sweet bread and variations on it in both Lebanon and Syria, where there are sizeable Christian communities, and in the Palestinian territories. As well as being baked for communion, it is also served on various saints' days – distributed to the congregation after it has been blessed by the priest. There is a fairly comprehensive description of the communion ritual in Helen Corey's *Syrian Cookery* – how the priest divides up the bread and what each part symbolises – although my main memory of these religious occasions is not so much the ritual but rather the sweet, slightly exotic taste of the cube of bread that the priest gave me to eat, followed by a delicious sip of sweet wine. Whenever I pass by a bakery where they are baking these breads, usually to order from one of the churches, I try to convince them to let me buy a loaf to make up for all those measly little bites I've been offered at communion. The following recipe is based on one in Corey's book, although mine is sweeter and possibly softer. I normally bake it to eat on its own as if it were a cake, and sometimes I use it to make sweet-savoury sandwiches filled with either mortadella or *kashkaval*, a hard, mild cheese made from sheep's milk.

Makes 6 individual breads

500g (1lb 1oz) unbleached plain flour, plus
   extra for dusting
2¼ tsp (1 × 7g sachet) fast-action yeast
1½ tsp fine sea salt
¼ tsp ground *mahlab* (see page 332)
125g (4½oz) golden caster sugar
2 tbsp unsalted butter, softened
1 tbsp orange blossom water

Mix the flour, yeast, salt, *mahlab* and sugar in a large mixing bowl and make a well in the centre. Add the butter to the well and rub into the flour until well incorporated. Add the orange blossom water then gradually add 190ml (6½fl oz) and 1 tablespoon of warm water, mixing in the flour as you go. Knead until you have a rough ball of dough.

Lightly sprinkle your work surface with flour. Transfer the dough onto it, dust with a little flour and knead for 3 minutes, then roll into a ball. Invert the bowl over the dough and leave to rest for 15 minutes. Knead for a few more minutes or until the dough is smooth and elastic. Roll into a ball and transfer to a clean, lightly floured bowl. Cover with cling film and leave to rise in a warm, draught-free place for 2 hours. Fold the dough after the first hour (see page 235). It should be double the original volume by the end.

Transfer the dough to your work surface and divide into six equal-sized pieces. Roll each into a ball. Cover with cling film and leave to rest for 15 minutes.

Roll out the balls of dough into discs about 15cm (6in) in diameter. Transfer to non-stick baking sheets (or ones lined with baking parchment or a silicone mat). Cover with a tea towel that is wet but not dripping and leave to rise for 1 hour.

Twenty minutes before the breads are ready, preheat the oven to 200°C (400°C), gas mark 6.

Uncover the breads about 5 minutes before they are ready for baking to allow the surface to dry. Sift a thin film of flour over each, then lightly score a geometric design in the middle of each bread using the tip of a knife – or, if you have one, stamp with the special stamp that is used for holy bread. With a pointed chopstick, make five holes at regular intervals around the outer rim of the design to stop the bread from puffing up during baking. Bake in the oven for 15–20 minutes or until golden. Allow to cool on a wire rack, then serve at room temperature, or reheated, and spread with very good unsalted butter.

Ramadan Bread with Dates

KHOBZ RAMADAN

Ramadan, which is the month of Muslim fast, is a time of contrasts: no food or water allowed to pass anyone's lips from sunrise to sunset, followed by lavish feasting throughout the night. These breads are one of the many specialities that are made throughout the month. Sold from carts and bakeries throughout the souks of Tripoli (northern Lebanon), Damascus and Aleppo, they are also made at home. They vary in size, too, from small to very large and pricked all over to achieve a decorative effect. The following recipe comes from a charming baker in Byblos, Lebanon, who makes them either filled with dates, as below, or plain as a kind of brioche-like loaf. His recipe is perfect except that my version puffs up in the oven while his stays pretty flat. I'm not quite sure what his trick is, but the texture and taste are pretty much the same. The breads freeze very well, and I usually make a batch to freeze and have for breakfast every now and then.

Makes 6 individual breads

500g (1lb 1oz) unbleached plain flour, plus
    extra for dusting
¾ tsp (⅓ × 7g sachet) fast-action yeast
⅛ tsp fine sea salt
½ tsp powdered milk
¾ tsp baking powder
30g (1oz) icing sugar

cont. 243

½ tbsp unsalted butter, softened

4 tsp extra-virgin olive oil

Toasted sesame seeds (to toast them yourself,
   see page 329) for sprinkling

1 egg yolk beaten with 1 tsp water, for brushing

For the filling

225g (8oz) pitted Medjool dates (about 10–11 in total)

4 tbsp unsalted butter

Mix the flour, yeast, salt, powdered milk, baking powder and sugar
in a large mixing bowl and make a well in the centre. Add the
butter and oil to the well and, with the tips of your fingers, rub into
the dry ingredients until well incorporated. Gradually add 250ml
(9fl oz) and 2 tablespoons of warm water, incorporating the flour
as you go. Knead until you have a rough ball of dough.

Transfer the dough onto a work surface lightly dusted in flour and
knead for 3 minutes. Invert the bowl over the dough and leave to
rest for 15 minutes. Knead for 3 more minutes or until the dough
is smooth and elastic. Shape into a ball and place in a clean, lightly
floured bowl. Set aside to rise in a warm, draught-free place for
2 hours. Fold after the first hour (see page 235). By the end, the
dough should have doubled in size.

Meanwhile, make the filling. Put the dates in a food processor and
process until coarsely chopped, then add the butter and process
until you have a fine paste. Roll the mixture into a ball, wrap in
cling film and refrigerate while the dough is rising.

Transfer the dough to your work surface and divide into six
equal-sized pieces, each weighing about 130g (4½oz). Roll each
into a ball, cover with cling film and let the balls of dough rest for
15 minutes.

Divide the date paste into six equal-sized pieces and roll each into
a ball.

Roll out each piece of dough into a disc about 15cm (6in) in
diameter and flatten each ball of date paste into a circle about 10cm
(4in) in diameter. Place each date disc in the middle of a circle of
dough and fold the dough over to completely cover the date filling.

Pinch the edges to seal and, with your hands, flatten further to mould into an even disc.

Scatter sesame seeds all over a couple non-stick baking sheets (or ones lined with baking parchment or a silicone mat). Transfer the filled breads onto the baking sheet, placing them seam side down. Cover with a tea towel that is wet but not dripping and leave to rise for 30–45 minutes. Uncover 5 minutes before baking to let the surface to dry.

About 20 minutes before the breads are ready for baking, preheat the oven to 220°C (425°F), gas mark 7.

Brush the top of the breads with the beaten egg yolk and sprinkle liberally with sesame seeds. Bake in the oven for 12–15 minutes or until golden brown all over. Cool on a wire rack and serve at room temperature.

Lebanese Fatayer

FATAYER BI-SABANEGH

Homemade *fatayer* (savoury pastries) are small and dainty, baked to serve with drinks or as part of a mezze spread. My mother and grandmother spent whole mornings shaping *fatayer* into the most perfect tiny triangles, and I often annoyed my mother by stealing one or two as I passed the tray on which she'd arranged them ready to be taken to the table or served to guests. *Fatayer* made in bakeries, on the other hand, are much bigger and sold to eat on the hop as a snack or quick lunch. Whether made at home or commercially, the filling is the same – either greens (spinach, Swiss chard, purslane or fresh thyme), *labneh* (strained yoghurt – see page 104) or *qarisheh* (curd cheese) – although the pastries from bakeries may be less generously filled and the ingredients not as fine.

I often drove from Beirut to Damascus before the Syrian revolution and I remember once stopping for lunch at a modest-looking bakery on an ugly stretch of road just before the border.

Not my kind of place, but my driver and I were hungry and I liked the look of the veiled lady who was standing in the doorway next to an old man who turned out to be her father. I expected pleasant service if not great *fatayer*. But as soon as the lady lifted the cotton sheet covering the last of her pastries (it was quite late), I knew we were in for a treat; and despite the rudimentary set-up and the rickety gas-fired oven, crudely welded from thin metal, her *fatayer* were just perfect, filled with a succulent combination of Swiss chard, diced tomatoes and onion, seasoned with sumac and very good olive oil. A revelation. I hope I find her there, still making excellent *fatayer*, when the situation in Syria improves and I am able to go to that bakery again.

You can use the dough, filled in various ways, to make either baked triangles, as in the recipe below, or fried crescents known as *sambusak* that in Syria confusingly describes triangles made with a very thin filo-like pastry, which you see being made in the streets of Damascus. The pastry-makers pour a thin layer of batter in overlapping rings on a wide metal hotplate, starting at the outer edge and slowly and meticulously working their way towards the centre, until the hotplate is covered with a very large, thin sheet of pastry. They then peel off the sheet, lay it on a piece of cloth and start again in a process that is just as complicated and skilled as making filo. In the recipe below, you can vary the filling by substituting the spinach with the same quantity of purslane (leaves only), sorrel, Swiss chard, young dandelion leaves or fresh thyme.

Makes 18–20 small or 4 large pastries

300g (11oz) plain flour, plus extra for dusting
Fine sea salt
60ml (2fl oz) extra-virgin oil, plus extra for brushing

For the filling
1 medium-sized onion, peeled and very finely chopped
½ tsp finely ground black pepper
2 tbsp ground sumac (see page 331)
400g (14oz) spinach (or other greens – see introduction above), shredded into very thin strips
2 tbsp pine nuts
Juice of 1 lemon or to taste

9cm (3½in) diameter pastry cutter

Mix the flour and 1 teaspoon of salt in a mixing bowl and make a well in the centre. Add the oil to the well and, with the tips of your fingers, work into the flour until well incorporated. Gradually add 125ml (4½fl oz) of warm water and mix until you have a rough dough.

Transfer the dough to a work surface lightly dusted in flour and knead for 3 minutes, then roll into a ball. Invert the bowl over it and leave to sit for 15 minutes. Knead for 3 more minutes or until the dough is smooth and elastic. Divide the dough into two, roll each piece into a ball and cover with a clean, damp tea towel. Let them rest while you make the filling.

Put the chopped onion in a small mixing bowl. Add a little salt, the pepper and sumac and, with your fingers, rub the seasonings in to soften the onion.

Put the chopped spinach in another bowl, sprinkle with a little salt and gently rub in with your fingers until the spinach is wilted. Squeeze the spinach until it is very dry with all excess moisture removed. Transfer to a clean mixing bowl and separate the leaves.

Add the onion to the spinach, together with the pine nuts, lemon juice and olive oil, and mix well. Taste and adjust the seasoning if necessary – the filling should be quite strongly flavoured to offset the rather bland dough. Cover with a clean tea towel and set aside.

Preheat the oven to 220°C (425°F), gas mark 7.

Roll out one ball of dough as thinly as you can, to about 2mm (1⁄16in), then use the pastry cutter to cut as many discs of dough as you can. Knead together any leftover dough and keep under the damp tea towel with the other ball of dough.

Place a little less than a tablespoon of the filling in the middle of each disc of dough – don't be tempted to add more or the filled pastry may split open during cooking. Pick up the sides of each disc and stick them together two-thirds of the way down. Next pick up the bottom part of the disk and stick the middle of it to the joint formed by the other two sides, then press each half to the loose edges to form a triangle with raised joints. Pinch the joints firmly together – these triangles have a tendency to open during baking and you want to make sure they remain well sealed.

Transfer to non-stick baking sheets (or ones lined with baking paper or a silicone mat). Make the remaining triangles and transfer to the baking sheet. Brush with oil and bake in the oven for about 15 minutes or until the triangles are golden.

While the first batch is baking, make the rest of the triangles in the same way using the remaining dough, including any leftover pieces from cutting out. You should end up with 18–20 triangles. Once they are all baked, serve warm or at room temperature.

If you want to make the larger triangles, divide your dough in four equal-sized pieces. Roll out each piece to a thin disc, then fill and shape in the same way, using a quarter of the filling for each triangle, and bake for slightly longer in the oven.

Syrian Fatayer

FATAYER JIBNEH SÜRIYEH

I used to have a routine in Damascus, always staying at the Talisman, a beautiful hotel with the most enchanting courtyard in the Jewish quarter behind Straight Street. It was once the palatial residence of a Jewish family but they, like many other Jewish families, left the country after the 1967 war and abandoned their beautiful home. Looking at the narrow lane and the tiny entrance door, you would never imagine such space and splendour behind it. And because the lanes are all quite similar, I often get lost returning to the hotel. Luckily, there is a welcome landmark a few doors up – a tiny *fatayer* bakery where a group of young men and boys, spend each day making some of the best *fatayer* in town. Syrian *fatayer* are mini versions of Turkish *pide* (see page 250), which describes both the flat, spongy Turkish bread and a whole range of savoury pastries made with the same dough. When *pide* is applied to a type of savoury pastry, the word is always preceded by the

248

name of the vegetable or ingredient used in the filling. What is interesting, though, is that I don't remember having these *fatayer* during my childhood summers in Syria. Neither my aunt nor my cousins made them at home and in those days Mashta el-Helou had no commercial bakery. I can only assume they were and still are a street speciality made and sold at tiny hole-in-the-wall places in the old city or from larger bakeries in the modern districts. They are the ultimate street food in Syria, at least in Damascus where you find specialist *fatayer* bakeries in the souks and on the main streets. The dough for these pastries is quite different from that of Lebanese *fatayer* (see page 245). Made with milk and a touch of ground *mahlab* (see page 322), it gives the pastries an exotic flavour. It is slightly sweet, too, with a softer texture than the Lebanese version.

Makes 8 pastries

225g (8oz) unbleached plain flour, plus extra for dusting
1 heaped tsp (½ × 7g) fast-action yeast
1 tsp caster sugar
⅛ tsp ground *mahlab* (see page 322)
Fine sea salt
1 small organic egg
60ml (2fl oz) full-cream organic milk, at room temperature

For the filling
250g (9oz) *akkawi* cheese (see page 313) or cow's milk
   mozzarella, chopped very small
1 small organic egg, beaten
Unsalted butter
Few sprigs of flat-leaf parsley, most of the stalk discarded,
   finely chopped
Finely ground black pepper

Mix the flour, yeast, sugar, *mahlab* and ½ teaspoon of salt in a large mixing bowl and make a well in the centre. Add the egg and the milk to the well and mix these together before slowly incorporating with the flour. Knead until you have a rough ball of dough.

Lightly dust your work surface with flour and transfer the dough onto it. Knead for 3 minutes, sprinkling with a little flour if the dough sticks. Invert the bowl over the dough and let it sit for

15 minutes. Knead for 3 more minutes or until the dough is smooth and elastic, then roll into a ball. Place in a clean, lightly floured bowl and leave to rise in a warm, draught-free place for 2 hours. Fold after the first hour (see page 235). By the end, the dough should have doubled in volume.

Meanwhile, mix the filling ingredients together, seasoning with salt and pepper to taste.

Transfer the risen dough to your work surface and divide into eight equal-sized pieces, each weighing just under 30g (1oz). Shape each piece into a ball, then cover with a clean tea towel that is wet but not wringing and let the balls of dough rest for 30 minutes.

Using your hands, flatten each ball into a thin disc about 12cm (5in) in diameter. Stretch each disc into an oval, then spread 1 tablespoon of filling down the middle. Fold one third of the oval over the filling, then fold over the other third, leaving a little of the filling showing, and pinch the sides together where they join at the tips. Transfer to a large non-stick baking sheet (or one lined with baking parchment or a silicone mat). Cover with the damp tea towel and allow to rest for 20 minutes.

Preheat the oven to its highest setting.

Bake in the oven for 10–12 minutes or until golden brown all over. Serve hot or warm.

Turkish Bread

PIDE

Pide is the type of bread that Turks eat most frequently – a soft, long, oval flat loaf, often sprinkled with sesame seeds. The bakeries making *pide* are dotted throughout the various neighbourhoods of a town. Most have large windows through which you can watch the bakers at work as they divide the dough into pieces and shape each part into a long flat loaf, stabbing it with their fingers to create the long indentations that are so characteristic of this bread. Sesame seeds are then sprinkled all over the loaves before they are loaded onto a peel to slide into the wood-fired oven. Beyond the wooden or marble counter on which the bakers work is a large area covered with wooden slats on which the baked bread is spread out to let it cool without steaming. Customers gather at the window to buy the freshly baked bread and you can tell who has a large family from the number of loaves he/she buys. As with Lebanese pita (see page 234), the same dough is used both for bread and to make savoury pastries, ones that are quite similar to Syrian *fatayer* (see page 248). Oddly enough, the same bakery won't make both: each bakery has its own speciality, either making the bread or the pastries.

Makes 1 loaf to serve 4

450g (1lb) unbleached plain flour, plus extra for dusting
2¼ tsp (1 × 7g sachet) fast-action yeast
2 tsp golden caster sugar
2 tsp fine sea salt
2 tbsp extra-virgin oil, plus extra for greasing
1 small organic egg beaten with 1 tsp water, for brushing
1–2 tbsp sesame seeds

Mix the flour, yeast, sugar and salt in a large mixing bowl and make a well in the centre. Pour the oil into the well and rub it into the flour, then gradually add just under 250ml (9fl oz) of warm water, incorporating the flour as you go. Knead until you have a rough ball of dough.

Transfer the dough to a work surface lightly dusted in flour and knead for 3 minutes. Invert the bowl over the dough and let it sit for 15 minutes. Knead for another 3 minutes or until the dough is smooth and elastic. Grease a large bowl with a little oil and place the dough in it, turning to coat in the oil. Cover with cling film and leave to rise in a warm, draught-free place for 2 hours. Fold after the first hour (see page 235). By the end, the dough should have doubled in volume.

Transfer the risen dough to your work surface and shape into a ball. Place on a non-stick baking sheet (or one lined with baking parchment or a silicone mat). Cover with clean tea towel that is

251

wet but not wringing and let the dough rest for 15 minutes. Using your hands, flatten it into a long oval loaf, about 1.5cm (⅝in) thick. Cover with the wet tea towel and leave to rise for 45 minutes.

Twenty minutes before the dough is ready for baking, preheat the oven to 200°C (400°F), gas mark 6.

Uncover the dough about 5 minutes before baking to let the surface dry. Brush with the egg mixture, then using your fingertips make dimples all over the top of the loaf and sprinkle with the sesame seeds. Bake in the oven for 30 minutes or until golden all over. Cool on a wire rack and serve at room temperature or reheat to serve later.

Aubergine Pastries
PATLICANLI PIDE

Pide (the pastries, that is, and not the bread (see page 250) – using the same name can be confusing) are quite similar to Syrian *fatayer* (see page 248) but made much larger. In some places a little of the filling is left showing in the middle while in others it is completely encased, but the shape remains the same – long and oval, a little like a boat. You won't see many of these pastries on sale in bakeries in Turkey, certainly not the way you see them in bakeries abroad like those on Green Lanes in north London. Most are filled with cheese or spinach, the latter often with eggs baked on top. The recipe below is for aubergine *pide* adapted from a wonderful version in Ayla Algar's *Classic Turkish Cooking*. You can make the pastries large, as suggested below, or small to serve with drinks. For small pastries, you'll need to divide the dough into 12 pieces and shape in the same way but making them thinner and shorter.

Makes 4 pastries

265g (9½oz) unbleached plain flour, plus extra for dusting
¾ tsp (⅓ × 7g sachet) fast-action yeast
Fine sea salt
2 tbsp extra-virgin olive oil

For the topping
2–3 tbsp extra-virgin olive oil, plus extra for drizzling
1 medium-sized aubergine (about 200g/7oz), trimmed and
   diced into small cubes
½ red bell pepper, trimmed, deseeded and finely chopped
Finely ground black pepper
1 garlic clove, peeled and crushed
1 × 200g can of Italian chopped tomatoes
⅛ tsp dried chilli pepper flakes or to taste
Few sprigs of flat-leaf parsley, most of the stalk discarded,
   finely chopped
Few sprigs of coriander, most of the stalk discarded,
   finely chopped
Few fresh basil leaves, to garnish

Mix the flour, yeast and 1 teaspoon of salt in a large mixing
bowl and make a well in the centre. Pour the olive oil into the well
and, with the tips of your fingers, rub it into the flour until well
incorporated. Add 125ml (4½fl oz) of warm water and mix until
you have a rough ball of dough.

Sprinkle a little flour on your work surface and transfer the dough
onto it. Knead for 3 minutes, then invert the bowl over the dough
and let it rest for 15 minutes. Knead for 3 more minutes or until the
dough is smooth and elastic. Cover with a clean tea towel that is
wet but not dripping and let the dough rise in a warm, draught-free
place for 30 minutes.

Meanwhile, make the filling. Put the olive oil, aubergine and red
pepper in a saucepan and place over low heat. Season with salt and
pepper, cover with a lid cook for 15 minutes, stirring regularly.

Add the garlic, tomatoes and pepper flakes and cook, covered with
the lid, for another 15 minutes, stirring occasionally, or until the
vegetables are done and the sauce is very thick. Add the parsley and

253

coriander and cook, uncovered, for another minute or so, then take off the heat and let the mixture cool.

Preheat the oven to 220°C (425°F), gas mark 7.

Divide the risen dough into four equal-sized pieces. Roll each piece into a ball, then cover with a clean, damp tea towel and let the balls of dough rest for 15 minutes. With your hands, flatten each ball into a circle about 12.5cm (5in) in diameter. Then stretch the circles into ovals and flatten further. Transfer to a large non-stick baking sheet (or one lined with baking parchment or a silicone mat).

Make indentations inside the edge of each pastry to raise it slightly, then place a quarter of the filling inside each one, spreading it up to the raised edge. Bake for 10–15 minutes or until golden. Serve hot or warm, garnished with basil.

Yufka

Turkey has probably the biggest selection of savoury pies of all the Levantine countries, including many types of *börek*, savoury pastries made with multiple thin sheets of *yufka*. This is like filo but varies in thickness depending on the type of pastry (it would be very thin for baklava, for example). Before being used in savoury dishes, *yufka* is either blanched in boiling water or very lightly baked on a *saj* (a special domed hotplate set over a gas fire). The recipe I give here is for *yufka* as bread rather than pastry to roll around a filling. The bread is often made in large quantities and left to dry so that it lasts a long time. Then when people want to serve it, it is moistend with a little water wrapped in a clean cloth and left to soften for about half an hour when it goes back to being as if it had been freshly baked. You can reheat it at that stage or serve as is.

Not so long ago and by sheer luck, I stumbled across a *yufka* factory in Gaziantep, in south-eastern Turkey. I had just been to my favourite ice-cream maker, Özgüler (see page 309), to have a mastic ice cream and I was about to jump into a taxi to return to my hotel when I noticed a big sign for *yufka* on the ground floor of the building next door. I walked up the few steps leading to the sign and pushed open a large double door to find a large man stacking huge round sheets of pastry. I asked if I could go in. He beamed a broad smile at me and waved me inside. The place had been someone's flat once, with large airy rooms and lovely big windows giving out onto greenery. In the main room sheets of *yufka* were being hung up to dry by a beautiful young boy who dunked each sheet into a metal tub full of water, then carefully lifted it out and draped it over rods that lined the walls of the room, each rod wrapped in foam so that the wet *yufka* didn't stick. There was a magical quality to the scene: this tanned creature in his white cotton vest and trousers rolled to the knee, bathed in light as he worked slowly and methodically, lifting the wafer-thin sheets of *yufka* from the water and draping them over the rods without ever tearing one. And even though what he was doing had nothing to do with Omm Youssef or my life in Beirut, the scene reminded me of her and brought back memories of the family flat in Beirut where all the rooms were filled with light, just like the one I was standing in.

In the next room were two men who rolled the sheets of *yufka*. They were older than the boy and they worked side by side, each with a marble slab in front of him and a thin metal rolling pin or *oklava*. One of them had a stack of small thick discs of dough to his right, which he took, one by one, to roll out. He then lifted the flattened disc of dough onto his rolling pin and laid it on his colleague's slab for him to roll out further into a very thin, perfect circle. This man then draped the dough over his rolling pin and slapped it against a large *saj* to his left, leaving it on the hot surface for a few seconds to dry out and bake but without browning. They both worked quickly, with the man baking the sheets building them into a stack on top of the *saj*; every time he added a new sheet, he would flip the stack to make sure that at least one side of each sheet came into contact with the heat.

I love the fact that, even today, with all the modernisation going on throughout the world, I can still come across masters of their craft working in the way their fathers and grandfathers did using specialist skills passed down from one generation to the next. Gaziantep is worth visiting for this reason alone, not to mention its many other attractions such as the bazaars and the wonderful cuisine. If you happen to be there in the autumn, everyone in the town will be busy preserving or drying or harvesting the bountiful produce in fields nearby. Whether in the old or modern part of the town, you will come across groups of women, both young and old, sitting by their doorway coring aubergines to dry on their roof, or trimming and deseeding peppers to have them minced in a gigantic food processor before the pepper purée is carried up to the roof in buckets to spread out to dry in the sun (see page 119).

Makes 10 individual breads

50g (2oz) unbleached plain flour, plus extra
  for dusting
50g (2oz) bread flour
3 tbsp wholewheat flour
½ tsp fine sea salt

Mix the flours and salt in a large mixing bowl and make a well in the centre. Gradually add 80ml (3fl oz) and 2 teaspoons of warm water and knead until you have a rough ball of dough.

Transfer the dough onto a work surface lightly dusted in flour and knead for 3 minutes. Invert the bowl over the dough and leave to rest for 15 minutes. Knead for 3 more minutes or until the dough is smooth and elastic.

Divide the dough into ten equal-sized pieces, each weighing about 20g (¾oz). Shape each into a small ball, rolling the dough between the palms of your hands and pressing on the joint with the side of your palm to seal. Sprinkle a tray or part of your work surface with flour and place the balls of dough on the floured surface. Cover with a clean, damp tea towel and leave to rest for 30 minutes.

Roll out each ball of dough – ideally with a thin rolling pin like the Turkish *oklava* (see introduction above) – sprinkling with flour every now and then, until you have a disc about 20cm (8in) in diameter. Turkish women can roll the dough into a thinner, larger circle, but this is as far as I can go. Place the discs of dough in between floured baker's couches or layer them between floured tea towels.

Place a large non-stick frying pan over a medium heat, and when the pan is very hot, cook the discs of dough, one after the other, for a minute or so on each side. They should be lightly golden with small burned spots where they have bubbled up. Layer the cooked breads between clean tea towels.

You can use these immediately to make wraps; or you can stack them in a dry place, wrapped in a tea towel, where they will keep for weeks. When you are ready to serve the breads, sprinkle each sheet with a little water to soften it, fold in half and wrap in a clean tea towel. Let it rest for 30 minutes so that it becomes soft and pliable, then serve as bread.

Tannur Bread

Even though Lebanon and Syria were one country for centuries – Lebanon was not given its independence by the French until 1943 – the choice of bread and savoury pastries is quite different in each place. Last time I drove from Aleppo to Beirut, I asked my driver to stop somewhere simple to eat – there are seriously extravagant road-stop restaurants in Syria. He suggested a bakery where they make *tannur* bread, a large flat loaf baked in a pit oven (see 'bread' on page 315).

    The idea appealed to me. My Syrian aunt baked *tannur* bread for us when we stayed with her, but the place suggested by my driver was not at all what I had expected. It was quite unlike the roadside *tannur* bakeries I had stopped at with wood-fired ovens like my aunt's, often manned by cheerful ladies whose method – flattening the dough by hand into a large disc – was the same as hers except for when it came to putting the loaves in the oven. While my aunt simply draped the dough over her hand and slapped it against the wall of the oven, not minding the fierce heat, the roadside ladies, by contrast, draped the dough over a cushion before slapping it against the oven wall. Once in the oven, the bread would be watched closely – like bread cooked on a domed hotplate or *saj*, *tannur* bread bakes in seconds – but as it started to peel off the wall, my aunt just lifted it with her hand while the ladies used a metal hook.

Everything at my driver's bakery was different, however. There were several ovens lined up on a platform, each of them industrially moulded out of clay and lit by a gas fire. The bakers were men and they worked in even more primitive conditions than my roadside ladies. Their breads were smaller and thicker, and instead of leaving them plain, they topped them with cheese or pepper paste to make a cross between *fatayer* (see page 232) and *manaqish* (see page 231), but not as good as either. Still, the place was fun and the atmosphere friendly, with mostly taxi and lorry drivers gathered in lively groups, discussing everything from politics to jobs. I was the only woman there and I tried to ignore their oblique glances. They must have been wondering what an Arabic-speaking, foreign-looking (my years abroad have made me look more foreign than Arab) creature was doing sharing their modest fare and chatting with her driver, all of which are definite no-nos for a respectable Arab lady.

Makes 8 individual breads

300g (11oz) unbleached plain flour, plus extra for dusting
1 tsp fine sea salt

Mix the flour and salt in a large mixing bowl and make a well in the centre. Gradually add 170ml (6fl oz) and 1½ tablespoons of warm water, incorporating the flour as you go, and knead until you have a rough ball of dough.

Dust your work surface with a little flour and place the dough on it. Knead for 3 minutes, then invert the bowl over the dough and leave to rest for 15 minutes. Knead for 3 more minutes or until the dough is smooth and elastic. Divide the dough into eight equal-sized pieces, shaping each into a ball. Sprinkle a tray or part of your work surface with flour and place the balls of dough, seam side down, on top. Cover with a tea towel that is wet but not dripping and allow to rest for 30 minutes.

Roll out each ball of dough, sprinkling with flour every now and then, until you have a disc 20cm (8in) in diameter. Place the discs of dough in between floured baker's couches or tea towels.

Place a large non-stick frying pan over a medium heat, and when the pan is very hot, cook the discs of dough, one at a time, for a minute on each side. They should be lightly golden with small burned spots where they have bubbled up. They will puff up, as with pita (see page 234), but will deflate as soon as you remove them from the heat; you could try pricking them with a fork here and there to stop them puffing up. Layer them between clean tea towels to keep soft and warm. Serve immediately or let the breads cool and freeze for later use.

Turkish Cheese Pie

Su Böreği

According to Evliya Çelebi, author of a seventeenth-century travel book, there were no less than 4,000 *börek* shops in Ottoman Turkey as against only 1,000 bakeries. I am pretty sure that nowadays there are still more *börek* shops than bakeries. This is not to say all of them will be good; indeed, I am always careful about which ones I go to. I love one particular tiny bakery in Sarıyer on the Bosphorus where the golden pastries are piled high in the window. Some are shaped in a figure of eight, others in large rectangles of lasagne-like pies, with bright green spinach sandwiched between the buttery layers, and others in long flat rolls filled with crumbly cheese or minced meat; and all are made with flaky layers of thin *yufka* (like filo – see page 246). As I don't speak Turkish, I ask for my favourite types by just pointing at them, then spreading my hands to indicate the size of the piece I want the vendor to cut for me. Every single one of their pastries is delectable. And the added attraction of the bakery being near the waterfront makes it a must for me to visit whenever I am in Istanbul.

After purchasing my pastries, I settle on a bench near a tea vendor who sells piping hot tea or coffee from a lovely cart and I gesture to him to pour me a cup of tea. The moment is always perfect as I sit with the Bosphorus at my feet and everything just how I like it: the *börek* as crisp and flaky as when I last ate it, the tea hot and sweet without being cloying, and the tea vendor and passers-by just as charming. The traditional way to make *su böreği* is by using *yufka* that is rolled out even thinner than described in the recipe on page 254 then boiled for a few seconds before being layered in a baking tin with a cheese or spinach filling – a sort of Turkish lasagne. However, it is quite a skill to boil large sheets of very thin dough and so I always use filo for my *su böreği*, which I buy from Turkish shops because it is thinner than Greek filo, not to mention the supermarket ones. Despite being thinner, it is easier to handle because it is softer.

It was far from the Sarıyer bakery that I first watched a woman preparing the boiled *yufka* for *su böreği*. That was at a restaurant near Safranbolu in the Black Sea region – a wonderfully preserved old town which is now a UNESCO world heritage site – where we had stopped with a group of foodies (all of us guests of the local government who had organised a food festival) on the way to a *rahat loukoum* (Turkish delight) factory. The restaurant was closed but they agreed to let us in for coffee, and as luck would have it, there was a young lady making *su böreği*. Working quite differently from the men I had seen in Gaziantep (see page 254), she rolled out the sheets of *yufka* on a wooden board with her rolling pin. Then she carried the sheets to a large pot full of boiling water and carefully dropped one sheet of *yufka* at a time into the water, gently immersing it with the help of a wooden spoon. She then lifted it into a colander and from there into a buttered baking dish where she smoothed it out to cover the bottom of the dish. She worked quickly and painstakingly, sprinkling melted butter on each sheet, until she had eight layers in the dish. She then spread crumbled cheese all over the *yufka* and resumed boiling and spreading the sheets of pastry until she had eight more layers covering the cheese. She tucked the sides in before covering the pie with a sheet of *yufka* that wasn't boiled to give the pie a crisp top. Sadly, we never got to taste her pie as we were rushing so as not to miss watching *rahat loukoum* being made. I still regret not tasting what must have been a very superior *su böreği*.

Serves 6

1 × 400g packet of Greek or Turkish filo pastry (about
    14 sheets, measuring 28 × 43cm/11 × 17in)
125g (4½oz) unsalted butter, melted

For the filling

150g (5oz) good feta cheese, crumbled

Few sprigs of flat-leaf parsley, most of the stalk discarded, finely chopped

1 medium-sized organic egg

Pie dish about 25cm (10in) in diameter

Preheat the oven to 200°C (400°F), gas mark 6.

Mix the ingredients for the filling together in a bowl.

Brush the pie dish with a little of the melted butter. Lay the sheets of filo, one at a time, in the dish and using half the packet. Brushing each with melted butter and cross the sheets over to cover the sides equally. Trim the corners.

Spread the filling evenly over the filo layers. Cover with the remaining sheets of filo, not forgetting to brush each sheet with butter and cross them over. Trim the corners and tuck any loose filo inside the dish.

Pour any leftover butter all over the top and, with a very sharp knife, cut into the top layers of filo to make six triangles. *Su böreği* is normally served cut into squares, but I prefer to serve it in triangles.

Bake in the oven for 15–20 minutes or until golden brown all over, and serve hot or warm.

Spinach Börek

Ispanakli Tepsi Böreği

Börek is probably the most ancient type of Mediterranean savoury pastry, brought by the Turks when they migrated west from Central Asia. Made with filo, *yufka* (like filo – see page 246) or rough puff pastry, it is served as part of a meal or eaten as a snack, either on the street or at home. Even though the choice of fillings is simply meat, greens or cheese, the variety is tremendous, depending on the region or particular family.

Serves 4

100g (3½oz) unsalted butter, melted, plus
    extra for greasing
1½ tbsp organic full-cream milk
1 medium-sized organic egg
12 sheets of Greek or Turkish filo pastry
    (measuring 28 × 43cm/11 × 17in)

For the filling
500g (1lb 1oz) spinach
2 medium-sized onions, peeled and finely
    chopped
1 tbsp extra-virgin olive oil
1 tbsp unsalted butter
2 medium-sized organic eggs, beaten
3 tbsp crumbled feta cheese
Fine sea salt
Finely ground black pepper

Baking dish measuring 22.5cm (9in) in diameter and
    2.5cm (1in) deep

First make the filling. Wash and drain the spinach and put in a large saucepan. Place over medium-high heat and cook for a few minutes, stirring regularly, until just wilted. Drain and allow to cool, then squeeze all the moisture from the spinach until it is very dry. Separate the leaves and set aside.

Put the chopped onions, oil and butter in a large frying pan and cook over medium-high heat, stirring occasionally, until lightly golden.

Add the spinach and cook for another minute or two. Take off the heat and stir in the eggs and the cheese. Season with salt and pepper and return to the heat. Cook for a couple of minutes, stirring all the time, until the eggs are very softly scrambled, then set aside while you prepare the filo pastry.

Preheat the oven to 200°C (400°F), gas mark 6, and grease the baking dish with a little butter.

Mix the melted butter with the milk and egg.

To assemble the pie, first lay one sheet of filo across the dish, leaving half hanging outside. Keep the other sheets of filo covered with cling film or a clean, damp tea towel so that they don't dry out. Brush the sheet in the dish with the butter, egg and milk mixture and fold the other half over it. You can leave the edges hanging over the sides of the dish, or you can trim them. I like leaving them – the pie looks very appealing with a crisp, golden skirt, as it were. Brush again with the milk/butter mixture, then repeat the operation with four more sheets of filo.

Spread the filling over the pastry. Cover with the remaining filo sheets, brushing each layer as you go. Pour any remaining butter mixture over the top and cut into quarters, slicing all the way to the bottom of the pie.

Bake in the oven for 25–35 minutes or until golden all over and serve hot or warm.

Turkish Meat Börek

KOL BÖREĞI

I always use Greek or Turkish brands of filo pastry as the sheets are bigger than the regular supermarket ones, and they are rolled out noticeably thinner, with less cornflour between the sheets. If you have a choice, select a Turkish variety as the filo is usually thinner than Greek or other Western brands.

Makes 20 pastries

10 sheets of Greek or Turkish filo pastry (measuring
     28 × 43cm/11 × 17in)
125g (4½oz) unsalted butter, melted

For the filling
1½ tbsp extra-virgin olive oil
½ tsp cumin seeds
1 large onion, peeled and finely chopped
2 tbsp pine nuts
1 garlic clove, peeled and finely chopped
½ red bell pepper, preferably Romano, trimmed,
     deseeded and diced into small squares
½ fresh red chilli pepper, trimmed, deseeded and finely
     chopped (scant 1 tbsp)
200g (7oz) freshly minced lean lamb, from the shoulder
     (either ask your butcher to mince the lamb or do it
     yourself using the fine attachment on a meat grinder)
1 × 200g can of Italian peeled tomatoes, drained and
     finely chopped
1½ tbsp sultanas
Few sprigs of flat-leaf parsley, most of the stalk discarded,
     finely chopped
2 tbsp finely chopped dill
½ tsp ground allspice
Fine sea salt
Finely ground black pepper

LEVANT

264

First make the filling. Put the oil in a large frying pan and place over a medium-high heat. Add the cumin seeds and stir until they become aromatic. Add the onion and pine nuts and cook, stirring regularly, until lightly golden, then stir in the garlic.

Add the peppers and lamb and stir – pressing on the meat with the back of the spoon to break up any lumps – until the meat is no longer pink. Add the tomatoes, sultanas, herbs and allspice and season with salt and pepper. Cook for a few minutes, stirring occasionally, until all liquid has evaporated. Set aside to cool while you prepare the pastry.

Preheat the oven to 200°C (400°F), gas mark 6.

Lay one filo sheet on your work surface. Keep the others covered with cling film or a clean, damp tea towel so that they don't dry out. Brush the filo sheet with melted butter, then cut it in half widthways. Turn both halves around so that the cut sides are nearest to you – the two filo halves are being filled at the same time. Place 2 teaspoons of filling in a thin line across each of the ends nearest to you, leaving 1.5cm (⅝in) free at the edges and from the top. Carefully fold the filo over the filling and roll, brushing with melted butter every two or three folds, to make a thin cylinder. Flatten one unfilled end, fold it over and roll the cylinder to make a coil. Brush with butter on both sides. Tuck the loose unfilled end under the coil and place on a large non-stick baking sheet (or one lined with baking parchment or a silicone mat). Make the other coils in the same way and transfer to the baking sheet.

Bake in the preheated oven for 15–20 minutes or until golden brown all over. Serve hot or warm.

At the Sweet-maker's

My parents moved houses often but always within West Beirut, the Muslim part of the city. I am not quite sure why because our homes were all the same style: large airy flats and all within walking distance of Hamra, which was then the Bond Street of Beirut. I liked everywhere we lived but I have particularly fond memories of our first home, on the top floor of a wonderful 1950's building with one curved corner that was my room. And I loved our last even though I had left Beirut by the time my parents moved there. It was on the ground floor of a 1920's building that had very high ceilings and a narrow garden that wrapped around one side that was full of gardenia trees. The street on which the building stood was narrow and right behind the underpass that became the boundary between West and East Beirut (which was the Christian part) during the civil war that lasted for more than 15 years, from the mid 1970s to the early 1990s.

Directly opposite was a tiny sweet shop where a delightful sweet-maker called Mustapha sold the best ever *k'nafeh*, a sweet cheese and semolina pie eaten hot inside a sesame galette that looked like a handbag. When a customer came in for *k'nafeh*, Mustapha would cut open the fat part of the galette, drizzle sugar syrup all over the inside then stuff pieces of *k'nafeh* into it using his spatula to contain the melting cheese. He then wrapped the handle part of the galette in paper and handed the bulging sweet sandwich to the customer. *K'nafeh* is, together with *manaqish* (see page 231), one of our great breakfasts and my absolute favourite despite the lethal calorie count.

Whenever I returned to visit my parents, I would have *k'nafeh* for my first breakfast back home even if I had to wake up early. Mustapha sold out quickly but all I had to do was to call out from the kitchen window – his shop was only a few metres on the other side of the street – to ask him to send me a *k'nafeh* 'sandwich' with the boy who helped in the shop. It took only a few minutes for my delicious treat to be delivered and I can still see the kitchen table where I sat, which my mother covered with a plastic tablecloth, taking one luscious bite after the other, getting my fingers and the tablecloth all sticky with the dripping syrup while listening to my mother asking me what I wanted for lunch – my home visits seemed to revolve around food long before I started writing about it! Sadly,

Mustapha is long gone, as is our home – the building was demolished shortly after the end of the civil war to make way for another high rise. Beirut is bristling with them now.

What is surprising though is that in all the years that I lived in Beirut, and for many years after, I never knew how *k'nafeh* or most other sweets for that matter were made. There was something mysterious about sweet-makers and their craft. Whereas you could see most of what went on in bakeries, the sweet-makers' kitchens were secret places where no one outside of the profession went and most of what we bought from sweet-makers, we never made at home. It wasn't until much later, when I started researching and writing about food, that I began to visit various sweet-makers' kitchens to unravel the secrets behind some of the world's most sophisticated and ancient sweets.

Sugar Syrup

You can divide the sweets of the Levant in two main categories: those that require sugar syrup (and not honey as many seem to think) and those that don't. And there are just as many that are sweetened with sugar syrup as those that are not. The basic ingredients for the syrup are sugar, water and lemon juice, although the proportions vary from country to country. The Iranians add fragrance with rose water, while the Syrians and Lebanese use a combination of rose and orange blossom water. The Turks prefer theirs plain, by contrast; their syrup is also thinner, with almost the same amount of water to sugar.

Below are the three basic types of syrup used with the different sweets included in this chapter:

Lebanese Sugar Syrup

350g (12oz) golden caster sugar
1 tsp lemon juice
1 tbsp rose water
1 tbsp orange blossom water

Put the sugar and lemon juice in a saucepan with 100ml (3½fl oz) of water and bring to the boil over a medium heat, stirring occasionally. Boil for 3 minutes, then add the rose and orange blossom water. Mix well and remove from the heat, letting the syrup cool down before you use it.

Iranian sugar syrup

250g (9oz) golden caster sugar
1 tsp lemon juice
1½ tbsp rose water

Put the sugar and 125ml (4½fl oz) of water in a saucepan and place over a medium heat. Bring to the boil, stirring occasionally, then reduce the heat to low and simmer for 10–15 minutes. Add the lemon juice and simmer for a minute or so before removing from the heat and adding the rose water. Let the syrup cool down before you use it.

Turkish sugar syrup

600g (1lb 5oz) golden caster sugar
1 tbsp lemon juice

Put the sugar and 500ml (18fl oz) of water in a saucepan. Add the lemon juice and place over a medium heat. Bring to the boil and allow to bubble gently for a few minutes, stirring regularly. Take off the heat and set aside to cool before using it.

Aniseed Fritters

MA'CARÛN

Throughout the Levant, it is rare for sweets to be served at the end of a meal unless it's a special occasion. Instead, people have fruit and coffee or tea while sweets are usually consumed separately in between meals. And most Levantine sweets are associated with religious feasts or special celebrations, with each boasting its own speciality. Some are shared between the two main religions, Islam and Christianity, while others are particular to one or the other. *Ma'carûn* comes into the former category. It is particularly associated with Epiphany (Gh'tass) and Ramadan, as well as the feast of breaking the fast (Eid el-Futr) that marks the end of Ramadan. At such times sweet-makers will have mounds of *ma'carûn* piled high on huge metal trays next to other fritters such as *'uwwamat* (see page 286) and *zûlabiyah*. These fritters are also made in Lebanon for the feast of the Virgin (Eid el-Saydeh) in mid-August. They can be made with flour or semolina, although I prefer using semolina for a crumblier texture.

Makes 25 fritters

250g (9oz) fine semolina
¼ tsp (⅛ × 7g sachet) fast-action yeast
1 tsp ground aniseed
¼ tsp ground cinnamon
3 tbsp extra-virgin olive oil
Vegetable oil for frying
1 quantity of Lebanese sugar syrup (see page 271)

Mix the semolina, yeast, ground aniseed and cinnamon in a mixing bowl. Add the olive oil and work it into the semolina mixture with your fingertips until fully incorporated. Pour in 125ml (4½fl oz) of water and knead by hand until you have a firm, elastic dough. Cover with cling film and let it rest for 45 minutes.

Divide the dough into 25 equal-sized pieces. Shape each into a fat sausage, about 7cm (2¾in) long. Place the rolled pastry against a flat perforated surface, like the bottom of a colander, and with your fingers press down on the dough, rolling it towards you to produce a knobbly surface all over. Place, groove side down, on a platter and continue shaping the remaining pieces of dough in the same way until you have finished all 25 fritters.

Pour enough vegetable oil in a large, deep-sided frying pan to deep-fry the *ma'carûn*, and set over a medium heat. To test whether the oil is hot enough, add a small piece of bread; if the oil bubbles around it, it is ready. Drop in as many fritters as will fit comfortably in the pan and fry until golden brown all over. Remove with a slotted spoon and drop into the sugar syrup. Let the *ma'carûn* soak up the syrup while the second batch is frying, then lift them out and drop the second batch into the syrup. Serve at room temperature.

Iranian 'Churros'

BÂMIEH

I like to call these 'churros' because they are not that different from the Spanish sweet except for the rose water, which makes them more interesting in my view. You'll find a variation on these in Turkey and India too.

Serves 4–6

30g (1oz) unsalted butter
150g (5oz) unbleached plain flour
2 large organic eggs
Vegetable oil for frying
1 quantity of Iranian sugar syrup (see page 272)

Piping bag with a large rosette nozzle

Put the butter in a saucepan and add 150ml (5fl oz) of water. Place over a medium heat and bring to the boil. Reduce the heat to low and add the flour, whisking it in quickly until you have a smooth but rather thick batter. Once the flour is fully incorporated, whisk in the eggs, one at a time, until the mixture is soft and shiny. Remove from the heat and cover with a cloth.

Pour enough vegetable oil into a large, deep-sided frying pan and place over a medium heat. To test whether the oil is hot enough, dip in a small piece of bread; if the oil bubbles around it, it is ready. Scoop the batter into the piping bag and pipe the batter into the oil to make sticks around 8cm (3in) long. Fry until golden brown all over.

Remove with a slotted spoon and drop into the cooled syrup, turning the churros in the syrup to coat them well. Place a wire rack over a baking sheet and transfer the syrupy churros onto the rack to get rid of the excess syrup. Serve at room temperature. These will last for a couple of days if kept in an airtight container.

Iranian Elephant's Ears

Gûsh-e Fil

Here is a very simple and incredibly moreish dessert whose delightful name comes from the way the little wavy squares of fried pastry are supposed to look like the ears of an elephant. Traditionally, Iranian women kneaded their own dough and rolled it out very thinly, but I have learned from the late Margaret Shaida, whose recipe I have adapted here, that filo pastry is just as effective as well as simpler to use. I have also successfully used *warqa* and *yufka* (Turkish filo – see page 254). If you are going to use filo, choose a brand that is slightly thicker than the Turkish or Greek varieties. This is one occasion when supermarket filo works better.

Serves 4–6

60g (2oz) filo pastry
Vegetable oil for frying
1 quantity of Iranian sugar syrup (see page 272)

Unroll the sheets of filo and make sure they are well aligned. Cut them into 5cm (2in) squares and cover with cling film to prevent the pastry from drying out. Then pick up every two squares together and pinch the sides tight. By having two layers and pinching the edges together, the middle will puff while frying and you will get pillowy fritters. Lay on a clean tea towel and cover with another. It is important to keep the pastry covered all the time or it will dry up and crumble before you even get a chance to fry it.

Pour enough vegetable oil into a large, deep-sided frying pan to deep-fry the squares and have the syrup ready by the pan to drop them into it. To test whether the oil is hot enough, add a small piece of bread; if the oil bubbles around it, it is ready. Fry as many squares as will fit comfortably in the pan, turning them over in the oil until golden on both sides.

Remove each square with a slotted spoon and drop into the cold syrup. Carefully turn in the syrup and transfer to a wire rack placed over a baking sheet for any excess syrup to drain. Serve immediately as these are too delicate to keep for any length of time.

The Lady's Wrists

Z'NUD EL-SITT

Hallab is the great sweet-maker in Tripoli in northern Lebanon. There are several going by this name, all brothers or cousins, but the most famous is the one who owns the Palace of Sweets, an art deco building with a shop and café on the ground floor and kitchens on the floors above. The atmosphere in the kitchens is a little more chaotic than at other sweet-makers, but their sweets are very good and in particular their *z'nud el-sitt* (or 'lady's wrists'). I love the name even though I don't particularly see the resemblance between that part of a lady's anatomy and the sweet itself. Still, they are perfectly scrumptious and fairly simple to make once you have mastered the trick of rolling filo pastry over the squidgy cream. In the shop, they are garnished with orange blossom jam and more cream, both adding to the sinfulness of the sweet but making it even more irresistible! You can be relatively virtuous, however, and serve them without the jam and extra cream, which is what I do.

Serves 4–6

Twice the amount of homemade *kaymak* on page 303
1 × 400g packet filo pastry
125g unsalted butter, melted
Vegetable oil for frying
1 quantity of Lebanese sugar syrup (see page 271)

Make the homemade *kaymak* following the instructions on page 303 and leave to cool.

Preheat the oven to 180°C (350°F), gas mark 4.

Lay one sheet of filo on your work surface. Brush with butter and cut in half lengthways. Place 2 tablespoons *kaymak* in a fat line at the top end nearest to you, leaving 1.5cm (½in) free at the top and about 2cm (¾in) free at the edges. Fold the sides over to make a long strip. Brush with butter, then fold the top over the filling and roll into a neat fattish cylinder, brushing with butter every two or three folds. Brush with butter all over and place, loose side down, on a non-stick baking sheet. Make the remaining rolls in the same way until you have used up both filo and cream filling.

You can bake the rolls in a preheated oven for 15–20 minutes, or until crisp and golden brown all over then pour the syrup over them. Or you can fry them as they are traditionally but if you do, scoop them out of the oil once crisp and golden and drop them in the syrup. Turn them over a few times and remove with a slotted spoon onto a serving platter. Serve immediately.

Kellage

The most important time for sweets in the Islamic world is during the month of Ramadan, when Muslims fast all day and feast all night. Throughout that month and during the feast that follows, people eat and offer vast quantities of sweets and, as a result, many sweet-makers expand their operations, often onto the pavement outside their shops. What I remember most from that month is not so much the sweet-makers' street operations but rather the haunting sound of the *tabbal* (drum beater) as he went round our neighbourhood just before dawn, beating his drum to rouse people for their last meal before the day's fast began. It is very rare to hear this sound nowadays – I guess people rely on their mobiles to wake them up! But the street 'kitchens' are still there and one of the typical Ramadan sweets is *kellage*, known in Turkey as *gullaç*. The word describes both the large round sheets of pastry (about 50cm/20in in diameter), like very thin communion wafer, and the sweet that is made with them. The sheets are made by pouring a thin batter over a *saj* (concave hotplate), letting the excess slide off to leave a wafer-thin layer on the hotplate. The *saj* is then moved over different gas fires, starting with a very hot one and finishing with a lower flame, until the batter is cooked, at which point it is peeled off and laid over a large cloth. And because the sheets of pastry are dry, they last quite a long time.

The basic sheets of pastry may be made in the same way in Lebanon and Turkey, but the way they are used is very different. In Turkey, the sheets are dipped in sweetened milk, then layered in a dish and sprinkled with walnuts, pistachios and pomegranate seeds to serve as a kind of soggy pie. I have yet to acquire a taste for it, but I love the fried Lebanese version where the sheets are softened by brushing them with milk and wrapped around *qashtah* (clotted cream – see page 318) into squares that are fried then dipped in sugar syrup. You can have the same pastries unfried, but they are just as soggy and slippery as the Turkish version. During Ramadan many Lebanese sweet-makers fry *kellage* to order in the fryers outside their shops and I love seeing them in action. I can spend ages watching the squares of pastry sink into the oil, then slowly surface again, like fish rising to gobble up flies.

Serves 4

8 round sheets of *kellage* pastry
Small bowl of full-cream organic milk
200g (7oz) *qashtah* (clotted cream – see page 318)
Vegetable oil for frying
1 quantity of Lebanese sugar syrup (see page 271)

Lay one *kellage* sheet on your work surface and brush with milk. Fold in the sides of the circle to make a rectangle measuring about

15 × 20cm (6 × 8in), brushing the folds with more milk if they are too dry.

Place one rounded tablespoon of *qashtah* in the middle of the rectangle, spreading it out slightly, then fold over the long sides first, followed by the shorter ones, to make a smaller rectangle measuring about 6 × 10cm (2½ × 4in). Prepare and fill the other seven sheets in the same way and set aside.

Pour enough vegetable oil to deep fry into a large, deep-sided frying pan and place over a medium heat. To test whether the oil is hot enough, dip in a small piece of bread; if the oil bubbles around it, it is ready. Drop in as many pastries as will fit comfortably in the pan and fry until lightly golden on both sides. Remove each pastry with a slotted spoon and drop into the sugar syrup. Turn over a couple of times in the syrup then lift onto a serving platter. Serve at room temperature.

Baklava

Baklava is a generic term describing a whole range of sweets from different parts of the Levant. One of two main types is *kol wa shkor* (translated as 'eat and be grateful'), made with multiple layers of filo pastry and filled with nuts. *Kol wa shkor* come in different shapes, ranging from fingers to small squares to tiny 'baskets'. The other main type of baklava is made with 'hair' pastry (because the very thin long strands of pastry look like hair – see page 283) and is again filled with nuts but shaped into cylinders, squares or tiny bird's nests. Turkish baklava is different from the Lebanese/Syrian variety – bigger and softer and without much fragrance as the Turks don't use fragrant waters in their sugar syrup.

Güllüoğlu in Istanbul was the first baklava-maker I ever visited; I was taken there by my great friend Nevin Halıcı, author of the classic and indispensable *Turkish Cookbook*. The kitchens at Güllüoğlu are on several floors of a modern building in Karakoy.

279

The first floor is where the sheets of *yufka* (Turkish filo – see page 254) are rolled out over beautiful white marble table tops into the biggest, thinnest sheets imaginable. The room is shrouded in a cloud of cornflour, which the bakers use to stop the dough from sticking. It is here that Nadir Güllüoğlu, the flamboyant owner who shows us around, gives his first stock performance of the morning to demonstrate how thin the sheets are. He asks one of his men to hold one up and asks another to place a newspaper behind it. He beams when we marvel at how easily we can read the small print through the *yufka*. He then asks for the *yufka* to be backlit, and instructs his men to start a Thai puppet show behind the sheet, which makes for a very amusing spectacle.

Nadir Bey then leads us to where a group of men are making the baklava, some filling triangles with nuts and *kaymak* (Turkish clotted cream – see page 303), some making tiny rolls filled with pistachios, and others layering the sheets of dough with nuts before cutting them into rectangles or squares. Whatever activity they are engaged in, their movements are quick, precise and graceful, and totally mesmerising. We then climb to the next floor where the baklava is baked and the sugar syrup prepared. It is the only place where modern technology is used. The gas-fired, brick-lined ovens are similar to those of the big Western bakeries and the syrup is boiled in large gleaming catering kettles. However, as soon as the trays of crisp golden baklava came out of the oven, it is back to manual work. The man watching over the syrup scoops a large ladleful of boiling syrup that he pours over the baklava, which immediately started to bob up and down or, in Nevin's words, 'dance'!

When the kitchen tour is over, Nadir Bey invites us back to his office for a tasting. I have to admit that I much prefer Syrian/Lebanese baklava; it is drier and crunchier. But when Turkish baklava is straight out of the oven, it is almost as good, especially if you have it the way Nadir Bey tells you to – stabbing the baklava with your fork then lifting and biting into it upside down. He urged us to listen for the crunch – the sign of a perfect, fresh baklava. I never tire of this part of his performance, especially if he is serving the baklava filled with nuts and melting cream, which makes a wonderful counterpoint to the crisp pastry, everything blending together in the mouth in the most luxurious way. No other sweet-maker I have been to puts on such a show, but for a really dramatic ambience there is no better place to visit than the baklava kitchens

of İmam Çağdaş in Gaziantep (see page 208). Everything and

everyone is shrouded in white dust, including the old owner, who still wears the traditional *serwal* (trousers that are very baggy to the knees, then skin tight at the calves and ankles), adding to the rather medieval atmosphere, which is reinforced by the wood-fired oven in the baking room.

The recipe below is for the classic diamond-shaped baklava, but you can also use it to make rolled fingers. First cut the filo pastry in half lengthways, to create strips measuring 9 × 32cm (3½ × 13in). Lay six strips one over the other, brushing each with melted butter. Spread half of the nut filling, in a thin raised line, down the length of the pastry and near the edges, and roll into a thin sausage. Cut the roll into 4cm (1½in) pieces and arrange on a greased baking sheet. Do the rest in the same way then bake and add syrup as below.

Serves 4–6

100g (3½oz) unsalted butter, melted, plus extra for
    greasing
12 sheets of Greek or Turkish filo pastry (measuring
    18 × 32cm/7 × 13in)
½ quantity of Lebanese sugar syrup (see page 271)

For the filling
200g (7oz) shelled walnuts (or almonds, pine nuts,
    pistachios or cashews), finely ground
100g (3½oz) golden caster sugar
¾ tsp ground cinnamon
1 tbsp orange blossom water
1 tbsp rose water

Baking dish measuring about 18 × 32cm (7 × 13in) and
    3cm (1¼in) deep

Preheat the oven to 200°C (400°F), gas mark 6, and grease the baking dish with a little butter.

To make the filling, put the nuts in a mixing bowl, add the sugar, cinnamon and orange blossom and rose water and mix well.

Spread one sheet of filo pastry over the bottom of the baking dish. (Keep the other sheets covered with cling film and a clean tea towel to stop them from drying out.) Brush with melted butter and lay another sheet over it. Brush with more melted butter and lay over another four sheets, brushing each with butter, until you have six layers of filo pastry.

Spread the nut filling evenly over the pastry and cover with six more layers of filo, making sure you brush each with melted butter. Pour any leftover butter over the pastry and cut into either diamonds, each side measuring 5cm (2in), or thin rectangles about 5cm (2in) long and 2cm (¾in) wide.

Bake for 15–20 minutes or until crisp and golden. Take out of the oven and let it sit for a minute or so, then pour the cooled syrup all over the pastry. Serve at room temperature. If you can resist it for that long, baklava will keep for a few days if stored in an airtight container.

Sweet Pistachio Pie

BALLURIYEH

Most sweet-makers in Turkey still work by hand, and if you visit their kitchens you will see battalions of men rolling out pastry in one room or filling and shaping the different sweets in another. In Syria and Lebanon, on the other hand, they seem to have become more mechanised, using ingenious machines to roll out the pastry. One man works the machine while another prepares stacks of small, thick discs of dough, each liberally sprinkled with cornflour to stop the dough from sticking as it's being rolled out. The stacks are placed one after the other underneath a roller that goes back and forth over the stack, flattening and widening it with each motion. In between each movement, the man in charge rotates the stack slightly so that the sheets come out in a perfect circle or oval, depending on what they are being used for. When the sheets have expanded to the desired size, they are rolled around a wooden rolling pin and passed to a young apprentice who takes them to the men shaping the baklava.

The other pastry that is essential for baklava is *sha'r* or 'hair' pastry, so called because the pastry is in long thin strands. It is used in two of my favourite types of baklava, *balluriyeh* (from *ballur*, meaning 'light' because the pastry remains white) and *borma* (meaning 'turned' in Arabic because the pastry is rolled around the nuts in the shape of a cylinder). The Arab version of *borma* is made in long fat rolls filled with whole pistachios and then fried, while the Turkish version is made into thinner rolls that are filled with ground pistachios and baked. The frying is also partly mechanised, with trays of *borma* slotted onto an electric rack that is lowered into a deep-fryer filled with hot oil and lifted out, at the flick of a switch, when the pastries are done. The sweet-maker uses large pincers – the trays are obviously too hot to handle – to move the trays from the frying rack to a vat of sugar syrup into which the trays are then lowered to soak the pastries. Once they have absorbed enough syrup, the trays are removed and slotted onto yet another rack for the excess syrup and oil to drain away, leaving the *borma* crisp and scrumptious. You can make this kind of *borma* at home, deep-frying them in the same way as the sweets in the previous recipes, but it is much easier to make *balluriyeh* – the baked version.

Serves 6

750g (1lb 10oz) raw shelled pistachios, very coarsely
   ground
200g (7oz) golden caster sugar
3 tbsp rose water
100g (3½oz) unsalted butter, melted
250g (9oz) hair pastry
1 quantity of Lebanese sugar syrup (see page 271)

Baking dish measuring about 22 × 38cm (8½ × 15in) and
   4cm (1½in) deep

Put the pistachios, sugar and rose water in a mixing bowl and mix well.

Pour half the melted butter into the baking dish and spread all over the bottom. Spread half the hair pastry evenly all over the butter, pressing down with your hands to make sure the pastry forms an even layer with no gaps anywhere. Cover with an even layer of the

283

pistachio filling and another of hair pastry, pressing down with your hands once again to make sure it is the same level throughout. Pour the remaining melted butter all over the pastry.

Preheat the oven to 180°C (350°F), gas mark 4.

Bake the *balluriyeh* in the oven for 20 minutes or until barely coloured. Pour the syrup all over, then wait for a few minutes before cutting into 4–5cm (1½–2in) squares, or even smaller if you want them to be very dainty, then serve at room temperature. *Balluriyeh* will last at least two weeks if stored in a sealed container.

Candyfloss
GHAZL EL-BANAT

Ghazl el-banat, basically candyfloss, means 'to flirt with the girls' in Arabic. I wouldn't be surprised to find out that it was named after a caramel known as *sukkar banat* (meaning 'sugar of young girls' and used like wax to remove unwanted hair on the legs and arms) because the same caramel is used for the candyfloss. My mother and aunt used to make it for us when we were teenagers and I would always nab some to eat before they started the painful process of laying it on our skin and yanking it off with a million hairs attached to it. Watching *ghazl el-banat* being made at Pistache d'Alep, Aleppo's best sweet-maker, always brings back those long-gone 'beauty' days.

The set-up for *ghazl el-banat*, as for most other Levantine sweets, is fairly simple: a gas burner to boil the caramel; a thick marble slab for stretching it out; a gas-fired drum to toast the flour (an essential ingredient for the miraculous transformation of the caramel into a million sweet wisps); and a square table with raised edges, a little like a shallow box, for the final step of incorporating the flour into the caramel. When the caramel has reached the soft-ball stage, it is poured onto the greased marble slab and using a spatula – it is far too hot to touch – the master sweet-maker picks it up to stretch and fold it. He repeats this action again and again until the caramel starts to cool. He then sets the spatula aside and, with his hands (the caramel is still hot but sweet-makers all seem to have asbestos hands), he stretches and folds it, again and again – as it gets too hot for him to carry on handling it, another sweet-maker takes over and when it becomes too hot for him, he passes it back to the master – until the caramel turns a lustrous white and firms up without losing its malleability.

Then the master, who has a wondrous girth from sampling what he makes, prods the caramel to make sure it is ready for the next stage. When he signals that it is, his team all slap their hands together and call a few more sweet-makers to join them for some serious pulling and stretching. The master shapes the caramel into a fat ring and transfers it to the table, which is covered in toasted flour. The men take their place around the table and, with their hands, shovel some of the flour over the caramel. They then cup their hands over the part of the ring closest to them, look at each other and shout '*Allah Akbar!*' ('God is Great!'), invoking Him to give them strength and His blessing, before they start stretching the ring while slowly rotating it. When the ring has widened, the master twists it into a figure of eight, then folds it into two rings, one on top of the other. The men shovel more flour onto the caramel and pull again, repeating the process again and again until the ring becomes very large and the caramel starts separating into strands, fat ones at first, then thinner and thinner until the ring is the size of the table and made up of a million feathery white strands.

By then, the men are all sweating profusely and a young apprentice goes round the table dabbing their foreheads with a cloth so that the sweat does not fall onto the candyfloss. They finally stop, exhausted, and take a breath while the master breaks the candyfloss into sections, giving one to each. The young apprentice brings in a tray of whole pistachio nuts dusted with icing sugar which he places on a raised platform in the centre of the table, then he sets a round metal tray at each corner. Each man picks up some candyfloss, piles a handful of pistachios in the centre and rolls the candyfloss over the pistachios, chopping off the straggly strands with the side of his hand to form a shimmering, jewel-like ball that he lays on the tray nearest to him. Sometimes they make a truly luxurious version, using a mixture of pistachios and clotted cream, but only as a special order. I was fortunate enough to be there one day when they

285

were making these – it is truly a spectacular combination of ingredients.

I never knew it took such relentless effort to produce these balls of fluff that disappear almost as soon as you put them in your mouth. And I never suspected that the caramel Levantine women use as a beauty aid could be so miraculously transformed. What is interesting, though, is that the commercially produced *ghazl* has a long shelf life needing no refrigeration, while the hand-made version lasts only two or three days. If you forget it as I did once, you will find the gorgeous white balls collapsed into sticky puddles.

The Turkish version, which is called *pişmaniye*, is made in the same way except that the caramel is cooked to a darker stage. There is also an Iranian version, called *pashmak*, as well as an Asian variety known as dragon-beard candy. The latter is made in the same way but in smaller quantities – by sweet-makers on the street – using rice instead of wheat flour and filling the balls with ground peanuts instead of whole pistachios. I thought it would be interesting to explain the process here, but decided against giving a recipe as it is definitely not a sweet you can make at home without a tremendous amount of effort. You are better off buying it from a good sweet-maker and enjoying it all the more because you know how it is made.

Round Fritters

'UWWAMAT

Whenever I am in Damascus I make sure I visit Souk el-Tanabel (Souk of the Lazy People), not only because I love the displays of vegetables prepared by women in their homes during the night so that they are very fresh in the shops the next morning, but also because of a sweets stall where the sweet-maker displays a most extraordinary technique for making *'uwwamat*. Standing a few feet away from a gigantic frying pan, he takes a chunk of dough in his left hand and a small spoon in his right which he dips in water before scooping up a little of the dough and flicking it into the hot oil. He never misses and the soft dough never sticks to the spoon.

He is there every morning and every evening, making hundreds of these small round fritters, and whenever I am there, I stand and watch, fascinated by his technique. Most other *'uwwamat* makers simply stand over their frying pan dropping the dough straight into it. I had never seen anyone flicking it the way he does. Not only is he masterful but his fritters are also exquisite and always crisp as he seems to sell them as soon as he makes them. (These are best when eaten straight after they have been fried.) And he clearly knows he is the best because written in big letters at the back of his stall is a sign proclaiming *malak al-'uwwamat* – 'king of round fritters'!

Serves 4–6

150g (5oz) unbleached plain flour
300g (11oz) plain yoghurt
½ tsp bicarbonate of soda
Vegetable oil for frying
1 quantity of Lebanese sugar syrup (see page 271)

Put the flour in a mixing bowl. Add the yoghurt and bicarbonate of soda and whisk until you have a smooth batter. Cover with cling film and leave to rest for 45 minutes.

Pour enough vegetable oil into a large, deep-sided frying pan to deep-fry the fritters, and place over a medium heat. To test whether the oil is really hot, add a small piece of bread; if the oil bubbles around it, it is ready. Dip a rounded dessertspoon in a little cold oil, fill it with batter and drop this ball of batter into the hot oil. Drop in as many balls as will fit comfortably in the pan and fry them, stirring to brown them evenly, until golden all over.

Remove with a slotted spoon onto a double layer of kitchen paper to drain off some of the oil before dropping them into the syrup. Turn them in the syrup a few times and transfer to a serving dish. Make the rest of the fritters and serve at room temperature.

Pistachio Cookies with a Sweet Dip

KARABIJ HALAB MA' NATEF

One sweet that I remember from when my family went to the mezze restaurant in Zahleh, and which we used to buy on the bridge over the Berdawni river, was a hard white nougat with a strong taste of mastic (see page 322); and every time I eat *natef*, a lustrous white dip, I think of that sweet, wondering if it was made with soapwort (see page 330). I haven't yet found out as the sweet seems to have disappeared, but I suspect it may have been made with egg white like other nougat confections. As for soapwort, it is an unlikely ingredient to be used in an edible confection given that it is a natural soap that was traditionally used to wash carpets. When the soapwort roots are boiled, the saponin seeps into the water that can then be whisked into a brilliant white foam, something you may find hard to believe as you look into the boiling brown water. And whenever I prepare *natef*, I have a moment's doubt, wondering if the water will actually whip up into a white foam. Fortunately it always does, and when you add the sugar syrup, the foam turns into a lovely meringue-like sweet dip that is just as good on its own as with the pistachio (in Lebanon) or walnut (in Syria) cookies it is normally served with. In Lebanon, the cookies are served at room temperature, while their Syrian counterparts are served warm and the dip sprinkled with a little ground cinnamon.

Makes about 25 cookies

350g (12oz) semolina
40g (1½oz) unbleached plain flour
40g (1½oz) golden caster sugar
¼ tsp (⅛ × 7g sachet) fast-action yeast
150g (5oz) unsalted butter, softened
3 tbsp orange blossom water
3 tbsp rose water

For the filling

175g (6oz) raw shelled pistachios (or walnuts if you want
    to make this the Aleppine way), ground medium-fine
50g (2oz) golden caster sugar
½ tbsp rose water
½ tbsp orange blossom water

For the natef

60g (2oz) soapwort root (see page 330)
1 quantity of Lebanese sugar syrup (see page 271)

First make the *natef*. Rinse the soapwort under cold water to rinse off any soil that may be still clinging to it. Put in a saucepan with 600ml (1 pint) of water, place over a medium heat and bring to the boil. Watch the soapwort as it comes to the boil as it will foam up and may boil over. Simmer until the liquid is reduced by three-quarters. You should be left with 150ml (5fl oz) of brown water.

Strain the soapwort liquid into a large mixing bowl and, using a strong electric beater, whisk until the brown water has become a white, rather shiny foam – scarcely believable but true. The miraculous transformation is due to the saponin in the soapwort (see the introduction). Gradually add the sugar syrup to the foam while the beater is still whisking until you have a fluffy, stretchy dip/sauce. Transfer to a bowl, cover with cling film and refrigerate while you make the cookies.

Mix the semolina, flour, sugar and yeast in a mixing bowl. Add the softened butter and, with your fingertips, work it into the flour mixture until fully incorporated. Add the orange blossom and rose water and knead until the pastry is smooth and elastic. Cover with a tea towel that is wet but not wringing and leave to rest in a cool place for 1½ hours.

Meanwhile, make the filling for the cookies. Mix the ground pistachios (or walnuts) and sugar in a mixing bowl. Add the rose and orange blossom water and mix well before setting aside.

Preheat the oven to 200°C (400°F), gas mark 6.

Pinch off a small piece of dough and knead it into a ball the size of a walnut. Place it in the palm of one hand and flatten it with the index and middle fingers of your other hand – it needs to be thin but not so thin as to tear when you fold it over the filling.

Place 1 teaspoon of filling in a line down the middle of the dough, leaving the ends clear, and start pinching the edges of the dough together from one end to the other to close it over the filling. Carefully shape the filled pastry into a domed finger, leaving the pinched side on the bottom. Place the moulded cookie on a large non-stick baking sheet (or one lined with baking parchment or a silicone mat). Fill and shape the remaining dough in the same way. You should end up with about 25 cookies, each measuring about 8cm (3in) long and 2cm (¾in) high.

Bake the cookies for 12–15 minutes or until golden. Remove from the oven onto a wire rack to allow to cool, then serve with the *natef*. Kept in an airtight container, these cookies will last for a couple of weeks.

Walnut Cookies

MA'MUL BIL-JOZ

These are the Lebanese Easter cookies par excellence. My mother and grandmother made them by the dozen for two or three days leading up to Easter. Part of the yield was kept at home for us to eat or offer our guests while the other part was sent to friends and neighbours to share in the celebrations. Easter is more important than Christmas for Lebanese Christians. *Ma'mul* is also made in large quantities by Muslims during Ramadan along with *qrass bil-tamr* (see page 293). If you don't have a *tabe'*, or special mould for shaping the cookies, you can use a tea strainer instead, or simply mould them by hand, using tweezers or a fork to create the pattern on top. Traditionally the moulds are carved by hand out of one block of wood. If you walk down Straight Street in Damascus, there is one stretch that is the kitchen corner and there is one particular shop that I like to call the Syrian Divertimenti. They sell anything and everything to do with kitchens in there, both for the home and for restaurants with some gigantic utensils that seem to be made locally; and in one corner sits a young man carving these moulds. The oval shape is for the pistachio-filled pastry. The round shape with a pointed well inside is for the walnut-filled ones and the shallow round one is for the dates. The carving inside is quite intricate with deep grooves so that the pattern does not get lost during baking. You can also buy moulded plastic ones nowadays but I would never use those and am lucky enough to have my mother's moulds from way way back. She gave them to me when I moved to London and she'd already had them from when she was married.

Makes about 30 cookies

350g (12oz) semolina
40g (1½oz) unbleached plain flour, plus extra for
  dusting
40g (1½oz) golden caster sugar
¼ tsp (⅛ × 7g sachet) fast-action yeast
150g (5oz) unsalted butter, softened
3 tbsp orange blossom water
3 tbsp rose water
Icing sugar for dusting

For the filling
175g (6oz) shelled walnuts, ground medium-fine
50g (2oz) golden caster sugar
½ tsp ground cinnamon
½ tbsp rose water
½ tbsp orange blossom water

Tabe' or *ma'mul* mould (optional)

Mix the semolina, flour, sugar and yeast in a mixing bowl. Add the softened butter and, with your fingertips, work it into the flour mixture until fully incorporated. Add the orange blossom and rose water and knead until the pastry is smooth and elastic. If you find the pastry a bit stiff, add a little more rose water or just plain water. Roll into a ball, then place in a clean, lightly floured bowl and cover with cling film. Leave to rest in a cool place for 1½ hours.

Meanwhile, make the filling. Mix the ground walnuts with the sugar and cinnamon in a mixing bowl, Add the rose and orange blossom water and mix well, then set aside.

When the dough has finished resting, preheat the oven to 200°C (400°F), gas mark 6.

Pinch off a small piece of dough and roll into a ball the size of a walnut. Place it in the palm of one hand and, with the index finger of your other hand, burrow into it to form a hollow cone – being careful not to pierce the bottom – with walls about 5mm (¼in) thick. Fill the pastry shell with 1 teaspoon of the walnut filling and pinch the dough together to close it over the filling.

Carefully shape the filled pastry into a ball and lightly press into the *tabe'*, leaving the pinched side on top so that when you invert the cookie, it is on the bottom. Invert the mould over the fingertips of your other hand and tap it lightly against your work surface to release it onto your hand. Slide the moulded cookie onto a large non-stick baking sheet (or one lined with baking parchment or a silicone mat). Fill and shape the remaining dough in the same way. You may have to scrape the inside of the mould every now and then, in case some pastry has stuck to it. You should end up with about 30 pastries.

Bake the cookies for 12–15 minutes or until crisp on top, like shortbread, but not browned. Remove from the oven and place on a wire rack. Allow to cool for a few minutes then sprinkle with icing sugar. Serve immediately or store in airtight containers to serve later. These cookies will keep for a couple of weeks.

Date Cookies

Q'RASS BIL-TAMR

The pastry for these is the same as the one for *ma'mul* (see page 290) except the filling is made with dates and the mould or *tabe'* used is flat and round and slightly wider. You could otherwise mould these by hand, although they won't look as attractive.

Makes about 30 cookies

350g (12oz) semolina
40g (1½oz) unbleached plain flour, plus extra for dusting
40g (1½oz) golden caster sugar
¼ tsp (⅛ × 7g sachet) fast-action yeast
150g (5oz) unsalted butter, softened
3 tbsp orange blossom water
3 tbsp rose water
Icing sugar for dusting

For the filling
350g (12oz) date paste (see page 320)
½ tsp ground cinnamon
30g (1oz) unsalted butter, melted
Tabe' or *qrass bil-tamr* mould (optional)

Mix the semolina, flour, sugar and yeast in a mixing bowl. Add the softened butter and, with your fingertips, work it into the flour mixture until fully incorporated. Add the orange blossom and rose water and knead until the pastry is smooth and elastic. If you find the pastry a bit stiff, add a little more rose water or just plain water. Roll into a ball, then place in a clean, lightly floured bowl and cover with cling film. Leave to rest in a cool place for 1½ hours.

Meanwhile, make the filling. Mix the date paste with the ground cinnamon and the melted butter. It will take a little kneading to blend the ingredients together. Then divide the paste into 28–30 little pieces that you then roll into balls the size of small walnuts. Shape each ball into a small disc that is the size of the grooved circle inside the mould (if using) which should be about 3½cm (1½in).

Preheat the oven to 220°C (425°F), gas mark 7.

Divide the dough into the same number of date discs and flatten each piece into a circle about 1.5cm (⅝in) wider than a date disc. Put each date disc in the middle of each circle of pastry, and fold the pastry over the disc. Gently shape into a circle that is slightly smaller than the mould. Put the filled cookie, seam side uppermost, into the mould and gently press to fit the mould and get the impression. Tap the top part of the mould against your work surface, with your hand underneath to catch the cookie as it drops out. Slide onto a large non-stick baking sheet (or one lined with baking parchment or a silicone mat).

Bake like the *ma'mul* (see page 290), for about 15 minutes, but leaving them a little longer in the oven so that they turn golden. Remove from the oven and place on a wire rack to cool. Serve at once or store in an airtight container to serve later. They will keep for up to two weeks although they are at their best in the first few days.

Sesame Cookies

BARAZIQ

My father always brought us back edible gifts when he returned from his business trips. When he went to Iraq, we'd get huge wicker baskets filled with dates; if it was Damascus, we'd get boxes of *baraziq*. The cookies were light and crumbly, covered with sesame seeds on one side and flaked pistachios on the other. My father bought them from what was the best sweet-maker in Damascus, M'hanna in Marjah Square – a huge area that is the city's equivalent of Piccadilly Circus or Leicester Square. M'hanna is still there but no longer producing the delicious sweets of my childhood. For that taste and quality I go to Semiramis/Rose de Damas, who

have yet to allow me into their kitchens! The lovely owners of
Pistache d'Alep have allowed me into theirs, however. Indeed, I
spent a couple of hours there one day trying to master the art of
making *baraziq*. I watched as young men worked in a chain around
a spotless big table. At one end, two men divided the pastry into
tiny nuggets, which they threw to the two men at the centre of the
table who picked up the nuggets, one in each hand, and pressed on
both simultaneously to flatten them into small discs. They then
dipped these into pistachios on one side and toasted sesame seeds
on the other before laying them on a baking sheet, pistachio side
down, and starting on the next batch. When the baking sheet was
full, a young apprentice picked it up and slid it onto a rack; and
when the rack was full, he wheeled it over to the oven and slid the
trays inside to bake. While the baklava-makers work relatively
slowly because of the delicate pastry (see page 279), the *baraziq*
makers are like fast robots, by contrast, repeating the same actions
again and again at top speed and with incredible precision. They
need to work fast because of the high butter content in the pastry.
They must have a secret that they won't share because my cookies
are never as good as theirs, but it gives me pleasure to make them
at home, wishing that my father were still alive so he could taste
his daughter's handiwork.

Makes 18–20 small cookies or six large ones

4 tbsp golden caster sugar
4 tbsp unsalted butter
1 medium-sized organic egg
½ tsp white wine vinegar
150g (5oz) unbleached plain flour, plus extra for dusting
Pinch of sea salt
⅓ tsp baking powder

To garnish
100g (3½oz) sesame seeds, toasted until lightly golden
   (see page 329)
100g (3½oz) slivered pistachio nuts

Put the sugar and softened butter in a mixing bowl and work
together with a wooden spoon until completely blended. Add the
rest of the ingredients and blend with your hand until you have a
soft dough. If it is too soft to work with immediately, refrigerate

for 1 hour. Divide the dough into 18–20 portions to make small *baraziq* or six portions to make larger ones.

Preheat the oven to 180°C (350°F), gas mark 4, and line a large baking sheet with baking paper or a silicone mat, or use a non-stick baking sheet.

Shape each ball of dough with your hands until you have quite a thin disc, about 7cm (2¾in) wide to make the small cookies, and place on a large platter. Put the sesame seeds on one plate and the slivered pistachios on another. When you have shaped all the discs, dip each in the pistachios on one side and the toasted sesame seeds on the other, making sure it is well coated in the seeds. Place on the baking sheet with the nuts side down.

Bake for 25–35 minutes or until the biscuits are golden brown. Allow to cool on a wire rack before serving. *Baraziq* will keep for up to two weeks in an airtight container.

Iranian Almond Pastries

GHOTÂB

The Persian word *sanbuseh* encompasses a whole range of small stuffed pastries, both savoury and sweet. The word is at the origin of the Arab *sambusak*, which describes only savoury pastries, as well as the Indian samosa and the North African *samsa*, tiny sweet pastry triangles filled with almond paste. Oddly enough, *sanbuseh* are no longer that common in Iran and even these pastries, which would have been called *sanbuseh* a few centuries ago, have a different Persian name now. I like to think of them as the Iranian precursor to the Moroccan *cornes de gazelle*, based on the same principle of encasing almond paste in very thin pastry to make crescents. The flavour in the Iranian version is headier because of the cardamom, although it lacks the fragrance of the orange blossom water used in the North African version. The Moroccan pastries are also baked whereas the Iranian ones are fried.

Makes about 35 pastries

150g (5oz) unsalted butter, softened
150g (5oz) plain yoghurt (preferably goat's)
2 large organic egg yolks
225g (8oz) unbleached plain flour, plus extra for dusting
⅔ tsp baking powder
Vegetable oil for frying

For the filling
75g (2½oz) icing sugar, plus extra for dusting
150g (5oz) ground almonds
1¼ tsp ground cardamom, plus extra for dusting

8cm (3in) diameter pastry cutter

Put the butter, yoghurt and egg yolks in a mixing bowl and whisk together until very creamy. Mix the flour and baking powder before gradually adding them to the yoghurt and butter mixture. Knead in the bowl until you have a rough dough.

Dust your work surface with a little flour and transfer the dough to it. Knead until you have a smooth dough, then shape into a ball and place in a clean, lightly floured bowl. Cover with cling film and let the dough rise for 2½ hours.

Meanwhile, mix the filling ingredients together.

Divide the risen dough in two and shape them each into a ball. Place one under a clean, damp tea towel and roll out the other until quite thin but not so thin as it could risk tearing or bursting during frying. Use the pastry cutter to cut out as many circles as you can. Place 2 teaspoons of filling in the middle of each circle of dough. Dampen the edges and close the pastry around the filling to form a semicircle, pressing on the edges to seal them, then bend the ends around to shape into a crescent. Repeat until all the dough and filling have been used up, making about 35 pastries in total.

Pour enough vegetable oil into a large, deep-sided frying pan to deep-fry the pastries. To test whether the oil is hot enough, dip in a small piece of bread; if the oil bubbles around it, it is ready. Lower the pastries into the hot oil and fry until golden all over. Remove

297

with a slotted spoon onto several layers of kitchen paper to drain the excess oil.

Sift some icing sugar and a pinch of ground cardamom into a shallow bowl, then dip the fried pastries in the sugar, turning them over to coat evenly. Serve warm or at room temperature.

Turkish Semolina Cake

REVANI

Here is the Turkish version of the Lebanese *nammurah* (see page 72), a simpler cake with a plainer syrup. The Turks don't use rose or orange blossom water in their syrup, unlike the other countries of the Levant, and the syrup is thinner too. Still, the cake is easy and quick to make and you can vary it by adding spices such as saffron or cardamom to the mixture to give it an interesting flavour.

Serves 4–6

Unsalted butter for greasing
100g (3½oz) golden caster sugar
6 medium-sized organic eggs
100g (3½oz) self-raising flour
100g (3½oz) semolina
1 quantity of Turkish sugar syrup (see page 272)

Baking dish measuring 25cm (10in) in diameter and
   4cm (1½in) deep

Preheat the oven to 180°C (350°C), gas mark 4, and grease the baking dish with a little butter.

Put the sugar and eggs in a mixing bowl and whisk together until creamy and well blended. Combine the flours in another bowl, then add to the sugar and egg mixture and mix in well.

Spoon the batter into the baking dish, spreading it evenly across the dish. Bake in the oven for 25–30 minutes or until golden and springy to the touch.

Take out of the oven (leaving it on) and cut the *revani* into medium-sized squares (reserving any small rounded edges for eating before serving). Pour the syrup all over and return to the oven for a minute or two. Then remove and let the cake sit for a couple of hours to cool and soak up the syrup. Serve at room temperature topped with a little *kaymak* (Turkish clotted cream – see page 303) or standard clotted cream.

Halva

I was quite surprised to discover that *natef* (see page 289) is an essential ingredient in halva. Not that I knew how the genuine article was made, but because of its crumbly texture I assumed that the sesame seeds were ground then mixed with sugar syrup or honey. I did in fact make halva once this way, using a recipe from Leslie Kenton's 1980s bestseller *Raw Energy*. She suggested crushing the sesame seeds in a food processor then mixing them with honey. I nearly broke my food processor trying to do this. The hull on the tiny seeds is very hard and I did not learn until much later that they need to be soaked before they can be hulled and crushed, an important piece of information that Ms Kenton omitted to mention! The resulting halva was nothing like the one I was familiar with.

Then one day I was walking through the old souks of Aleppo with a friend who knew everyone there and he introduced me to Omar Akesh, halva-maker extraordinaire. Omar's large, rather medieval kitchens are hidden behind the small shop where he sells his tahini and halva. The kitchens occupy two floors connected by an ingenious gully system. On the upper floor, toasted sesame seeds are soaked in large stone troughs, then hulled and pressed to extract the tahini, which is channelled into the gully to drop into big vats on the ground floor. There the tahini is either packed into plastic containers to be sold in the shop or transferred to a deep metal-lined trough where it is mixed with *natef* (made in a machine that looks like a giant ice-cream maker) and churned into halva. The tahini is mixed with the *natef* using a massive electrically operated churner inside the trough. While the churner rotates, the halva-maker uses a wooden paddle to scrape the halva off the blades and back into the trough. He then stops the churner and attaches a gigantic wooden pestle (like those used to beat ice cream – see page 170) to a pulley high above the trough. Then, at the flick of another switch, the pestle starts beating down on the halva, with the halva-maker guiding it to reach every part of the mixture. When the halva reaches the right consistency, he transfers it to a number of very large, rather beautiful metal bowls with round bottoms. Holding a bowl in one hand, he kneads the halva with his free hand, rocking the bowl back and forth, until the halva becomes smooth. He then divides the mixture, weighing it and packing it into plastic boxes that are sold in the shop alongside the tahini.

The two classic types of halva are plain or mixed with pistachio nuts. Omar also makes one with chocolate that I don't much care for. I had never eaten freshly made halva until I met him and it was a revelation, far better than any I had had before and less cloying. I can't promise that the recipe below will produce as good a halva as his, but it is the nearest you will get to making your own halva using the right method!

Makes 1 kg (2lb 2oz)

500g (1lb 1oz) tahini
1 quantity of *natef* (see page 289)
Sunflower oil for greasing

Two 500g (1lb 1oz) round or rectangular
  plastic containers

Pour the tahini into a large mixing bowl and add the *natef*. Then, using a wooden paddle, mix well, lifting the mixture every now and then – you are trying to emulate the churning action of the machine (see introduction). You could otherwise use a food mixer with the kneading attachment. Once the two are properly blended and you have a mixture that is slightly textured, gently beat it with a large pestle, for a few minutes, then transfer to a clean mixing bowl.

Grease your hands with a little sunflower oil and knead the mixture very lightly. Transfer to the plastic containers – the classic shape is round – and press on the halva with your hands. Let it sit in a cool place until it hardens. Serve on its own or with pita bread. We used to make halva sandwiches as a sweet treat when we were young.

Cream Triangles
SH'AYBIYATT

If you are going to make these delicious crisp pastries using Arab-style clotted cream (see page 318), you will need to make the cream the day before. You'll also need to use the widest pan possible for your hob so as to maximise the amount of skin formed on top, which will be the cream. I have not yet been able to buy proper *qashtah* in London and I definitely don't advise using the one sold in tins. A friend once taught me to make a fast version by boiling the milk and cream with soft white breadcrumbs; others make it with cornflour. I don't really like either version and prefer to use the walnut filling if I don't have time to make the cream. In Turkey, they fill them with both ground pistachios and *kaymak* (which is their version of *qashtah*).

Makes 24

100g (3½oz) unsalted butter, melted
16 sheets of Greek or Turkish filo pastry (measuring 28 × 43cm/11 × 17in)
1 quantity of Lebanese sugar syrup (see page 271)

For the clotted cream (makes about 140g/5oz)
1 litre (1¾ pints) full-cream organic milk
300ml (½ pint) double cream

For the walnut filling
75g (2½oz) shelled walnuts, ground medium-fine
1 scant tbsp golden caster sugar

cont.

¼ scant tsp ground cinnamon
½ tsp orange blossom water
½ tsp rose water

To make the clotted cream (if using as a filling), pour the milk and cream into a wide, shallow saucepan and put over a low heat. Bring to the boil then reduce the heat to very low and leave to simmer for 1½–2 hours.

Remove the pan from the heat and cover with a lid. Let it sit undisturbed for about 6 hours, then place in the fridge and leave overnight. Skim off the thick skin and discard the leftover liquid.

To make the walnut filling (if using), put the ground nuts in a mixing bowl. Add the remaining ingredients and mix well.

Preheat the oven to 200°C (400°F), gas mark 6.

Use a little of the melted butter to grease a large baking sheet. Then lay one sheet of filo pasty on your work surface and brush with a little melted butter. Lay another sheet over it, brushing it with butter, followed by another two layers, brushing each with butter.

Cut the layered sheets into 9cm (3½in) squares. Separate one square and spread a heaped teaspoon of cream or walnut filling in the middle, leaving the edges clear. Fold the pastry over the filling to make a triangle and press the edges together. Brush the top and bottom with butter and place on the baking sheet. Continue making the rest of the triangles until you have finished both pastry and filling.

Bake in the oven for 10 minutes or until crisp and golden. Transfer to a serving platter, drizzle the syrup over the pastries and leave to cool. Serve at room temperature.

Turkish Pistachio and Cream Pie

KATMER

Katmer is one of Turkey's most splendid sweets. Made with incredibly thin pastry encasing a mixture of clotted cream and finely ground pistachios, it is baked until crisp and golden. The resulting pie is delicate and feels extremely light when you eat it even though it clocks in at around 1,000 calories a bite. But don't let this worry you. If you happen to be in Gaziantep, where *katmer* originates, you must go to Orkide to sample theirs – it is simply the best. If you want to try your hand at making it yourself, here is a recipe. I have to warn you, though, that homemade *katmer* is unlikely to be as delicate as that of a master *katmer*-maker. This is because of the way the dough is stretched. You will be rolling yours out with a rolling pin, while in Gaziantep the *katmer*-maker stretches the dough after rolling it out by flipping it in the air in a swirling motion. He does this a few times and, with each motion, the dough stretches wider and wider until it is about a metre in diameter, at which stage he slaps it against his marble worktop and gently stretches it further by pulling on the edges. It is unlikely that without any previous experience, you will know how to stretch the dough in this fashion, but you will still be able to achieve a respectable result using a rolling pin. Or even better, you can use filo pastry to make a fast version which is the recipe I give below where I have also changed the size to make mini *katmer* because they are easier to handle. And in this recipe, I recommend you use supermarket filo because it is thicker and easier to handle unless you are adept at handling the thinner Turkish or Greek brands.

Serves 4

For homemade *kaymak*
250ml (9fl oz) organic whole milk
50g (2oz) fine semolina
50ml (2fl oz) cream

cont.

For the katmer
250g (9oz) finley ground pistachios
125g (4oz) golden caster sugar
½ pack filo pastry (about 200g/7oz)

Put the milk in a saucepan and stir in the semolina and cream. Place over a medium-low heat and bring to the boil, stirring constantly to avoid having lumps. Continue stirring once it has come to the boil and boil for another 3–5 minutes until the mixture is thicker than crème fraîche.

Preheat the oven to 220°C (425°F), gas mark 7. Have 2 large non-stick baking sheets to hand or line regular ones with silicone mats or parchment paper.

Cut the filo into 21cm (8in) squares and stack them up under cling film and a clean kitchen towel so that the sheets don't dry up. Take one square of filo and brush with butter. Sprinkle about 2 tablespoons ground pistachios all over, then sprinkle as much sugar as you would like your *katmer* to be sweet – I use ½ tablespoon but this may not be sweet enough for you. Scatter dollops of cream here and there – don't overdo the cream – and lift one corner and bring it to the centre to cover part of the filling. Lift the other corners to do the same until you end up with about a 10cm (4in) square. Gently lift onto the baking sheet and make the remaining *katmers* in the same way. Bake in the oven for 10 minutes or until crisp and golden. Serve immediately.

Sweet Cheese and Semolina

HALAWET EL-JEBN

Halawet el-jebn is a very interesting sweet, a little like a sweet polenta that is spread thinly and left to set before being served with syrup, either plain or rolled around clotted cream. It is a speciality of the city of Homs, once the seat of the Syrian revolution before it was devastated by regime forces when they bombed many of the city's neighbourhoods. Bustling, modern and rather grimy, the city has never really interested me, but whenever I drove past it on the way to Lebanon from Aleppo I would stop at a sweet-maker just outside the city to buy *halawet el-jebn* for my mother. Fortunately, there is also a sweet-maker in Tripoli in northern Lebanon, Halawiyat el-Tom, that specialises in *halawet el-jebn* and makes an excellent version. They also make a very fine orange blossom jam, which is no longer so easy to find. The jam was once the classic garnish for all creamy or cream-filled sweets. Even though *halawet el-jebn* is a real sweet-maker's speciality, it is not so difficult to make at home. Just be sure to soak the cheese long enough and in enough changes of water to get rid of the salty taste.

Serves 4

100g (3½oz) unsalted butter
150g (5oz) semolina
150ml (5fl oz) Lebanese sugar syrup (see page 271), plus extra for brushing (optional) and to serve
500g (1lb 1oz) *akkawi* cheese (see page 313) or mozzarella, cut into slices and soaked in several changes of cold water until all the saltiness has gone

For the rolls (optional)
150g (5oz) *qashtah* (clotted cream – see page 318), for the filling
1 tbsp coarsely ground raw pistachios, to garnish (optional)

Melt the butter in a saucepan over a medium heat, then add the semolina and stir for a few minutes until it has absorbed all the butter. Add the sugar syrup and continue stirring until the mixture is smooth and well blended.

Drain the cheese slices and add to the saucepan. Stir, scraping the bottom of the pan to stop the cheese from sticking, until the cheese is completely melted and the mixture looks like a thick purée.

I like to eat it hot, which is rather tricky because the cheese will stretch for ever, but the classic way to serve *halawet el-jebn* is to spread the mixture rather thinly on a baking sheet brushed with sugar syrup, dipping your spatula in syrup every now and then so that it doesn't stick. Then when the *halaweh* is cool, peel it off and cut it into irregular pieces, which you layer and serve either plain or with clotted cream and more syrup on the side.

Another way to serve *halawet el-jebn* is to shape it into long rolls filled with clotted cream. Then you cut the roll into pieces about 5cm (2in) long to make one or two bites. Dust the rolls with coarsely ground pistachio nuts and serve chilled.

Fragrant Shortbread Biscuits

GH'RAYBEH

There are many things that I miss about Syria: the lovely people and their charming hospitality, the gorgeous landscapes and fabulous ruins, and most of all Semiramis/Rose de Damas, the best sweet-maker in the whole of the Middle East. Whenever I went to Damascus, I would stock up on the finest and tiniest baklava. I also bought boxes and boxes of tiny *baraziq* (see page 294) and *gh'raybeh*, which are basically shortbread although more crumbly than the Western version and fragrant with rose and orange blossom water. Semiramis's *gh'raybeh* are undoubtedly the best I have ever eaten. Sadly they were not forthcoming with their recipe, so I had to rely on my mother for the one below. Her biscuits are almost as good as Semiramis's.

Makes about 36 biscuits

100g (3½oz) unsalted butter, softened
125g (4½oz) icing sugar
250g (9oz) fine semolina
2 tbsp orange blossom water
2 tbsp rose water
50g (2oz) raw shelled pistachios

Preheat the oven to 170°C (325°F), gas mark 3.

Put the softened butter and icing sugar in a mixing bowl and work together with the back of a wooden spoon until you have a creamy, smooth white paste.

Work in the flour gradually with your hands until it is fully incorporated, then add the orange blossom and rose water and knead until the pastry is soft and smooth.

Pinch off a bit of dough the size of a walnut and roll it into a sausage about 10cm (4in) long and 1.5cm (⅝in) thick. Bring both ends together so that they overlap slightly and flatten the pastry a little. Press a pistachio nut into the pastry where the two ends join and place on a large non-stick baking sheet (or one lined with baking parchment or a silicone mat). Continue shaping the biscuits and adding the pistachios until you have finished the pastry and the nuts; you should end up with about 36.

Bake in the oven for 15 minutes or until cooked but not browned. Leave to cool completely before transferring to a serving platter or an airtight container.

You can shape gh'raybeh differently from the above, either in round biscuits about 5cm (2in) in diameter and 2cm (¾in) thick, each with a slightly depressed centre in which you press an almond or a pistachio nut; or in diamonds 2cm (¾in) thick and with 5cm (2in) sides, each diamond topped with a nut.

Iranian Chickpea Shortbread

NÂN-E NOKHODCHI

This is the Iranian equivalent of *gh'raybeh* (see page 306), very crumbly shortbreads that melt in the mouth but made instead with chickpea flour and flavoured with cardamom.

Makes 30

150g (5oz) chickpea flour
75g (2½oz) golden caster sugar
⅓ tsp ground cardamom
80g (2⅔oz) unsalted butter, very soft
plain flour to roll out the shortbreads

Mix the flour, sugar and cardamom in a mixing bowl and make a well in the centre. Add the butter to the well. Bring in the flour to mix with the butter. You may find it difficult to make the pastry bind at first – it is a very short pastry – but it should come together and if it doesn't, add a medium egg although the biscuits will not be as crumbly if you do.

Shape the pastry into a ball. Flatten it then roll out to a thickness of about 1cm (½in). Use a 20mm rosette shape cutter to cut the shortbreads and carefully transfer to a non-stick baking sheet or one lined with parchment paper. Put in the refrigerator while you heat the oven to 150°C (300°F), gas mark 2.

Bake in the preheated oven for 5–7 minutes. Let cool before decorating each with a sliver of pistachio (see page 326). Serve at room temperature. These shortbreads will keep for at least two weeks if you store them in an airtight container.

Pistachio Ice Cream

Buza 'ala Fustuq

Even though many sweet-makers produce ice cream, the best is usually to be obtained from specialist ice-cream makers. Hanna Mitri in Beirut, together with Özgüler in Gaziantep in south-eastern Turkey and Dimashq in Souk el-Hamidiyeh in Damascus, are my favourites. Hanna's ice cream is less dense and he has more choice than Özgüler, who offers only pistachio or mastic and makes his, like everyone else in that region, with goat's milk. Syrian ice cream – which is beaten rather than churned (see page 169) – is also dense but made with cow's milk and the choice is with or without cream. I don't remember which ice-cream maker I used to go to when I lived in Beirut. Whoever it was must have been near where we lived, somewhere in Hamra or perhaps in downtown Beirut. If I ever went to Hanna, it would have been when we visited my grandmother because his shop in Achrafiyeh on the Christian side is very near to where she lived, and it is still there 60 years on, although now run by his widow and their son. What I remember clearly is the rectangular biscuit 'cones' into which the vendor used to push the thick ice cream until the biscuit bulged, before piling more on top. Fortunately, they still use the same rectangular biscuits and, more importantly, they still make ice cream the same way that Hanna did, in the same tiny space right next door to the equally tiny shop, using the same antiquated equipment that would horrify any European health inspector. Hanna's widow helps out in the shop, and prepares the ingredients such as picking the pistachios clean and trimming seasonal fruit – they never use artificial flavourings. Her other children and even grandchildren chip in when they can. And for Easter, they make delicate walnut or pistachio cookies (*ma'mul* – see page 290) and date cookies (*q'rass bil-tamr* – see page 293). Whenever I go there, I order the same flavours as I used to all those years ago: plain milk, pistachio and the fruit flavour of the season.

Unlike many Levantine sweets, ice cream is easy to recreate at home. The principle of the domestic ice-cream churner is the same as the giant ones the late Hanna used and Özgüler still uses, and preparing the *salep*-thickened mixture is fairly easy to master, that is if you can source the best *salep* from Turkey, now banned from

309

export because it has become endangered. You can replace the *salep* with cornflour. You will not get the same texture nor the faint earthy flavour, but many makers of ice cream already mix their *salep* with cornflour, so your's wouldn't be too different if you use it.

Makes about 1 litre (1¾ pints)

600ml (1 pint) full-cream organic milk
½ tbsp *salep* (see page 000) or 3 tbsp cornflour
200g (7oz) golden caster sugar
200g (7oz) raw shelled pistachios, finely ground
300ml (½ pint) crème fraîche
2 tbsp rose water
¼ tsp ground mastic (see page 322)

Pour the milk into a saucepan and place over a medium heat. Slowly sprinkle in the *salep*, gradually whisking it into the milk. Carry on whisking the milk as you wait for it to come to the boil. Once it is boiling, reduce the heat to medium-low, add the sugar and continue whisking for another 7 minutes.

Pour the milk into a large jug. Add the nuts, crème fraîche, and the rose water and mix well. Sir in the mastic and cover with cling film. Let the mixture cool before you pour it into your ice-cream maker to churn it into ice cream following the manufacturer's instructions. Transfer to a freezerproof container and freeze until you are ready to serve it.

Mango Ice Cream
BUZA 'ALA MANGA

The best mangoes to use for this recipe are Alphonso mangoes. They have a beautiful intense colour and an equally intense flavour that works very well with the milk/cream mixture. You can vary this recipe by using any other fruit that is in season. Some work better than others, however: the more watery the fruit, the less successful the combination. Raspberries and strawberries work very well.

Makes about 1.2 litres (2 pints)

300ml (½ pint) full-cream organic milk
500g (1lb 1oz) ripe mango flesh
250ml (9fl oz) double cream (preferably goat's) or
    300g (11oz) crème fraîche
175g (6oz) golden caster sugar

Pour the milk into a saucepan, place over a medium heat and bring to the boil, then take off the heat and allow to cool.

Put the mango flesh in a blender and process until you have a smooth purée.

Transfer the puréed mango to a wide jug. Strain the cooled milk over the fruit and add the cream (or crème fraîche) and sugar. Stir until the sugar has dissolved and the cream is fully incorporated. Pour into your ice-cream maker to churn the mixture into ice cream following the manufacturer's instructions. Transfer to a freezerproof container and freeze until you are ready to serve it.

Glossary

akkawi

A semi-hard white cheese that is softer and less salty than hallumi cheese, it is eaten as is and it is used in sweet-making, especially in K'nafeh and Halawet el-Jebn (see pages 269 and 304). You can find it in Middle Eastern shops and you need to soak it in several changes of cold water before using in sweets.

ALEPPO PEPPER (*fleifleh*)

Cultivated in Turkey and Syria, Aleppo pepper (named after the city in Syria) is similar to the Turkish *pul biber*, which comes in different varieties, including *isot* or *Urfa biber*, and *Marash biber*, both named after the places in which the peppers are grown. All are fairly mild types of pepper; *Urfa biber* is darker because of the way it is processed: dried in the sun during the day and wrapped at night to let it sweat and restore some of its moisture. When dried, all these varieties of pepper are deseeded and crushed into small flakes, or they are ground fresh and left to dry in the sun to become a thick paste (see page 326), a little like **tomato paste**. Both flakes and paste are used to flavour **bread** and savoury dishes.

ALLSPICE (*b'har helû*)

Called *b'har helû* ('sweet spice') in Arabic, and also known as Jamaica pepper, allspice is the dried unripe berry of *Pimenta dioica*, a tree native to the Greater Antilles, southern Mexico and Central America. Now cultivated in many warm parts of the world, it is an essential spice in Lebanese, Syrian and Turkish cooking because of its subtle flavour that hints of **cloves**, **cinnamon** and nutmeg.

313

ALMONDS (*loz*)

Eaten fresh when in season, and sold as 'green almonds'. You can eat the nut whole, shell and all or, when it matures to what I like to call the second stage, you crack open the green shell to extract the tender nut inside, which you need to peel before eating. Green almonds are pickled in Turkey and used in stews in Iran. In dried form, the shelled nuts are left plain or either roasted and salted, or soaked to rehydrate them and make them taste fresh again. In Middle Eastern cooking, almonds are also toasted or sautéed in butter and used in dishes or as a garnish. Blanched almonds can also be ground and soaked to make almond milk or ground with sugar to make marzipan to use in various sweets.

ANGELICA (*golpar*)

Angelica, which is a member of the Apiaceae or Umbelliferae, commonly known as the carrot or parsley family, was once cultivated for its roots, which were regarded as an antidote to the plague. Over the years, the leaves, stem and seeds also came into use, although in the West it is now mainly known for the stem, which is crystallised and used to decorate sweets. In Iran, by contrast, the seeds are the part that is used. Viewed as a digestive, they are ground for use in various dishes, cooked with **pulses** to relieve flatulence. In northern Iran, where the plant grows easily, *golpar* is also used in soups and pickles.

ANISE (*yansûn*)

The seeds from a flowering plant in the Apiaceae family, native to the eastern Mediterranean and south-west Asia. Tasting of liquorice and fennel, anise is used in both seed and ground form to flavour **bread** and puddings.

BARBERRIES (*zereshk*)

The berries of the *Berberis vulgaris* shrub, these were once used in English cooking and they remain an essential flavouring as well as garnish in many Iranian dishes, adding a brilliant note of red and an intriguing sour flavour. You can buy them dried in Iranian shops and they will keep for a long time if properly stored in sealed containers away from the light. Barberries are also juiced, or cooked to make barberry 'leather' (see **fruit leather**).

BAY LEAVES (*waraq ghar*)

Added to stuffings, soups and stews to impart an elusive aromatic flavour. Bay oil is also used in the famous **olive oil** soap made in Aleppo and in the south of Lebanon.

BREAD (*khobz*)

Bread is an essential part of meals throughout the Levant. Indeed, it is unthinkable not to have bread laid on the table alongside the meal, whether at breakfast, lunch or dinner. Levantine breads are flat, some layered and others spongy. Pita is the main bread of Lebanon, Syria, Egypt, Jordan and the Palestinian territories, while *pide*, a soft, spongy oval loaf (see page 5), is the staple of Turkey and *nan-e lavash* or *nan-e taftun*, a large rectangular flatbread cooked against the wall of a *tandur* or over a hot metal plate, is what is chiefly used in Iran. Then there are the regional breads as well as those that are specific to meals. In Lebanon, *marqûq* is the mountain bread par excellence. I like to call it handkerchief bread because it is paper-thin and unfolds like one. The making of *marqûq* requires a special technique which was, and still is, passed from mother to daughter. The method is similar to that used by a *pizzaiolo* (pizza maker) in that the dough is passed from one hand to the other and with each movement it stretches until the circle of dough has become very thin and wide. *Shraak* is a Palestinian bread that is similar to *marqûq* and used to make *mussakhan* (see page 68). *Tabuneh* is a speciality of the north: larger and thinner than pita, as well as longer lasting and with a slightly different flavour, it is leavened with the 'yeast of Christ' (*khamiret al-Massih*), which is nothing more than a day-old piece of dough, kept from the previous batch. (The reason it is called the yeast of Christ is because the initial piece of dough that is made every year is traditionally hung on a tree for the spirit of Christ to pass over it.) Once the loaves are baked and cooled, they are sprinkled with a little water, then left to dry and packed in plastic bags to send to the shops. In the south of Lebanon, *mishtah*, a textured bread, flavoured with different spices (see page 236), is the bread that everyone likes to eat. Long and oval in shape, it is often made like Roman focaccia – cut up and sold in separate pieces. It is also made in individual round loaves In Syria, *tannur* bread (see page 257) is cooked in a pit oven or *tannur*, believed to have been the earliest type of oven and from which the Indian 'tandoor' derives. It is the favoured option in rural communities. For further detail on bread from the different countries of the Levant, see the Introduction (page 4).

Nan-e sangak, is my favourite Iranian bread. It is made with a mixture of white and wholewheat flour and baked over pebbles lining the floor of wood-fired ovens, which leave deep indentations on the bottom of the loaf. The loaves are rounded at one end and square at the other, and when they are not sold straight out of the oven, they are hung against a wall on something like a coat rack to keep them from steaming against each other.

Pita in the Middle East is very different from the pita you buy in the supermarket, which is quite thick and often oval in shape whereas traditional pita is always round. It normally comes in two sizes, medium (around 15cm/6in) and large (around 30cm/12in). I recommend the medium in the recipes. You can also make your own by following the recipe on page 234.

BURGHUL

Made from wheat that has been parboiled, dried then finely or coarsely ground. A staple ingredient in Lebanon, Turkey and Syria, although not Iran, it is used in stuffings and salads as well as in main dishes, whether vegetarian or meat-based. In Lebanon and Syria, people favour brown burghul, whereas in Turkey the pale variety is preferred. Until not so long ago, mountain people made their own from newly harvested wheat. The women spent hours picking the wheat clean of stones and wild grasses. Then they sorted and washed the grain before parboiling it, after which the wheat was drained, spread on cotton sheets and left to dry in the sun. The wheat was left out for several days, with the women turning it over regularly, until it was completely dry, at which stage the men took it to special stone mills to have it ground. The ground wheat was then sifted by the women to produce the different grades – from fine to coarse – before being packed in canvas bags, labelled according to the grade and stored for up to one year. This 'artisanal' way of preparing burghul has mostly vanished. It is now industrially processed. After the wheat has been parboiled, it is kiln-dried, then passed through two different-grade mills to achieve fine and coarse grains.

Burghul has a long shelf life if stored properly, and it is worthwhile buying a good-quality one, if you can, to have at hand in your pantry.

CARAWAY (*karaweyah*)

Also known as Persian cumin, probably because it resembles **cumin**, the seeds of *Carum carvi* taste a little like **anise**. They are used mostly in desserts like *meghli* (see page 168), where it is the main flavouring, and certain **spice mixtures**.

CARDAMOM (*hal*)

Native to India, Nepal and Bhutan, cardamom is the second most expensive spice in the world. Part of the ginger family, it is obtained from several plants of the similar genera *Elettaria* and *Amomum*. In Lebanon cardamom is mostly used in Turkish coffee, whereas in Iran it has wider culinary application, featuring in both sweet and savoury dishes.

CINNAMON (*qerfeh*)

Obtained from two different types of cinnamon tree, both from the laurel or Lauraceae family. The thin sheets of the inner part of the bark of *Cinnamomum zeylanicum* are dried and rolled in thin quills to produce 'real' cinnamon. These are sold in the West, usually cut to the same short length, whereas in Lebanon they are left uncut and can be found measuring as much as 30cm (12in) in length. The thick, dark bark of *Cinnamomum cassia* is known as cassia and is the variety chiefly used in the Levant because of its stronger flavour. It is a required addition to most soups, stocks and stews in Lebanon and Syria as well as in Turkey. Ground cinnamon is also commonly used in both savoury and sweet dishes. Cinnamon sticks of the standard supermarket length (5cm/2in) are intended in this book.

CITRUS PEEL (*qeshrat al-laymûn*)

Featuring mostly in Iranian cooking, orange peel is used dried when oranges are not in season and fresh when they are; the peel is sliced into very thin strips and used to garnish **rice** dishes. In Lebanon, both orange and lemon peel are added to stews, such as the pea and

317

carrot stew on page 39, to give an intriguing citrusy flavour. Citrus peel is also used in soups and in some sweets.

CLARIFIED BUTTER (*samneh*)

Known as *samneh* or *samna* in Arabic, clarified butter (or ghee) is, as the term indicates, butter that has been stripped of its milk solids, making it a purer fat and one that lasts longer and can be cooked at a higher temperature without burning. Despite all these qualities, few people use *samneh* now, favouring non-clarified butter or **olive oil** as a healthier fat. You can easily make it yourself, however, by heating butter in a saucepan until it melts and starts foaming. Skim the foam from the top and let the milk solids settle at the bottom of the pan, then carefully pour the clarified butter into a clean jar with a lid and store in a cool place or in the refrigerator to use when you need it. Kept covered in the fridge, it will last for several months.

CLOTTED CREAM (*kaymak* and *qashtah*)

Known as *kaymak* in Turkey or *qashtah* in the Arab world, the Levantine versions having a grainier texture. In some parts of Turkey clotted cream is made using the milk of water buffaloes, whereas the best *qashtah* in Lebanon and Syria is made with sheep's milk. The milk is poured into a very wide pan with one edge placed over a very low flame. As the milk simmers it forms a skin that is pushed away from the edge by the bubbling milk. The skin is skimmed off and put to drain to produce the very thick cream that does not quite melt during baking the way normal cream does. It is served for breakfast or as a pudding drizzled with honey; it is also used in various desserts and/or served with them. Because the cream doesn't melt during cooking, it makes an ideal filling in stuffed pancakes (see page 164). It is difficult to get hold of here in the West, however, so you will have to make your own – see page 302.

CLOVES (*qrûnfûl*)

The dried flower buds of a tree in the Myrtaceae family. Cloves are very aromatic and used in both sweet and savoury preparations, either whole or ground. They are also incorporated in the various Levantine **spice mixtures**. Because of their strong aroma, cloves should be used in moderation and not exceeding the quantity specified in a particular recipe.

CORIANDER (*kûzbûrah*)

Coriander (seeds and ground) may not be such an essential spice as **cinnamon** and **allspice,** but it is still an important component of the Levantine spice cupboard and appears in various **spice mixtures.** Dried coriander is often used together with fresh coriander in various stews. Sometimes the seeds are toasted before use but more often they are not. They come in two sizes, the larger seeds from a variety known as *Coriandrum sativum vulgare* and the smaller ones from *C. s. microcarpum.* The larger seeds are the ones most commonly used as a spice, while the smaller seeds are valued for their essential oil. Coriander was cultivated in antiquity for the manufacture of perfume and for culinary purposes, used then, as now, both as a spice (the seeds) and a flavouring (the fresh leaves). In the late seventeenth century, it was one of the first spices cultivated by early settlers in North America, where the fresh herb is known as cilantro.

CORNFLOUR (*nashah*)

Used as a thickener in milk puddings, *rahat lokum* (Turkish delight) and yoghurt sauces, cornflour is the white powdered starch of the maize grain. I like to use it in milk puddings but not to thicken yoghurt as it can make the sauce too thick and rather coarse. Instead, I use egg yolks to stabilise the yoghurt, even if there is a risk that it may curdle.

'BURNED' GREEN CRACKED WHEAT (*frikeh, firik*) AND *cracked wheat* (*jrish*)

Frikeh is made from the same wheat that is used for **burghul** except that it is picked green and burned in the fields before being dried and cracked coarsely (see page 87). *Frikeh* is actually delicious eaten still tender, with the lovely smoky flavour at its most pronounced, and I can imagine making a crunchy salad with it freshly picked and just burned, but it is near impossible getting it at that stage unless you happen to be on hand just before the farmers dry the hulled grain, then crack and store it for the year. In the south of Lebanon, they leave the grain whole and, if I am not

319

mistaken, they don't pick the wheat as green. Turkish *firik* seems to be a little less smoky, and they don't normally burn it in Egypt – there they use *frika* (as they pronounce it) to stuff pigeons, one of their special delicacies. *Jrish* is simply cracked wheat and it is used to give texture to *mishtah*, the regional bread from southern Lebanon (see page 236).

CUMIN (*kammûn*)

The dried seeds of *Cuminum cyminum*, a member of the parsley family, cumin looks very similar to **caraway** seeds but the flavour is different. It is an essential spice in Levantine cooking, used either as whole seeds or ground in soups and stews and as a last-minute seasoning, notably in *fûl medammes* (see page 216).

DAIRY PRODUCTS (*ajban wa alban*)

Very important in the Levantine diet, dairy products can be made from the milk of cows, sheep, goats or buffalo, and many home cooks still make their own yoghurt at home. Once the yoghurt is set, some of it is strained to make *labneh* (see page 104), which is strained further before being shaped into balls, which are then dried and preserved in **olive oil**. Turkey has a greater variety of cheese than Lebanon, Syria or Iran, where people favour fresh cheeses, especially in spring and summer when both goats and sheep have plenty to graze on and as a result produce a richer milk and plenty of it. A typical Syrian/Lebanese cheese is one called *majduleh*. It is basically a halloumi that has been stretched until the cheese separates into filaments that are then gathered into tresses. You eat the cheese by undoing the tresses and separating the strips of cheese, which are then piled in a tangle on a plate and served for breakfast or as part of a mezze spread. It tends to be a little salty, but a brief soaking in fresh water will soon fix that. As for milk and cream, they are used to make a range of delectable sweets that are often flavoured with fragrant waters.

DATE PASTE

Used in sweets and breads, it is made of stoned mashed-up dates and shaped into a cake. You buy it from Middle Eastern shops and simply knead it with a little butter to use according to the recipe instructions.

DRIED ROSEBUDS (*ward jouri m'yabbass*)

Used in Iranian cooking more than in any other type of Levantine cuisine, dried rose petals are added to various **spice mixtures** (as they are, too, in Tunisia and southern Lebanon) or used as a garnish. They have a heady aroma that imparts an intriguing and rather mysterious flavour to **rice** and/or meat dishes, as well as stews, salads and savoury pastries.

DRIED YOGHURT (*jamid, kashk, kishk* and *tarhana*)

Each Levantine country has its own way of drying yoghurt to preserve it. *Jamid* is the Jordanian version where the yoghurt is shaped into balls and dried (see page 89) before being rehydrated in water and used to cook such dishes as *mansaf* (see page 89). *Kashk* (see page 132) is the Iranian answer to *jamid*, but made with buttermilk, while *kishk* (see page 120) is the Lebanese one. As for *tarhana*, it is the Turkish version and the most diverse, available plain or mixed with other ingredients – such as tomato or different vegetables, depending on the region or family – and ranging from coarsely ground to blocks shaped like irregular rocks with holes in them.

FILO PASTRY (*reqaqat* and *yufka*)

Known as *yufka* in Turkish and *reqaqat* ('thinned' or 'rolled out') in Arabic, filo pastry is more or less the same throughout the Levant, but it is rolled out thinner when used to make baklava (see page 279), for instance, and a little thicker for *börek* (see pages 189). And sometimes it is lightly seared on a *saj* or domed hotplate. I have seen *reqaqat* made with batter in the souks of Damascus, with the resulting sheets made into savoury triangles called *sambusak* (a bit like samosas) – different from the Lebanese version of the dish, which are made with regular dough and shaped into half moons.

FRUIT LEATHER (QAMAR EL-DIN AND *malban*)

Our lollipop when we were children was a torn sheet of apricot leather known in Arabic as *qamar el-din* (meaning moon of the religion). *Qamar el-din* is also used to make drinks or a sweet juice to soak dried fruit for the *khoshaf*. *Malban* (which I describe on page 110) is a fruit leather made with grapes whereas in Iran, they use pomegranate juice to make a sour leather rolled like quills and used to flavour fish dishes among others. The sight of these bright red quills standing in bowls in Iranian markets is quite stunning.

HERBS (*al-a'shab*)

Both fresh and dried herbs are important in Levantine cooking. Fresh herbs such as parsley, mint, **coriander** and purslane are often used as an ingredient in a dish rather than as a garnish, as are tarragon, dill and basil. Dried mint is used to flavour tomato or yoghurt sauces, while dried thyme is mixed with **sumac** and **sesame seeds** to make *za'tar*. It is also used fresh in salads and to make a filling for *fatayer* (see page 232)

KELLAGE

A wafer-like dry pastry used to make the sweet of the same name (see page 277). In Lebanon, it is brushed with milk before it is used, whereas in Turkey, where it is known as *gullaç*, it is first layered and milk is then poured over the layers to produce a kind of soggy pie. It is one of the great specialities of Ramadan, the Muslim month of fast.

mahlab

A spice made from the kernel of a black cherry (*Prunus mahaleb*) native to Asia Minor. You can buy the kernels whole or ground to use in **bread** and cookies. The flavour is very pronounced, nutty with a hint of bitterness, and a little *mahlab* goes a long way.

MASTIC (*miskeh*)

A dried resin obtained from the bark of the *Pistacia lentiscus* (the same genus as **pistachios**), an evergreen tree native to the

Mediterranean basin. Mastic is harvested in July and August. Producers go to the fields very early in the morning and make incisions in the trees for the resin to seep out – a process called *kentima*. The transparent resin is then collected and rinsed in barrels, after which it is spread out and left to dry before being sorted by hand. There are two kinds of mastic: the clear, tiny crystals which are called *dahtilidopetres* (flintstones) and the larger, spotted soft ones known as *kantiles* (blisters). The latter being a coarser grade is normally used for chewing – the resin being a natural chewing gum ('mastic' derives from the ancient Greek for 'to chew') – while the finer grade is traditionally used in cooking. These days, however, it seems to be more difficult to purchase the 'flintstones', most mastic now available being the 'blisters' type.

meqteh

Known in Los Angeles as Armenian cucumbers, no doubt because they are found in Armenian stores, *meqteh* are thinner and longer than regular cucumbers, with a paler skin that is ridged and furry; they are also drier and crunchier. In the Lebanon, they are very sought after when they come into season and used in salads. They are also used for pickling (see page 102).

MINCED LAMB

Minced lamb is seen as a cheap option in the west whereas in the Levant it is used to produce elegant dishes such as *kibbeh* or cherry kebabs (see pages 41 and 217). No self-respecting home-cook would buy the meat ready-minced. Instead he/she would ask for a specific cut, usually from the leg, to be trimmed before being minced. You can use a food processor to mince meat but it is preferable to use a proper meat mincer, using the fine attachment for *kibbeh* or *kafta* (see pages 41 and 52). They are not so expensive and are now much lighter than the old-fashioned all-metal ones.

moghrabbiyeh

Meaning 'Moroccan' or 'from the Maghreb' in Arabic, *moghrabbiyeh* describes a large-grain type of couscous that is basically pasta made with flour and water and no eggs. It is known as *m'hamssa* in Morocco. In Lebanon, the term also applies to a

323

ATON

whole dish in which these small pellets of pasta are either poached
and steamed or simply boiled like pasta before being sautéed with
cinnamon and **allspice** and mixed with chickpeas and baby onions
together with the sauce in which the lamb and/or chicken that are
served with it have been cooked. In the northern city of Tripoli, not
far from the Syrian border, *moghrabbiyeh* refers to a snack sold
on the street, in which the cooked pasta is wrapped in pita bread
(see **bread** and page 143).

na'nâ DÂGH

A typical Iranian garnish made by frying dried mint in a little oil or
clarified butter and pouring the mixture over soups to add a musky
flavour that reminds diners of summer days.

NIGELLA SEEDS (*habbet el-barakeh*)

Often wrongly referred to as black **cumin**, this spice is obtained
from *Nigella sativa* (*Nigella* deriving from the Latin *niger*, 'black'),
also known as black **caraway**, among other names. They are used
mostly in baking, to both garnish and give **bread** and savoury
pastries a pungent, nutty taste.

NOODLES (*erişte*, *reshteh* and *sh'ayriyeh*)

Noodles are not that common in the Levant, confined to specific
dishes. In Lebanon and Syria, *sh'ayriyeh* (vermicelli) are toasted
and cooked with **rice** to serve with certain stews, while in Iran
reshteh (a kind of eggless linguine) are added to *ash-e reshteh*
(a typical soup served at tea time and sold in bazaar cafés – see
page 132). *Erişte* (also known as *kesme*) is Turkey's answer to
reshteh, although the Turkish version has a small percentage of egg
and a little **olive oil** added to the dough. Both Turks and Syrians
add noodles to lentil dishes (see *haraq osba'u* on page 203).

OLIVE OIL (*zeyt zaytûn*)

Olive oil is as essential to the Levant as **bread** is, although more
prevalent in Turkey, Syria, Lebanon, Jordan and Palestine than in
Iran, even though olives are grown in the northern province of
Gilan. Many Lebanese buy their yearly supply directly from trusted
producers who are often relatives or friends. My mother bought

324

our yearly supply from her uncle, who hand-picked the green olives and carefully selected them to produce three different grades of extra-virgin oil: *khadir* (green), the best grade, extracted from totally unblemished olives; *bab awal* (first door), the second best, pressed from slightly blemished olives; and *bab thani* (second door), extracted from the remainder of the crop. The olives that fall off the trees are collected and pressed to produce oil for soap. I always use extra-virgin olive oil, to cook with and to finish dishes or season them, but it makes sense to have at least two different types in your kitchen cupboard: a regular one for cooking – the heat takes away most of the flavour – and as good as you can afford for drizzling over dips, soups or grilled vegetables and for seasoning salads. The quality of the oil you use in these dishes will make a huge difference to the final taste. Like my mother, I buy my oil directly from a friend in Sicily, Mary Taylor Simeti, whose book *Sicilian Food* is my culinary bible for the island. Mary's husband Tonino goes to the olive press to make sure that no one tampers with his olives during pressing.

ORANGE BLOSSOM WATER (*ma zaher*)

A fragrant water distilled from macerated blossom of the Seville orange (*bou-sfayr*). The taste is slightly bitter and, as a result, it is used only sparingly in desserts. It is also used as a delicate, aromatic substitute for real coffee, called 'white coffee' (*qahwah baydah*). To make this yourself, add a teaspoon of orange blossom water to a small coffee-cupful of boiling water.

pekmez (OR *dibs*)

Pekmez is the Turkish word for grape molasses. When the molasses is made with carob, it is known as *keçiboynuzu* or *harnup pekmezi*. *Pekmez* is used as a sweetener or mixed with **tahini** to eat for breakfast. In Arabic the molasses is known as *dibs* and it can be made with grapes (*dibs 'enab*), carob (*dibs kharrub*) or dates (*dibs tamer*). The latter is used, at least in Lebanon and Syria, to make a refreshing drink called *jellab* (see page 172), while in the Arabian Gulf it is drizzled over fritters called *l'geimat*.

PEPPER FLAKES

See **Aleppo pepper**.

PEPPER PASTE (*rûbb el-fleifleh*)

Found both in northern Syria and in Turkey, the paste comes in different degrees of heat, depending on the region: mild, medium and hot in Syria, and mild and hot in Turkey. It makes a wonderful addition to soups, stews and some salads, imparting a slight kick and a lovely reddish hue. The paste is made by first trimming, deseeding and mincing fresh peppers, then spreading the resulting mash in the sun (see page 118). Every day, the mashed peppers are stirred until most of the moisture has evaporated and all that is left is a thick red paste that looks like **tomato paste** but obviously tastes very different. To have a go at making it yourself, see page 118.

PINE NUTS (*snûbar*)

Nuts feature large in both savoury and sweet Levantine dishes, and none are more important than pine nuts, the edible seeds of about 20 different species of pine (family Pinaceae, genus *Pinus*). The two most common types available to buy are those produced in Europe from the Stone Pine (*Pinus pinea*), which are long and rather slim, and those produced in Asia from the Korean Pine (*Pinus koraiensis*), which are short and rather fat. I prefer the European variety, grown from anywhere in the Mediterranean, whether it is Lebanon, Spain or Italy. They are nicer-looking, in my view, and taste nuttier than the Asian ones. They are also more expensive and this is why most restaurants use the latter. Unshelled, they have a long shelf life, but this reduces considerably once they have been shelled. For this reason, I keep mine, alongside other nuts, in the freezer and take them out about half an hour before I need to use them.

PISTACHIOS (*festûq halabi*)

The pistachio is one of two types of nut mentioned in the Bible (the other is **almonds**), and Pliny the Elder writes about them in his Natural History, mentioning how they were once unique to Syria but introduced into Italy by the Roman consul to Syia in AD 35. The pistachio tree (*Pistacia vera*, in the Anacardiaceae family, to which cashews and **sumac** also belong) is in fact originally from Greater Iran (both Iran and Iraq), but is now grown in parts of Asia, North Africa and America (in particular California), as well as southern Europe. In the Levant, the nut is used in both savoury and sweet preparations and has a particular place in the making of baklava (see page 279), when the favoured type is that picked early when the nut is still very green. I tend to prefer the Syrian, south-eastern Turkish, Sicilian and Iranian pistachios over those grown in California.

PITA BREAD

See **bread**.

POMEGRANATE SYRUP OR MOLASSES (*dibs al-rûmman*)

The flavour of Syria and Iran, pomegranate syrup or molasses (see also *pekmez*) is used in all kinds of dishes, from salad dressings to dips, soups and stews. It is also used to a lesser extent in Lebanon and Turkey. The syrup is made by reducing the juice of sour pomegranates (*abu leffan*) until it thickens and turns dark. It is then left to cool and bottled to use throughout the year until the next pomegranate season. If properly stored in a cool place, the syrup will last longer: I have kept mine for over two years without it losing any flavour. The taste of the syrup varies quite noticeably depending on the type of pomegranates used and whether it is adulterated or not. Mymouné is a very good artisanal Lebanese variety; if buying a more commercial brand, I tend to go for Iranian ones.

PULSES

Dried pulses are an important element in the Levantine diet. Chickpeas and fava (or broad), cannellini and butter beans are also eaten fresh when in season, whereas lentils are only used dried. Green lentils are normally mushier than brown, with the exception of those from the Le Puy region in France. For the brown variety, I like to use Spanish Pardina lentils or Italian ones from Umbria. Both keep their shape during cooking and work well with any recipe calling for lentils. I have learned from Nevin Halıcı, author of *Nevin Halıcı's Turkish Cookbook* and my guru on all things Turkish, to soak lentils before cooking, which cuts cooking time and also helps keep the shape.

qarisheh

See *shanklish*.

RICE (*rezz*)

There is a noticeable difference between the various kinds of rice used in the countries of the Levant and how they are cooked. In Lebanon, Syria and Turkey, for instance, short grain is favoured, cooked in double the amount of water so that the liquid is completely absorbed by the time the rice is done. In Iran, long-grain rice is preferred except in puddings or soups, in which case short grain is used. It is generally parboiled first and then steamed (see page 41), but in northern Iran, which could be considered as part of the Levant proper, rice is also boiled in enough water so that it is fully absorbed by the time the rice is cooked. This method is called *kateh*, the rice being left for long enough on the heat to develop a crust all over, which is not done in Syria or Lebanon. I like to use bomba from Spain for short grain, and for long grain I try to buy *dom-e sia*, the best Iranian rice, grown in Gilan Province. The grain is longer than basmati and has a wonderful fragrance.

ROSE WATER (*ma el-ward*)

A fragrant water distilled from the Damascus rose (*Rosa damascena*, or *ward jouri* in Arabic) and used in many sweets, including milk puddings and ice cream. It is combined with **orange blossom water** to flavour the Lebanese sugar syrup used in a range of sweets, including baklava (see page 279). If you can't buy a homemade variety, as I do, it is very important to use a good brand. I recommend Mymouné, as well as several Iranian brands. Rose water and **dried rosebuds** are highly prized in Iran, with the water sometimes sprinkled over **rice** at the end of cooking to give it a heady scent.

SAFFRON (*za'faran*)

Saffron is the most expensive spice in the world, obtained from the stigmas of the crocus flower (*Crocus sativus*), which are picked by hand. As each flower has only three stigmas, a large number of flowers have to be picked to produce a few grams of saffron. Saffron is used extensively in Iran but less so in Lebanon, Syria or

Turkey, and its quality varies, with the costliest spice grown in Kashmir. I normally alternate between saffron that is grown in La Mancha, Spain, and saffron produced in Iran. As long as the stigmas are not mixed with anything else, any variety will be fine, however. Beware of fake saffron that is sold cheaply in souks; it is made from safflower and all it will do is give you a yellow colour but no flavour. Because saffron can be bitter, you need to be careful not to overdo the quantity you add to a dish. Iranians always soak the stigmas in water or **rose water** before using it. They also crush it first, which makes it easier to measure. I prefer to use the stigmas whole as I love seeing them dotted over rice or scattered inside milk puddings. And the interesting thing is that the flavour is more intense in the bite that has the stigma in it, at least in the case of *muhallabiyeh* (see page 167), as the saffron continues to bleed into the pudding.

SALEP (*sahlab*)

Still a mysterious ingredient for many, *salep* is 'flour' made from the dried tubers of *Orchis mascula* or *O. militaris*, which are ground and used to thicken milk to produce either a warming drink in winter (see page 173) or ice cream in summer (see pages 169 and 171). The drink was very popular in France and England in the seventeenth century.

SEMOLINA (*smid*)

Ground from durum wheat, semolina, in both fine and regular grades, is used in sweets to create a pastry that is crumblier and has more texture than that of regular flour. Semolina is also boiled with milk to make a custard-like filling for pastries.

SESAME SEEDS (*semsûm*)

Considered to be the oldest oilseed crop known to humankind, sesame (*Sesamum indicum*) was first domesticated over 5,000 years ago. In some places, it is known as a survivor crop because it is very drought tolerant and can grow where most crops fail. With the highest oil content of any seed, it is widely used throughout the world. In the Levant, the raw or toasted seeds are added to both savoury and sweet dishes. The roasted seeds are also used to make **tahini**. You can buy them ready-toasted or you can dry-toast them yourself in a pan over a medium heat. You need to stir them all the time, to ensure they do not burn, taking the pan off the heat just before they reach the desired colour while continuing to stir because they will keep browning from the heat of the pan. The taste is more pronounced when the seeds are toasted.

SEVEN-SPICE MIXTURE (*sabe' b'harat*)

See **spice mixtures**.

shanklish

A very interesting fermented cheese that is a speciality of Akkar, in northern Lebanon, and various regions in Syria. The curds (*qarisheh* – also the term for curd cheese) are kneaded with chilli pepper and salt, then rolled into balls roughly the size of a tennis ball or a little larger and left to dry for a day or two. The balls of cheese are then stored in earthenware jars that have already been used to ferment the previous batch and left until they develop a coat of mould, which is then rinsed off before the cheeses are rolled in dried thyme (see **herbs**) and stored to serve either on their own or in a salad, such as the one on page 223. To make your own, see page 121.

SOAPWORT (*shirsh el-halaweh*)

The dried roots of either *Saponaria officinalis* or *Gypsophila struthium* and known as *shirsh el-halaweh* in Arabic. The roots are boiled until the water is reduced by three-quarters, at which point the mixture is whisked into a stiff white foam – quite an extraordinary transformation, due to the saponin (soap) content of the root. The foam is mixed with sugar syrup and whisked to make *natef*, a soft meringue-like sweet dip served with *karabij halab ma natef* (see page 288). Soon after the publication of my book on Lebanese cuisine, Helen Saberi, Esteban Pombo-Villar, Alan Davidson and myself embarked on an investigation to establish whether *shirsh el-halaweh* was soapwort or *bois de Panama* (a South American bark that can be used as a substitute). The results of our investigation were first published in a series of articles in the journal *Petits Propos Culinaires*, then reprinted in *The Wilder Shores of Gastronomy* (2002). And we came to the conclusion that *shirsh el-halaweh* was indeed soapwort although

you can use *bois de panama* (which is a bark and not a root) to
make *natef*.

SPICE MIXTURES (*b'harat*)

Each country has its own spice mixture. In Lebanon and Syria,
the mixture (which can differ slightly depending on who makes it)
is made up of seven different spices – black pepper, nutmeg,
cinnamon, allspice, cloves, ginger and **coriander** – hence the name
sabe' b'harat or 'seven-spice mixture', while in Turkey they have
baharat karisimi, which includes dried mint and spices such as
nutmeg, cinnamon, **cumin** and black pepper. In Iran, the mixture is
called *advieh* ('medicines' in Arabic) and it is composed along the
lines of Indian masala, varying according to the dish it is used in
or the region or family, although it is never hot and contains no
chillies, ginger or garlic. There is also a mix from southern Lebanon
called *daqqat ka'k*, mainly used in baking, and another called
kammuniyeh, which is made up of dried **herbs**, spices and **dried
rosebuds** and used primarily in raw *kibbeh* dishes.

SUMAC

A lemony seasoning that is made with the dried berries of the *Rhus
coriaria* (Tanner's or elm-leafed sumac, not to be confused with
other poisonous plants of the same family, Anacardiaceae, to which
pistachios also belong). The purplish-brown berries are harvested
and left on the branch to dry in the sun, after which they are
ground to produce a coarse-textured powder, ranging in colour
from deep maroon to a brighter red, which is used to season salads,
stuffings, fried eggs and grilled fish or meat.

TAHINI

A paste made from roasted and hulled **sesame seeds** and used in
both savoury and sweet preparations. It is mixed with *natef* to
make halva (see page 299), and with lemon juice, garlic and water
to make *tarator*, a lemony sauce served with fish, falafel or
shawarma (see pages 147 and 150). The sauce can be made thicker
and mixed with chopped herbs to become a dip. And tahini is, of
course, used with chickpeas to make hommus or with mashed
grilled aubergines for *baba ghannuge as well as with* other
vegetables to make similar dips.

331

TAIL FAT (*liyeh*)

Fat-tailed sheep are an ancient breed characterised by their enormous tails in which a very pure soft fat is stored that is highly prized in the Levant. It was once melted and used in cooking in lieu of **clarified butter** or vegetable oil, although people are more health conscious nowadays and use the fat from the tail chiefly to make *qawarma* (see page 115) or to eat with raw liver or grill with kebabs. They also mince the fat and mix it with the meat for *kafta* or *kibbeh* (see **minced lamb**); in the latter instance, the fat is also chopped and seasoned with spices to use as a stuffing for grilled *kibbeh* balls.

TOMATO PASTE (*rûbb el-banadûrah*)

There are two ways of making tomato paste. One is to dry tomato purée in the sun like the Sicilians do, stirring it regularly until it is very thick and very dark, while the other way is to cook the tomatoes (after first peeling and deseeding them) until they reduce to a slightly thinner paste, which is what my mother and grandmother did (see page 117) and which is what most Levantines do. Traditionally the paste was used only when there were no fresh tomatoes, but now it is used together with fresh tomatoes to give a sauce a more intense flavour.

TURMERIC (*kurkum* OR *'eqdeh safrah*)

A ground spice or fresh root that is used both to flavour and colour dishes, turmeric is obtained from the rhizomes of *Curcuma longa* (from the ginger family) and is not often used in Lebanese cooking, except in *sfuf*, a yellow rather dry type of sponge cake that is a favourite snack of Lebanese children (see page 71).

VERJUICE (*'assir hosrum*)

The sour juice of unripe grapes (*hosrum*) used in the place of lemon juice in salad dressings and cooked dishes. The fresh juice is boiled with a little salt so that it keeps throughout the year.

za'tar

Za'tar ('thyme' in Arabic) is a mixture of powdered dried thyme, **sumac** and toasted or raw **sesame seeds**, made up of two-thirds thyme to one-third sumac, with raw or toasted sesame seeds to taste, although the seeds rarely exceed one-quarter of the quantity of thyme and sumac mixture. The blend is salted and sautéed in a pan over a low heat to warm it up and make it last longer. *Za'tar* is mixed with **olive oil** and spread on flatbread (see **bread**) to make the quintessential Lebanese breakfast, *manaqish* (see page 240). It is also used to flavour *labneh* (see **dairy products** and page 104). Syrian *za'tar* has added spices, seeds and nuts.

Select Bibliography

GENERAL:
Ibn al-Mabrad or Ibn al-Mubarrad, *Kitab al-Tibakhah* (*The Book of Cookery*)

PALESTINIAN & JORDANIAN:
Afyouni, Izdihar Al-Farkh, *Wa La Atyab Min Sahn Al-Dar (Nothing is Better than Home-Cooking)*, Al-Wataniya 2002
Hourani, Cecil, Jordan, *The Land & the Table*, David Brown Book Company, 2004

IRAN:
Margaret Shaida, *The Legendary Cuisine of Persia*

LEBANON & SYRIA:
Corey, Helen, *The Art of Syrian Cookery*, Doubleday & Co, 1962
Ollivry, Florence, *Les Secrets d'Alep*, Actes Sud 2006
Helou, Anissa, *Lebanese Cuisine*, Grub Street, 1994
Mediterranean Street Food, HarperCollins US, 2002
Savory Baking from the Mediterranean, William Morrow, 2007
Khayat, Marie Karam & Keatinge, Margaret Clark, *Food from the Arab World*, Khayats, 1959
Mouzannar, Ibrahim, *La Cuisine Libanaise*, Librairie du Liban, 1981

TURKEY:
Algar, Ayla, *Classical Turkish Cooking*, HarperCollins, 1991
Evliya Çelebi, 17th-century travel book
Ertürk, Ilyas, *Turkish Kitchen Today*, Istanbul Mastabaasi, 1967
Halıcı, Nevin, *Turkish Cookbook*, Dorling Kindersley, 1989
Halıcı, Nevin, *Classical Turkish Cuisine*, Gategourmet, 1999

Index

Acknowledgements

As with every book I have published, I was helped in the research and writing of this one by many people, some already friends and others who have become friends. Indeed, even if it is somewhat of a cliché to say so, it is easier to make friends over food than over any other subject. When I worked in art, I made friends attending auctions, previews and exhibitions but the connections were never as immediate as those I make with people I meet when I'm researching recipes and culinary traditions, be they home cooks, street vendors or artisan food producers or simply friends of friends helping me find the dishes I am looking for or the cooks or sweet-makers to prepare them. There is hardly a Levantine person who doesn't love to talk about food, and wherever I travel in the region, it never feels awkward accosting people in the street, at a restaurant or in the souk to ask about what they are eating, ordering or buying. They almost always respond warmly despite never having met me before. And it always makes me happy when I have these friendly encounters with total strangers. So, here are the friends, new and old, who I would like to thank.

In Syria, Pierre and Irene Antaki, Lena Antaki and Georges Husni for talking to me about Aleppine cuisine and arranging for me to taste an extraordinary range of dishes cooked at home (at Lena's and Georges's) or in the restaurant and in particular the Club d'Alep. Majed Krayem and Bassam Mawaldi for letting me into the kitchens of Pistache d'Alep to watch the sweet-makers perform miracles, at least as far as *ghazl el-banat* (candyfloss) is concerned. Lina Sinjab for brilliant restaurant recommendations in Damascus. Chef Emad at Bazar el-Sharq for making the most amazing dishes for me and explaining how he prepares them, and Maria Gaspard for teaching me what has become one of my favourite dips made with beetroot. Also Sonia Khandji for generously sharing some of her recipes with me. Not to mention the many people I have met in markets, on the road and in small villages with whom I have shared marvellous moments over a piece of bread or something more. Sadly, Syria has changed in the last two years and much has been destroyed. I have not been back since the beginning of the uprising but I hope that when I do, I will be able to find some if not all the people that I have befriended as well as the various food places that I loved to visit.

In Lebanon, Jacquot and Marco Ayoub – Jacquot always takes me on wonderful culinary trips of discovery to taste an exceptional goat meat *kibbeh nayeh*, or a goat's cheese matured in goatskin; Huda and Elie Broudi and her sister Mona Za'tari, who is an amazing traditional cook while Huda is a fantastic modern one. Both have cooked for me, generously sharing their culinary secrets. Nayla Audi and her father Abdullatif el-Zeyn and her mother Alice for receiving me so warmly in their home down south and introducing me to specialities of the region that I was unfamiliar with. Amal Bohsali, my favourite place for *k'nafeh* (a sweet cheese pie eaten at breakfast), for allowing me into their kitchens to watch it and other sweets being made and for getting me a huge stock of the mysterious soapwort root (*shirsh le-halaweh*) to experiment with making *natef* (a sweet dip served with walnut or pistachio cookies). Youmna Ghorayeb and her sister Leila for showing me around their Mymouné kitchens where they produce some of the best artisanal preserves. And of course my wonderful mother, Laurice Helou, who remains an invaluable fount of knowledge as far as the country's cooking is concerned.

In Istanbul, Hande Bozdogan and Kaya, her husband, for being wonderful hosts and taking me to great places to eat. Banu Özden for introducing me to the best stuffed mussels vendor in Istanbul as well as other places. Musa Dağdeviren and his wife Zeynep for the delicious food at their restaurant Çiya. Nevin Halıcı, my guru on all things Turkish, who arranged for me to go with her brother Feyzi Bey and his delightful wife Bahar to an amazing lunch cooked by Bahar's sister, Lale, which unfortunately will remain unrecorded – Jason Lowe lost all the pictures from our trip due to a break-in at his place. Also Nadir Güllüoğlu for opening his baklava kitchens to us. Sabahat and Fahri Küpelikılıç and their daughter Gökçe for receiving us into their homes and serving *kormenli* pilaf and *tarhana çorba* (soup made with dried yoghurt) and village cheese, and Hale for sending over delicious *yaprak sarması* (stuffed vine leaves). And finally Aylin Öney Tan.

In Gaziantep, my adopted sister Filiz Hösükoğlu, who is the perfect guide to all things culinary in that city. Mustafa and Murat Özgüler for letting me see how the best *katmer* (pistachio and cream pie) in the world is made and allowing me to film their *katmer* master; Mustafa Hasırcı at Metanet for the best *beyran* (lamb stew eaten boiling hot for breakfast) in Gaziantep. Mr Bayram Sarıbaş at Güllü Baklava who makes scrumptious *kourebyeh* (pistachio shortbread); Özgüler ice cream. Belgin Yetkin, a wonderful home cook who taught me several typical south-eastern Turkish dishes, including *omaç*, a very interesting salad shaped into balls. Ali Gürbüz, the owner of Ciğerci Ali Haydar Usta restaurant, where the speciality is liver kebabs, the best you will ever eat. Şevket Kılıç at Kılıç Kadayıf and his *kadayıf*-makers for allowing us into their back kitchen to watch the mesmerising process of making *kadayıf* ('hair' pastry) by hand. Older Talat Bey, his son Burhan Bey and young Talat Bey of İmam Çağdaş for their hospitality and help and for opening their kitchens for me to see how they prepare their kebabs and baklava. Ferhat Almacı (apple seller) who arranged for us to go and watch *bastik* and *ceviz sucuğu* (grape leather and sweet walnut 'sausages') being made. Resul Bayhan and his team for letting us into their *bastik*-making hangar. Vakkas Azrak for connecting us to families drying vegetables. Kamil Sarpkaya at the Pistachio Research Centre and all the wonderful pickers in the pistachio groves. Also all the lovely people who let us into their homes to watch them prepare various specialities and take photographs which sadly are now all gone. Derman Tuzlu for translating and accompanying us at the Kahkeci. Hanımeli Yufka for opening their doors and letting me watch the men make *yufka* (the Turkish equivalent of filo pastry). Ali, our wonderful driver, who started out by being very sullen but ended up cheerfully trying to speak English with us. Şirvan Payaslı at Şirvan restaurant. Cevdet Güllü at Güllüoğlu Mahmut Güllü in Elmacı Pazarı for pistachio *kurabiye* (shortbread) and his lovely bald chef Arap Usta.

In Iran, Nasrine Faghih for receiving me so warmly in her beautiful house and Ali Farboud for being a perfect companion on our travels together. Mrs Akbar and her daughter who have shown me how to prepare various Gilaki (from Gilan province) dishes and all those who have helped me with information, introductions to friends and whose names I sadly never wrote down.

In London, Jenny Heller, Lizzy Gray, Helen Wedgewood, Elen Jones and the design team HarperCollins as well as Nada Menzalji for going over the transliteration. Caspian Dennis for being a perfect agent, and the late Abner Stein for his wonderful company and advice while he was alive. Amir Amirani for introducing me to his wonderful friends in Tehran and Jane Levi for testing some of my recipes so brilliantly. And to all those I have forgotten to mention. Sadly, I do this with each book and however hard I try to keep track of all those who have helped me, I always miss a few. I hope you will forgive me if you are among the forgotten ones!